I0015771

Go Recipes for Developers

Top techniques and practical solutions for real-life Go
programming problems

Burak Serdar

Go Recipes for Developers

Group Product Manager: Kunal Sawant

Publishing Product Manager: Samriddhi Murarka

Book Project Manager: Prajakta Naik

Lead Editor: Kinnari Chohan

Technical Editor: Vidhisha Patidar

Copy Editor: Safis Editing

Proofreader: Kinnari Chohan

Indexer: Pratik Shirodkar

Production Designer: Alishon Mendonca

DevRel Marketing Coordinator: Sonia Chauhan

First published: December 2024

Production reference: 2171224

Published by Packt Publishing Ltd.

Grosvenor House

11 St Paul's Square

Birmingham

B3 1RB, UK.

ISBN 978-1-83546-439-7

www.packtpub.com

Contributors

About the author

Burak Serdar is a software engineer with over 30 years of experience designing and developing distributed applications. He has used Go to create backend software, data processing platforms, interactive applications, and automation systems. Burak has worked for both startups and large corporations as an engineer and technical lead. He holds B.Sc. and M.Sc. degrees in Electrical and Electronics Engineering, as well as an M.Sc. degree in Computer Science.

About the reviewer

Dylan Meeus is a software engineer with over a decade of experience in various functional and non-functional programming languages. He has used Go to develop systems across diverse domains, including healthcare, machine learning frameworks, and digital signal processing software. Dylan developed a passion for functional programming while learning Haskell and has applied this knowledge to traditionally non-functional languages like Java. In recent years, he has spoken at various Go- and Java-oriented conferences, such as GopherCon and Devoxx.

Table of Contents

3

Working with Date and Time   53

6

Working with Generics   111

7

Concurrency   121

8

Errors and Panics   133

9

The Context Package   147

10

Working with Large Data   159

11

Working with JSON   181

12

Processes   201

13

Network Programming   213

14

Streaming Input/Output   251

15

Databases   275

16

Logging   291

17

Testing, Benchmarking, and Profiling   301

Preface

Go, with its straightforward syntax and pragmatic conventions, has solidified its position as the language of choice for developers tackling network programming, web services, data processing, and beyond. This book is designed to empower engineers by providing up-to-date, practical recipes for solving common programming challenges.

The journey begins with foundational principles, including effective approaches to organizing packages and structuring code for various project types. From there, the book delves into real-world engineering challenges, offering practical solutions in network programming, process management, database interactions, data pipelines, and testing. Each chapter presents working solutions and production-ready code snippets, tailored for both sequential and concurrent programming environments.

Leveraging Go's most recent language features—such as generics and structured logging—the recipes in this book primarily rely on the Go standard library, ensuring minimal reliance on third-party packages and maximizing compatibility.

By the end of this book, you'll have a wealth of proven, hands-on solutions to accelerate your Go development journey and tackle the complexities of modern software engineering with confidence.

Who this book is for

This book is intended for developers with a basic understanding of the Go language. More experienced developers can also use it as a reference, offering practical examples that can be applied to a variety of use cases.

What this book covers

Chapter 1, Project Organization, covers modules, packages, source tree organization, importing packages, versioning modules, and workspaces.

Chapter 2, Working with Strings, contains recipes showing how to work with strings, internationalization, encoding, regular expressions, parsing, and generating formatted text using templates.

Chapter 3, Working with Date and Time, shows how to work with date, time, and duration values correctly with time zone considerations, formatting/parsing date and time values, performing periodic tasks, and scheduling functions to run later.

Chapter 4, Working with Arrays, Slices, and Maps, introduces the basic container types that are the building blocks for many data structures.

Chapter 5, Working with Types, Structs, and Interfaces, shows how to define new types, extending existing types to share functionality, interfaces, and their uses. In particular, this chapter includes the two approaches to using interfaces, namely, interfaces as contracts and defining interfaces where they are used.

Chapter 6, Working with Generics, introduces the basic recipes for writing generic functions and generic types with examples.

Chapter 7, Concurrency, includes basic recipes to write concurrent programs using goroutines and channels. Mutual exclusion using mutexes is also discussed here.

Chapter 8, Errors and Panics, shows generating errors, passing errors around, handling them, and organizing errors in a project. It also discusses how to generate and deal with panics.

Chapter 9, The Context Package, introduces the Go's Context which is useful for controlling request lifecycle and passing request-scoped values within an application in a concurrent program.

Chapter 10, Working with Large Data, includes recipes for working with large amounts of data in a concurrent setting using worker pools and concurrent pipelines.

Chapter 11, Working with JSON, includes recipes for encoding and decoding JSON, marshaling/unmarshaling simple and complex data types, working with custom serialization logic, encoding/decoding polymorphic structures, and streaming JSON data.

Chapter 12, Processes, shows how to run and interact with external programs, working with environment variables, working with pipes, and graceful termination using signals.

Chapter 13, Network Programming, gives recipes for TCP and UDP servers and clients, working with TLS, deadlines, HTTP client/servers, request multiplexing, and HTML forms.

Chapter 14, Streaming Input/Output, includes recipes using reads and writers, working with files and the file system, and pipes.

Chapter 15, Databases, shows how to interact with an SQL database using the standard library packages in a secure way.

Chapter 16, Logging, has recipes showing the common uses of the standard library log and slog packages.

Chapter 17, Testing, Benchmarking, and Profiling, gives recipes on writing and running unit tests, testing HTTP servers, benchmarking, and profiling

To get the most out of this book

You need a recent version of Go (anything newer than 1.22 will do) integrated with your favorite development environment. Some of the example programs use Docker.

If you are using the digital version of this book, we advise you to type the code yourself or access the code via the GitHub repository (link available in the next section). Doing so will help you avoid any potential errors related to the copying and pasting of code.

Download the example code files

You can download the example code files for this book from GitHub at `https://github.com/PacktPublishing/Go-Recipes-for-Developers`. In case there's an update to the code, it will be updated on the existing GitHub repository.

We also have other code bundles from our rich catalog of books and videos available at `https://github.com/PacktPublishing/`. Check them out!

Conventions used

There are a number of text conventions used throughout this book.

`Code in text`: Indicates code words in text, database table names, folder names, filenames, file extensions, pathnames, dummy URLs, user input, and Twitter handles. Here is an example: "Note the capitalization of `InitDB`."

A block of code is set as follows:

```
ctx:=context.Background()
cancelable, cancel:=context.WithCancel(ctx)
defer cancel()
```

> **Tips or important notes**
> Appear like this.

Sections

In this book, you will find several headings that appear frequently (*Getting ready, How to do it…, How it works…*).

To give clear instructions on how to complete a recipe, use these sections as follows:

Getting ready

This section tells you what to expect in the recipe and describes how to set up any software or any preliminary settings required for the recipe.

How to do it...

This section contains the steps required to follow the recipe.

How it works...

This section usually consists of a detailed explanation of what happened in the previous section.

Get in touch

Feedback from our readers is always welcome.

General feedback: If you have questions about any aspect of this book, mention the book title in the subject of your message and email us at customercare@packtpub.com.

Errata: Although we have taken every care to ensure the accuracy of our content, mistakes do happen. If you have found a mistake in this book, we would be grateful if you would report this to us. Please visit www.packtpub.com/support/errata, selecting your book, clicking on the Errata Submission Form link, and entering the details.

Piracy: If you come across any illegal copies of our works in any form on the Internet, we would be grateful if you would provide us with the location address or website name. Please contact us at copyright@packt.com with a link to the material.

If you are interested in becoming an author: If there is a topic that you have expertise in and you are interested in either writing or contributing to a book, please visit authors.packtpub.com.

Share Your Thoughts

Once you've read *Go Recipes for Developers*, we'd love to hear your thoughts! Scan the QR code below to go straight to the Amazon review page for this book and share your feedback.

https://packt.link/r/1835464394

Your review is important to us and the tech community and will help us make sure we're delivering excellent quality content.

Download a free PDF copy of this book

Thanks for purchasing this book!

Do you like to read on the go but are unable to carry your print books everywhere?

Is your eBook purchase not compatible with the device of your choice?

Don't worry, now with every Packt book you get a DRM-free PDF version of that book at no cost.

Read anywhere, any place, on any device. Search, copy, and paste code from your favorite technical books directly into your application.

The perks don't stop there, you can get exclusive access to discounts, newsletters, and great free content in your inbox daily

Follow these simple steps to get the benefits:

1. Scan the QR code or visit the link below

https://packt.link/free-ebook/978-1-83546-439-7

2. Submit your proof of purchase
3. That's it! We'll send your free PDF and other benefits to your email directly

1

Project Organization

This chapter is about how you can start a new project, organize a source tree, and manage the packages you need to develop your programs. A well designed project structure is important because when other developers work on your project or try to use components from it, they can quickly and easily find what they are looking for. This chapter will first answer some of the questions you may have when you are starting a new project. Then, we will look at how you can use the Go package system, work with standard library and third-party packages, and make it easy for other developers to use your packages.

This chapter includes the following recipes:

- Creating a module
- Creating a source tree
- Building and running programs
- Importing third-party packages
- Importing specific versions of packages
- Using internal packages to reduce API surface
- Using a local copy of a module
- Workspaces
- Managing the versions of your module

Modules and packages

First, a few words about modules and packages would be helpful. A **package** is a cohesive unit of data types, constants, variables, and functions. You build and test packages, not individual files or modules. When you build a package, the build system collects and also builds all dependent packages. If the package name is `main`, building it will result in an executable. You can run the `main` package without producing a binary (more specifically, the Go build system first builds the package, produces the binary in a temporary location, and runs it). To use another package, you import it. Modules help with organizing multiple packages and the resolution of package references within a project. A **module** is simply a collection of packages. If you import a package into your program, the module containing that package will be added to go.mod, and a checksum of the contents of that module will be added to go.sum. Modules also help you to manage versions of your programs.

All files of a package are stored under a single directory on the filesystem. Every package has a name declared using the package directive, shared by all source files in it. The package name usually matches the directory name containing the files, but this is not necessarily so. For example, the main package is not usually under a directory named main/. The directory of the package determines the package's "import path." You import another package into your current package using the import <importPath> statement. Once you import a package, you use the names declared in that package using its package name (which is not necessarily the directory name).

A module name points to the location where the module contents are stored in a version control system on the Internet. At the time of writing, this is not a hard-and-fast requirement, so you can actually create module names that do not follow this convention. This should be avoided to prevent potential future incompatibilities with the build system. Your module names should be part of the import paths for the packages of those modules. In particular, module names whose first component (the part before the first /) does not have . are reserved for the standard library.

These concepts are illustrated in *Figure 1.1*.

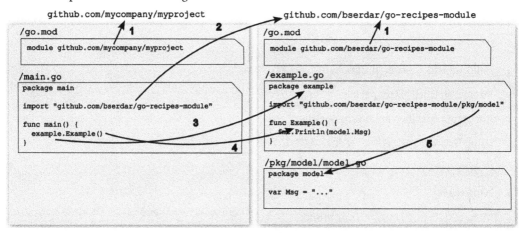

Figure 1.1 – Modules and packages

1. The module name declared in go.mod is the repository path where the module can be found.

2. The import path in main.go defines where the imported package can be found. The Go build system will locate the package using this import path, and then it will locate the module containing the package by scanning the parent directories of the package path. Once the module is found, it will be downloaded to the module cache.

3. The package name defined in the imported module is the package name you use to access the symbols of that package. This can be different from the last component of the import path. In our example, the package name is `example`, but the import path for this package is `github.com/bserdar/go-recipes-module`.

4. The `Example` function is located in the `example` package.

5. The `example` package also imports another package contained in the same module. The build system will identify this package to be part of the same module and resolve the references, using the downloaded version of the module.

Technical requirements

You will need a recent version of Go on your computer to build and run the examples in this chapter. The examples in this book were tested using **Go version 1.22**. The code from this chapter can be found at `https://github.com/PacktPublishing/Go-Recipes-for-Developers/tree/main/src/chp1`.

Creating a module

When you start working on a new project, the first thing to do is to create a module for it. A module is how Go manages dependencies.

How to do it...

1. Create a directory to store a new module.

2. Under that directory, use `go mod init <moduleName>` to create the new module. The `go.mod` file marks the root directory of a module. Any package under this directory will be a part of this module unless that directory also has a `go.mod` file. Although such nested modules are supported by the build system, there is not much to be gained from them.

3. To import a package in the same module, use `moduleName/packagePath`. When `moduleName` is the same as the location of the module on the internet, there are no ambiguities about what you are referring to.

4. For the packages under a module, the root of the module is the closest parent directory containing a `go.mod` file. All references to other packages within a module will be looked up in the directory tree under the module root.

5. Start by creating a directory to store the project files. Your current directory can be anywhere on the filesystem. I have seen people use a common directory to store their work, such as `$HOME/projects` (or `\user\myUser\projects` in Windows). You may choose to use a directory structure that looks like the module name, such as `$HOME/github.com/mycompany/mymodule` (or `\user\myUser\github.com\mycompany\mymodule` in Windows). Depending on your operating system, you may find a more suitable location.

> **Warning**
>
> Do not work under the `src/` directory of your Go installation. That is the source code for the Go standard library.

> **Tip**
>
> You should not have an environment variable, `GOPATH`; if you have to keep it, do not work under it. This variable was used by an older mode of operation (Go version <1.13) that is now deprecated in favor of the Go module system.

Throughout this chapter, we will be using a simple program that displays a form in a web browser and stores the entered information in a database.

After creating the module directory, use `go mod init`. The following commands will create a `webform` directory under `projects` and initialize a Go module there:

```
$ cd projects
$ mkdir webform
$ go mod init github.com/examplecompany/webform
```

This will create a `go.mod` file in this directory that looks like this:

```
module github.com/PacktPublishing/Go-Recipes-for-Developers/chapter1/
webform

go 1.21.0
```

Use a name that describes where your module can be found. Always use a URL structure such as the `<host>.<domain>/location/to/module` format (e.g., `github.com/bserdar/jsonom`). In particular, the first component of the module name should have a dot (`.`) (the Go build system checks this).

So, even though you can name the module something such as `webform` or `mywork/webform`, do not do so. However, you can use something such as `workspace.local/webform`. When in doubt, use the code repository name.

Creating a source tree

Once you have a new module, it is time to decide how you are going to organize the source files.

How to do it...

There are several established conventions, depending on the project:

- Use a standard layout, such as `https://github.com/golang-standards/project-layout`.

- A library with a narrow focus can put all the exported names at the module root, with implementation details optionally stored under internal packages. A module that produces a single executable with relatively few or no reusable components can also use the flat directory structure.

For a project like ours that produces an executable, the structure laid out in `https://github.com/golang-standards/project-layout` fits. So, let's follow that template:

```
webform/
  go.mod
  cmd/
    webform/
      main.go
  web/
    static/
  pkg/
    ...
  internal/
    ...
  build/
    ci/
    package/
  configs/
```

Here, the `cmd/webform` directory will contain the `main` package. As you can see, this is one instance where the package name does not match the directory it is in. The Go build system will create executables using the directory name, so when you build the `main` package under `cmd/webform`, you get an executable named `webform`. If you have multiple executables built within a single module, you can accommodate them by creating a separate `main` package under a directory matching the program name, under the `cmd/` directory.

The `pkg/` directory will contain the exported packages of the program. These are packages that can be imported and reused in other projects.

If you have packages that are not usable outside this project, you should put them under the `internal/` directory. The Go build system recognizes this directory and does not allow you to import packages under `internal/` from other packages that are outside the directory containing the `internal/` directory. With this setup, all the packages of our `webform` program will have access to the packages under `internal/`, but it will be inaccessible to packages importing this module.

The web/ directory will contain any web-related assets. In this example, we will have a web/static directory containing static web pages. You can also add web/templates to store server-side templates if you have any.

The build/package directory should have packaging scripts and configuration for cloud, container, packaging systems (dep, rpm, pkg, etc.).

The build/ci directory should have continuous integration tool scripts and configurations. If the continuous integration tool you are using requires its files to be in a certain directory other than this, you can create symbolic links, or simply put those files where the tool needs them instead of /build/ci.

The configs/ directory should contain the configuration file templates and default configurations.

You can also see projects that have the main package under the module root, eliminating the cmd/ directory. This is a common layout when the module has only one executable:

```
webform/
    go.mod
    go.sum
    main.go
    internal/
        ...
    pkg/
        ...
```

Then there are modules without any main package. These are usually libraries that you can import into your projects. For example, https://github.com/google/uuid contains the popular UUID implementation using a flat directory structure.

Building and running programs

Now that you have a module and a source tree with some Go files, you can build or run your program.

How to do it...

- Use go build to build the current package
- Use go build ./path/to/package to build the package in the given directory
- Use go build <moduleName> to build a module
- Use go run to run the current main package
- Use go run ./path/to/main/package to build and run the main package in the given directory
- Use go run <moduleName/mainpkg> to build and run the module's main under the given directory

Let's write the `main` function that starts an HTTP server. The following snippet is `cmd/webform/main.go`:

```
package main

import (
    "net/http"
)

func main() {
    server := http.Server{
        Addr:    ":8181",
        Handler: http.FileServer(http.Dir("web/static")),
    }
    server.ListenAndServe()
}
```

Currently, `main` only imports the standard library's `net/http` package. It starts a server that serves the files under the `web/static` directory. Note that for this to work, you have to run the program from the module root:

```
$ go run ./cmd/webform
```

Always run the `main` package; avoid `go run main.go`. This will run `main.go`, excluding any other files in the main package. It will fail if you have other `.go` files that contain helper functions in the `main` package.

If you run this program from another directory, it will fail to find the `web/static` directory; because it is a **relative path**, it is resolved relative to the current directory.

When you run a program via `go run`, the program executable is placed in a temporary directory. To build the executable, use the following:

```
$ go build ./cmd/webform
```

This will create a binary in the current directory. The name of the binary will be determined by the last segment of the main package – in this case, `webform`. To build a binary with a different name, use the following:

```
$ go build -o wform ./cmd/webform
```

This will build a binary called `wform`.

Importing third-party packages

Most projects will depend on third-party libraries that must be imported into them. The Go module system manages these dependencies.

How to do it...

1. Find the import path of the package you need to use in your project.

2. Add the necessary imports to the source files you use in the external package.

3. Use the go get or go mod tidy command to add the module to go.mod and go.sum. If the module was not downloaded before, this step will also download the module.

> **Tip**
> You can use https://pkg.go.dev to discover packages. It is also the place to publish documentation for the Go projects you publish.

Let's add a database to our program from the previous section so that we can store the data submitted by the web form. For this exercise, we will use the SQLite database.

Change the cmd/webform/main.go file to import the database package and add the necessary database initialization code:

```go
package main

import (
    "net/http"
    "database/sql"

    _ "modernc.org/sqlite"

    "github.com/PacktPublishing/Go-Recipes-for-Developers/src/chp1/
    webform/pkg/commentdb"
)

func main() {
    db, err := sql.Open("sqlite", "webform.db")
    if err != nil {
        panic(err)
    }
    commentdb.InitDB(db)
    server := http.Server{
        Addr:    ":8181",
```

```
            Handler: http.FileServer(http.Dir("web/static")),
        }
        server.ListenAndServe()
    }
```

The _ "modernc.org/sqlite" line imports the SQLite driver into the project. The underscore is the **blank** identifier, meaning that the sqlite package is not directly used by this file and is only included for its side effects. Without the blank identifier, the compiler would complain that the import was not used. In this case, the modernc.org/sqlite package is a database driver, and when you import it, its init() functions will register the required driver with the standard library.

The next declaration imports the commentdb package from our module. Note that the complete module name is used to import the package. The build system will recognize the prefix of this import declaration as the current module name, and it will translate it to a local filesystem reference, which, in this case, is webform/pkg/commentdb.

On the db, err := sql.Open("sqlite", "webform.db") line, we use the database/sql package function, Open, to start a SQLite database instance. sqlite names the database driver, which was registered by the imported _ "modernc.org/sqlite".

The commentdb.InitDB(db) statement will call a function from the commentdb package .

Now, let's see what commentdb.InitDB looks like. This is the webform/pkg/commentdb/initdb.go file:

```
package commentdb

import (
    "context"
    "database/sql"
)

const createStmt=`create table if not exists comments (
email TEXT,
comment TEXT)`

func InitDB(conn *sql.DB) {
    _, err := conn.ExecContext(context.Background(), createStmt)
    if err != nil {
        panic(err)
    }
}
```

As you can see, this function creates the database tables if they have not been created yet.

Note the capitalization of `InitDB`. If the first letter of a symbol name declared in a package is a capital letter, that symbol is accessible from other packages (i.e., it is *exported*). If not, the symbol can only be used within the package it is declared (i.e., it is *not exported*). The `createStmt` constant is not exported and will be invisible to other packages.

Let's build the program:

```
$ go build ./cmd/webform
   cmd/webform/main.go:7:2: no required module provides package
modernc.org/sqlite; to add it:
       go get modernc.org/sqlite
```

You can run `go get modernc.org/sqlite` to add a module to your project. Alternatively, you can run the following:

```
$ go get
```

That will get all the missing modules. Alternatively, you can run the following:

```
$ go mod tidy
```

`go mod tidy` will download all missing packages, update `go.mod` and `go.sum` with updated dependencies, and remove references to any unused modules. `go get` will only download missing modules.

Importing specific versions of packages

Sometimes, you need a specific version of a third-party package because of API incompatibilities or a particular behavior you depend on.

How to do it...

- To get a specific version of a package, specify the version label:

    ```
    $ go get modernc.org/sqlite@v1.26.0
    ```

- To get the latest release of a specific major version of a package, use this:

    ```
    $ go get gopkg.in/yaml.v3
    ```

    Alternatively, use this:

    ```
    $ go get github.com/ory/dockertest/v3
    ```

- To import the latest available version, use this:

    ```
    $ go get modernc.org/sqlite
    ```

- You can also specify a different branch. The following will get a module from the `devel` branch, if there is one:

  ```
  $ go get modernc.org/sqlite@devel
  ```

- Alternatively, you can get a specific commit:

  ```
  $ go get modernc.org/sqlite@
  a8c3eea199bc8fdc39391d5d261eaa3577566050
  ```

As you can see, you can get a specific revision of a module using the `@revision` convention:

```
$ go get modernc.org/sqlite@v1.26.0
```

The revision part of the URL is evaluated by the version control system, which, in this case, is `git`, so any valid `git` revision syntax can be used.

> **Tip:**
> You can find which revision control systems are supported by checking out the `src/cmd/go/alldocs.go` file under your Go installation.

That also means you can use branches:

```
$ go get modernc.org/sqlite@master
```

> **Tip**
> The `https://gopkg.in` service translates version numbers to URLs compatible with the Go build system. Refer to the instructions on that website on how to use it.

Working with the module cache

The module cache is a directory where the Go build system stores downloaded module files. This section describes how to work with the module cache.

How to do it...

The module cache is, by default, under `$GOPATH/pkg/mod`, which is `$HOME/go/pkg/mod` when `GOPATH` is not set:

- By default, the Go build system creates read-only files under the module cache to prevent accidental modifications.

- To verify that the module cache is not modified and reflects the original versions of modules, use this:

  ```
  go mod verify
  ```

- To clean up the module cache, use this:

  ```
  go clean -modcache
  ```

The authoritative source for information about the module cache is the Go Modules Reference (https://go.dev/ref/mod)

Using internal packages to reduce an API surface

Not every piece of code is reusable. Having a smaller API surface makes it easier for others to adapt and use your code. So, you should not export APIs that are specific to your program.

How to do it...

Create internal packages to hide implementation details from other packages. Anything under an internal package can only be imported from the packages under the package containing that internal package – that is, anything under myproject/internal can only be imported from the packages under myproject.

In our example, we placed the database access code into a package where it can be accessed by other programs. However, it does not make sense to expose the HTTP routes to others, as they are specific to this program. So, we will put them under the webform/internal package.

This is the internal/routes/routes.go file:

```
package routes

import (
    "database/sql"
    "github.com/gorilla/mux"
    "net/http"
)

func Build(router *mux.Router, conn *sql.DB) {
    router.Path("/form").
        Methods("GET").HandlerFunc(func(w http.ResponseWriter, r
        *http.Request) {
        http.ServeFile(w, r, "web/static/form.html")
```

```
    })

    router.Path("/form").
        Methods("POST").HandlerFunc(func(w http.ResponseWriter, r
        *http.Request) {
        handlePost(conn, w, r)
    })
}

func handlePost(conn *sql.DB, w http.ResponseWriter, r *http.Request)
{
    email := r.PostFormValue("email")
    comment := r.PostFormValue("comment")
    _, err := conn.ExecContext(r.Context(), "insert into comments
    (email,comment) values (?,?)",
    email, comment)
    if err != nil {
        http.Error(w, err.Error(), http.StatusInternalServerError)
        return
    }
    http.Redirect(w, r, "/form", http.StatusFound)
}
```

Then, we change the main.go file to use the internal package:

```
package main

import (
    "database/sql"
    "net/http"

    "github.com/gorilla/mux"
    _ "modernc.org/sqlite"

    "github.com/PacktPublishing/Go-Recipes-for-Developers/src/chp1/
    webform/internal/routes"
    "github.com/PacktPublishing/Go-Recipes-for-Developers/src/chp1/
    webform/pkg/commentdb"
)

func main() {
    db, err := sql.Open("sqlite", "webform.db")
```

```
if err != nil {
    panic(err)
}
commentdb.InitDB(db)

r := mux.NewRouter()
routes.Build(r, db)

server := http.Server{
    Addr:    ":8181",
    Handler: r,
}
server.ListenAndServe()
}
```

Using a local copy of a module

Sometimes, you will work on multiple modules, or you download a module from a repository, make some changes to it, and then want to use the changed version instead of the version available on the repository.

How to do it...

Use the `replace` directive in `go.mod` to point to the local directory containing a module.

Let's return to our example – suppose you want to make some changes to the `sqlite` package:

1. Clone it:

    ```
    $ ls

    webform

    $ git clone git@gitlab.com:cznic/sqlite.git
    $ ls

    sqlite
    webform
    ```

2. Modify the `go.mod` file under your project to point to the local copy of the module. `go.mod` becomes the following:

    ```
    module github.com/PacktPublishing/Go-Recipes-for-Developers/
    chapter1/webform
    ```

```
go 1.22.1

replace modernc.org/sqlite => ../sqlite

require (
    github.com/gorilla/mux v1.8.1
    modernc.org/sqlite v1.27.0
)
...
```

3. You can now make changes in the `sqlite` module on your system, and those changes will be built into your application.

Working on multiple modules – workspaces

Sometimes you need to work with multiple interdependent modules. A convenient way to do this is by defining a workspace. A workspace is simply a set of modules. If one of the modules within a workspace refers to a package in another module in the same workspace, it is resolved locally instead of that module being downloaded over the network.

How to do it...

1. To create a workspace, you have to have a parent directory containing all your work modules:

    ```
    $ cd ~/projects
    $ mkdir ws
    $ cd ws
    ```

2. Then, start a workspace using this:

    ```
    $ go work init
    ```

    This will create a `go.work` file in this directory.

3. Place the module you are working on into this directory.

    Let's demonstrate this using our example. Let's say we have the following directory structure:

    ```
    $HOME/
        projects/
            ws/
                go.work
                webform
                sqlite
    ```

Now, we want to add the two modules, `webform` and `sqlite`, to the workspace. To do that, use this:

```
$ go work use ./webform
$ go work use ./sqlite
```

These commands will add the two modules to your workspace. Any `sqlite` reference from the `webform` module will now be resolved to use the local copy of the module.

Managing the versions of your module

Go tooling uses the semantic versioning system. This means that the version numbers are of the `X.Y.z` form, broken down as follows:

- `X` is incremented for major releases that are not necessarily backward compatible.
- `Y` is incremented for minor releases that are incremental but backward-compatible
- `z` is incremented for backward-compatible patches

You can learn more about semantic versioning at `https://semver.org`.

How to do it...

- To publish a patch or minor version, tag the branch containing your changes with the new version number:

  ```
  $ git tag v1.0.0
  $ git push origin v1.0.0
  ```

- If you want to publish a new release that has an incompatible API with the previous releases, you should increment the major versions of that module. To release a new major version of your module, use a new branch:

  ```
  $ git checkout -b v2
  ```

  Then, change your module name in `go.mod` to end with `/v2`, and update all references in the source tree to use the `/v2` version of the module.

For example, let's say you released the first version of the `webform` module, `v1.0.0`. Then, you decided you would like to add new API endpoints. This would not be a breaking change, so you simply increment the minor version number – `v1.1.0`. But then it turns out some of the APIs you added were causing problems, so you removed them. Now, that is a breaking change, so you should publish `v2.0.0` with it. How can you do that?

The answer is, you use a new branch in the version control system. Create the v2 branch:

```
$ git checkout -b v2
```

Then, change go.mod to reflect the new version:

```
module github.com/PacktPublishing/Go-Recipes-for-Developers/chapter1/
webform/v2

go 1.22.1

require (
   ...
)
```

If there are multiple packages in the module, you have to update the source tree so that any references to packages within that module also use the v2 version.

Commit and push the new branch:

```
$ git add go.mod
$ git commit -m "New version"
$ git push origin v2
```

To use the new version, you now have to import the v2 version of the packages:

```
import "github.com/PacktPublishing/Go-Recipes-for-Developers/chapter1/
webform/v2/pkg/commentdb"
```

Summary and further reading

This chapter focused on the concepts and mechanics of setting up and managing Go projects. It is by no means an exhaustive reference, but the recipes presented here should give you the basics of using the Go build system effectively.

The definitive guide for Go modules is the Go Modules Reference (https://go.dev/ref/mod).

Check out the *Managing dependencies* link (https://go.dev/doc/modules/managing-dependencies) for a detailed discussion on dependency management.

In the next chapter, we will start working with textual data.

2

Working with Strings

String is one of the fundamental data types in Go.

Go uses immutable UTF-8-encoded strings. This might be confusing for a new developer; after all, this works:

```
x:="Hello"
x+=" World"
fmt.Println(x)
// Prints Hello World
```

Didn't we just change x? Yes, we did. What is immutable here are the `"Hello"` and `" World"` strings. So, the string itself is immutable, but the string variable, x, is mutable. To modify string variables, you create slices of bytes or runes (which are mutable), work with them, and then convert them back to a string.

UTF-8 is the most common encoding used for web and internet technologies. This means that any time you deal with text in a Go program, you deal with UTF-8 strings. If you have to process data in a different encoding, you first translate it to UTF-8, process it, and encode it back to its original encoding.

UTF-8 is a variable-length encoding that uses one to four bytes for each codepoint. Most codepoints represent a character, but there are some that represent other information, such as formatting. This may cause some surprises. For instance, the length of a string (i.e., the number of bytes it occupies) is different from the number of characters. To find the number of characters in a string requires you to count them sequentially. When you slice a string, you have to be careful about codepoint boundaries.

Go uses the `rune` type to denote codepoints. So, a string can be seen as a sequence of bytes as well as a sequence of runes. This is illustrated in *Figure 2.1*. Here, x is a string variable that has a pointer to the immutable string, which is a sequence of bytes and can also be seen as a sequence of runes. Even though UTF-8 is a variable-length encoding, `rune` is a fixed-length 32-bit type (`uint32`). Smaller codepoints, like the following character, H, is a 32-bit decimal, 72, whereas the byte, H, is an 8-bit value.

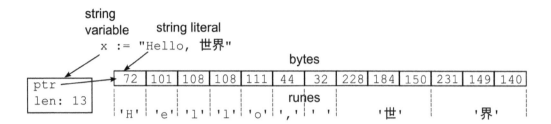

Figure 2.1 – A string, byte, and rune

In this chapter, we will look at some common operations involving strings and text. The recipes included in this chapter are as follows:

- Creating strings
- Formatting strings
- Combining strings
- Uppercase, lowercase, and title case comparisons
- Dealing with internationalized strings
- Working with encodings
- Iterating bytes and runes of strings
- Splitting
- Regular expressions
- Reading strings line by line or word by word
- Trimming
- Templates

Creating strings

In this recipe, we will look at how to create strings in a program.

How to do it...

- Use a string literal. There are two types of string literals in Go:
  - Use interpreted string literals, between the double quotations:

    ```
    x := "Hello world"
    ```

- With interpreted string literals, you must escape certain characters:

```
x:="This is how you can include a \" in your string literal"
y:="You can also use a newline \n, tab \t"
```

- You can include Unicode codepoints or hexadecimal bytes, escaped with ' \ ':

```
w:="\u65e5本\U00008a9e"
x:="\xff"
```

You cannot have newlines or an unescaped double-quote in an interpreted string:

- Use raw string literals, using backticks. A raw string literal can include any characters (including newlines) except a backtick. There is no way to escape backticks in a raw literal.

```
x:=`This is a
multiline raw string literal.
Backslash will print as backslash \`
```

If you need to include a backtick in your raw string literal, do this:

```
x:=`This is a raw string literal with `+"`"+` in it`
```

Formatting strings

The Go standard library offers multiple ways to substitute values in a text template. Here, we will discuss the text formatting utilities in the fmt package. They offer a simple and convenient way to substitute values in a text template.

How to do it...

- Use the fmt.Print family of functions to format values
- fmt.Print will print a value using its default formatting
- A string value will be printed as is
- A numeric value will be first converted to a string as an integer, a decimal number, or by using scientific notation for large exponents
- A Boolean value will be printed as true or false
- Structured values will be printed as a list of fields

If a Print function ends with ln (such as fmt.Println), a new line will be output after the string.

If a Print function ends with f, the function will accept a format argument, which will be used as the template into which it will substitute values.

fmt.Sprintf will format a string and return it.

fmt.Fprintf will format a string and write it to io.Writer, which can be a file, network connection, and so on.

fmt.Printf will format a string and write it to standard output.

How it works...

All these functions use the %[options] <verb> format to consume an argument from the argument list. To produce a % character in the output, use %%:

```
func main() {
    fmt.Printf("Print integers using %%d: %d|\n", 10)
    // Print integers using %d: 10|

    fmt.Printf("You can set the width of the printed number, left
    aligned: %5d|\n", 10)
    // You can set the width of the printed number, left
    // aligned:    10|

    fmt.Printf("You can make numbers right-aligned with a given
    width: %-5d|\n", 10)
    // You can make numbers right-aligned with a given width: 10    |

    fmt.Printf("The width can be filled with 0s: %05d|\n", 10)
    // The width can be filled with 0s: 00010|

    fmt.Printf("You can use multiple arguments: %d %s %v\n", 10,
    "yes", true)
    // You can use multiple arguments: 10 yes true

    fmt.Printf("You can refer to the same argument multiple times :
    %d %s %[2]s  %v\n", 10, "yes", true)
    // You can refer to the same argument multiple times : 10 yes
    // yes   true

    fmt.Printf("But if you use an index n, the next argument will be
    selected from n+1 : %d %s %[2]s %[1]v  %v\n", 10, "yes", true)
    // But if you use an index n, the next argument will be selected
    // from n+1 : 10 yes yes 10   yes

    fmt.Printf("Use %%v to use the default format for the type: %v %v
    %v\n", 10, "yes", true)
```

```go
    // Use %v to use the default format for the type: 10 yes true

    fmt.Printf("For floating point, you can specify precision:
    %5.2f\n", 12.345657)
    // For floating point, you can specify precision: 12.35

    fmt.Printf("For floating point, you can specify precision:
    %5.2f\n", 12.0)
    // For floating point, you can specify precision: 12.00

    type S struct {
        IntValue    int
        StringValue string
    }

    s := S{
        IntValue:    1,
        StringValue: `foo "bar"`,
    }

    // Print the field values of a structure, in the order they are
    // declared
    fmt.Printf("%v\n", s)
    // {1 foo "bar"}

    // Print the field names and values of a structure
    fmt.Printf("%+v\n", s)
    //{IntValue:1 StringValue:foo "bar"}
}
```

Combining strings

The Go standard library offers multiple ways to build strings from components. The best way depends on what type of strings you are dealing with, and how long they are. This section shows several ways that strings can be built.

How to do it...

- To combine a few fixed numbers of strings, or to add runes to another string, use the + or += operators or string.Builder
- To build a string algorithmically, use strings.Builder
- To combine a slice of strings, use strings.Join

- To combine parts of URL paths, use `path.Join`
- To build filesystem paths from path segments, use `filepath.Join`

How it works...

To build constant values, or for simple concatenations, use the + or += operators:

```
var TwoLines = "This is the first line \n"+
"This is the second line"
```

```
func ThreeLines(newLine string) string {
    return TwoLines+"\n"+newLine
}
```

You can add runes to a string the same way:

```
func AddNewLine(line string) string {
   return line+string('\n')
}
```

Tip

Using the + operator for strings can be controversial among performance-conscious teams. It is correct that the + operator may become inefficient because multiple additions may create unnecessary temporary strings to store intermediate results. It is also correct that, for some use cases, the compiler can generate better code than you can write manually. However, unless you use the + operator to create strings in `for`-loops, they are rarely the cause of your performance problems. For example, x+y will almost always outperform `fmt.Sprintf("%s%s",x,y)`. When in doubt, write a benchmark and measure. Here's how it appears on my laptop:

```
BenchmarkXPlusY-12          98628536           11.31 ns/op

BenchmarkSprintf-12         12120278           97.70 ns/op

BenchmarkBuilder-12         33077902           34.89 ns/op
```

For non-trivial cases where you have to add many short strings to build a longer one, use `strings.Builder`. Even though `strings.Builder` looks like a convenient frontend to a byte slice, it does more than that. It creates strings from the underlying byte slice without copying, so it almost always outperforms using a byte slice and then creating a string from it.

> **Tip**
>
> This is an example showing why you should prefer standard library functions to third-party libraries or manual optimizations. These functions are aggressively optimized and rely on Go internals without creating portability issues:

```
builder := strings.Builder{} // Zero-value is ready to use
for i:=0; i< 10000; i++ {
    builder.WriteString(getShortString(i))
}
fmt.Println(builder.String())
```

Use `strings.Join` to combine a slice of strings. If you are dealing with filenames and you need to combine multiple levels of directories, use `filepath.Join` to avoid platform-specific separator characters. `filepath.Join` will use \ on Windows platform and / on Linux-based platforms. If you are dealing with URLs and need to combine multiple segments, use `path.Join`, which will always use / to combine parts:

```
package main

import (
    "fmt"
    "path"
    "path/filepath"
    "strings"
)

func main() {
    words := []string{"foo", "bar", "baz"}
    fmt.Println(strings.Join(words, " "))
    // foo bar baz

    fmt.Println(strings.Join(words, ""))
    // foobarbaz

    fmt.Println(path.Join(words...))
    // foo/bar/baz

    fmt.Println(filepath.Join(words...))
    // foo/bar/baz or foo\bar\baz, depending on the host system

    paths := []string{"/foo", "//bar", "baz"}
    fmt.Println(strings.Join(paths, " "))
    // /foo //bar baz
```

```
    fmt.Println(path.Join(paths...))
    // /foo/bar/baz

    fmt.Println(filepath.Join(paths...))
    // /foo/bar/baz or \foo\bar\baz depending on the host system
}
```

Working with string cases

When working with textual data, problems related to string cases arise often. Should a text search be case-sensitive or case-insensitive? How do we convert a string to lowercase or uppercase? In this section, we will look at some recipes to deal with these common problems in a portable way.

How to do it...

- Convert strings to uppercase and lowercase using the `strings.ToUpper` and `strings.ToLower` functions, respectively.

- When dealing with text in languages with special uppercase/lowercase mappings (such as Turkish, where "İ" is the uppercase version of "I"), use `strings.ToUpperSpecial` and `strings.ToLowerSpecial`

- To convert text to uppercase for use in titles, use `strings.ToTitle`

- To compare strings lexicographically, use comparison operators

- To test the equivalence of strings ignoring case, use `strings.EqualFold`

How it works...

Converting a string to uppercase or lowercase is easy:

```
greet := "Hello World!"
fmt.Println(strings.ToUpper(greet))
fmt.Println(strings.ToLower(greet))
```

This program outputs the following:

```
HELLO WORLD!
hello world!
```

But the uppercase/lowercase may differ from language to language. For example, there are special cases for some of the Turkic languages:

```
word := "ilk"
fmt.Println(strings.ToUpper(word))
```

This will print the following:

```
ILK
```

However, that is not the correct uppercase use for Turkish. Let's try the following:

```
import (
    "fmt"
    "strings"
    "unicode"
)

func main() {
  word := "ilk"
  fmt.Println(strings.ToUpperSpecial(unicode.TurkishCase,word))
}
```

The preceding program will print the following:

```
İLK
```

The title case differs from uppercase or lowercase mainly when dealing with ligatures and digraphs –
that is, more than one character represented as a single character, such as LJ (U+01C7):

```
package main

import (
    "fmt"
    "strings"
)

func main() {
    fmt.Println(strings.ToTitle("LJ")) // U+01C7
    fmt.Println(strings.ToUpper("LJ"))
    fmt.Println(strings.ToLower("LJ"))
}
```

This program prints the following:

```
LJ
LJ
lj
```

Uppercase, lowercase, and title case define how to print a string using a particular case mapping.
These are **case mappings**. **Case folding** is the process of transforming text into the same case for
comparison purposes.

For lexicographical case-sensitive comparisons, use the relational operators:

```
fmt.Prinln("a" < "b") // true
```

To compare two Unicode strings in a case-insensitive way, use `strings.EqualFold`:

```
fmt.Println(strings.EqualFold("here", "Here")) // true
fmt.Println(strings.EqualFold("here", "Here")) // true
fmt.Println(strings.EqualFold("GÖ", "gö")) // true
```

There's more...

While the standard library `strings` package includes most of the string comparison functions you need, they may not be sufficient when dealing with internationalized strings. For example, in many cases, you would want to have Montréal and montreal be considered equal. `strings.EqualFold` will not do that. Many of the supporting functions to deal with internalized text processing are in the packages under `golang.org/x/text`.

Unicode offers multiple ways to represent a given string. The é in Montréal can be represented as a single rune, \u00e9 or e, followed by an acute accent, e\u0301. \u0301 is the "combining acute accent," ◌́, and it modifies the codepoint that comes before it. According to the Unicode standard, é and e + ◌́ are "canonically equivalent." There is also a compatibility equivalence, such as \ufb00, representing ff as a single codepoint, and the ff sequence. Canonically equivalent sequences are also compatible, but not all compatible sequences are canonically equivalent.

So, if you need to remove diacritics (i.e., nonspacing marks) from text, you can decompose it, remove the diacritics, and then compose it as follows:

```
// Based on the blog post https://go.dev/blog/normalization
package main

import (
    "fmt"
    "io"
    "strings"
    "unicode"

    "golang.org/x/text/transform"
    "golang.org/x/text/unicode/norm"
)

func main() {

    isMn := func(r rune) bool {
        return unicode.Is(unicode.Mn, r) // Mn: nonspacing marks
```

```
    }
    t := transform.Chain(norm.NFD, transform.RemoveFunc(isMn), norm.
    NFC)
    rd := transform.NewReader(strings.NewReader("Montréal"), t)
    str, _ := io.ReadAll(rd)
    fmt.Println(string(str))
}
```

The above program will print the following:

```
Montreal
```

Working with encodings

If there is a chance that your program will have to work with data produced by disparate systems, you should be aware of different text encodings. This is a huge topic, but this section should provide some pointers to scratch the surface.

How to do it...

- Use the `golang.org/x/text/encoding` package to deal with different encodings.

- To find an encoding by name, use one of the following:

  - `golang.org/x/text/encoding/ianaindex`

  - `golang.org/x/text/encoding/htmlindex`

- Once you have an encoding, use it to translate text to and from UTF-8.

How it works...

Use one of the indexes to find an encoding. Then, use that encoding to read/write data:

```
package main

import (
    "fmt"
    "os"

    "golang.org/x/text/encoding/ianaindex"
)

func main() {
    enc, err := ianaindex.MIME.Encoding("US-ASCII")
```

```go
    if err != nil {
            panic(err)
    }
    b, err := os.ReadFile("ascii.txt")
    if err != nil {
            panic(err)
    }
    decoder := enc.NewDecoder()
    encoded, err := decoder.Bytes(b)
    if err != nil {
            panic(err)
    }
    fmt.Println(string(encoded))
}
```

Iterating bytes and runes of strings

Go strings can be seen as a sequence of bytes, or as a sequence of runes. This section shows how you can iterate a string either way.

How to do it...

To iterate the bytes of a string, use indexes:

```go
for i:=0;i<len(str);i++ {
   fmt.Print(str[i]," ")
}
```

To iterate the runes of a string, use `range`:

```go
for index, c:=range str {
   fmt.Print(c," ")
}
```

How it works...

A Go string is a slice of bytes, so you would expect to be able to write a for-loop to iterate the bytes and runes of a string. You might think that you can do the following:

```go
strBytes := []byte(str)
strRunes := []rune(str)
```

However, converting a string to a slice of bytes or a slice of runes is an expensive operation. The first one creates a writeable copy of the bytes of the `str` string, and the second one creates a writeable copy of the runes of `str`. Remember that `rune` is `uint32`.

There are two forms of for-loop to iterate the elements of a string. The following for-loop will iterate the bytes of a string:

```
str:="Hello 世界"
for i:=0;i<len(str);i++ {
  fmt.Print(str[i]," ")
}
```

The output is as follows:

```
72 101 108 108 111 32 228 184 150 231 149 140
```

Also, note that `str[i]` will give you the i'th byte, not the i'th rune.

The following form iterates the runes of a string:

```
for i,r:=range str {
  fmt.Printf("( %d %d %s)", i, r, string(r))
}
```

The output is as follows:

```
(0  72 H)(1 101 e)(2 108 l)(3 108 l)(4 111 o)(5 32   )(6 19990 世)(9
30028 界)
```

Note the indexes – they go in a sequence of 0, 1, 2, 3, 4, 5, 6, 9. This is because `str[6]` contains a rune of 3 bytes, and so does `str[9]`.

When you are dealing with `[]byte` instead of a string, you can emulate the rune iteration, as follows:

```
import (
  "unicode/utf8"
  "fmt"
)

str:=[]byte("Hello 世界")
for i:=0;i<len(str); {
  r, n:=utf8.DecodeRune(str[i:])
  fmt.Print("(",i,r, " ",string(r),")")
  i+=n
}
```

The utf8.DecodeRune function decodes the next rune from the byte slice and returns that rune and the number of bytes consumed. This way, you can decode the runes of a byte slice without first converting it to a string.

Splitting

The strings package offers convenient functions to split a string to get a slice of strings.

How to do it...

- To split a string into components using a delimiter, use strings.Split.
- To split the space-separated components of a string, use strings.Fields.

How it works...

If you need to parse a string delimited with a fixed delimiter, use strings.Split. If you need to parse the space-separated sections of a string, use strings.Fields:

```
package main

import (
        "fmt"
        "strings"
)

func main() {
    fmt.Println(strings.Split("a,b,c,d", ","))
    // ["a", "b", "c", "d"]

    fmt.Println(strings.Split("a, b, c, d", ","))
    // ["a", " b", " c", " d"]

    fmt.Println(strings.Fields("a    b    c  d  "))
    // ["a", "b", "c", "d"]

    fmt.Println(strings.Split("a---b---c--d--", "-"))
    // ["a", "", "", "b", "", "", "c", "", "d", "", ""]
}
```

Note that strings.Split may cause some surprises when the delimiter is repeated. For instance, with "-" as the delimiter, "a---b" splits into "a", "", "", and "b". The two empty strings are those between the first and second "-", and the second and third "-".

Reading strings line by line, or word by word

There are many use cases for processing strings in a stream, such as when dealing with large text or user input. This recipe shows the use of bufio.Scanner for this purpose.

How to do it...

- Use bufio.Scanner for reading lines, words, or custom blocks.
- Create a bufio.Scanner instance
- Set the split method
- Read scanned tokens in a for-loop

How it works...

The Scanner works like an iterator – every call to Scan() method will return true if it parsed the next token, or false if there are no more tokens. The token can be obtained by the Text() method:

```go
package main

import (
    "bufio"
    "fmt"
    "strings"
)

const input = `This is a string
that has 3
lines.`

func main() {
    lineScanner := bufio.NewScanner(strings.NewReader(input))
    line := 0
    for lineScanner.Scan() {
        text := lineScanner.Text()
        line++
        fmt.Printf("Line %d: %s\n", line, text)
    }
    if err := lineScanner.Err(); err != nil {
        panic(err)
    }
    wordScanner := bufio.NewScanner(strings.NewReader(input))
    wordScanner.Split(bufio.ScanWords)
```

```
    word := 0
    for wordScanner.Scan() {
            text := wordScanner.Text()
            word++
            fmt.Printf("word %d: %s\n", word, text)
    }
    if err := wordScanner.Err(); err != nil {
            panic(err)
    }
}
```

The output is as follows:

```
Line 1: This is a string
Line 2: that has 3
Line 3: lines.
word 1: This
word 2: is
word 3: a
word 4: string
word 5: that
word 6: has
word 7: 3
word 8: lines.
```

Trimming the ends of a string

User input is usually messy, including additional spaces before or after the text that matters. This recipe shows how to use the string trimming functions for this purpose.

How to do it...

Use the strings.Trim family of functions, as shown here:

```
package main

import (
        "fmt"
        "strings"
)

func main() {
        fmt.Println(strings.TrimRight("Break-------", "-"))
        // Break
```

```
    fmt.Println(strings.TrimRight("Break with spaces-- -- --", "- "))
    // Break with spaces

    fmt.Println(strings.TrimSuffix("file.txt", ".txt"))
    // file

    fmt.Println(strings.TrimLeft(" \t   Indented text", " \t"))
    // Indented text

    fmt.Println(strings.TrimSpace(" \t \n  Indented text  \n\t"))
    // Indented text
}
```

Regular expressions

A regular expression offers efficient methods to ensure that textual data matches a given pattern, searches for patterns, extracts, and replaces parts of text. Usually, you compile a regular expression once and then use that compiled regular expression many times to efficiently validate, search, extract, or replace parts of strings.

Validating input

Format validation is the process of ensuring that data coming from user input or other sources is in a recognized format. Regular expressions can be an effective tool for such validation.

How to do it...

Use precompiled regular expressions to validate input values that should fit a pattern.

```
package main

import (
    "fmt"
    "regexp"
)

var integerRegexp = regexp.MustCompile("^[0-9]+$")

func main() {
    fmt.Println(integerRegexp.MatchString("123"))    // true
    fmt.Println(integerRegexp.MatchString(" 123 ")) // false
}
```

To ensure an exact match, make sure you include the beginning (^) and end-of-text markers ($); otherwise, you will end up accepting input **containing** strings that match the regular expression.

Not all types of input are suitable for regular expression validation. Some inputs have complicated regular expressions (such as the one for emails or password policies), so custom validations may work better for those.

Searching patterns

You can use a regular expression to search through textual data to locate strings matching a pattern.

How to do it...

Use the `regexp.Find` family of methods to search for substrings matching a pattern.

```
package main

import (
        "fmt"
        "regexp"
)

func main() {
        re := regexp.MustCompile(`[0-9]+`)
        fmt.Println(re.FindAllString("This regular expression find
        numbers, like 1, 100, 500, etc.", -1))
}
```

Here is the output:

```
[1 100 500]
```

Extracting data from strings

You can use a regular expression to locate and extract text that occurs within a pattern.

How to do it...

Use capture groups to extract substrings that match a pattern.

How it works...

```
package main

import (
```

```
        "fmt"
        "regexp"
)

func main() {
    re := regexp.MustCompile(`^(\w+)=(\w+)$`)
    result := re.FindStringSubmatch(`property=12`)
    fmt.Printf("Key: %s value: %s\n", result[1], result[2])
    result = re.FindStringSubmatch(`x=y`)
    fmt.Printf("Key: %s value: %s\n", result[1], result[2])
}
```

Here is the output:

```
Key: property value: 12
Key: x value: y
```

Let's look at this regular expression:

- `^(\w+)`: A string composed of one or more word characters at the beginning of the line (capture group 1)

- `=`: An "=" sign

- `(\w+)$`: A string composed of one or more word characters (capture group 2), and then the end of line

Note that the capture groups are in parentheses.

The `FindStringSubmatch` method returns the matching string as the 0th element of the slice, and then each capture group. Using the capture groups, you can extract data as above.

Replacing parts of a string

You can use a regular expression to search through text, replacing parts that match a pattern with other strings.

How to do it...

Use the `Replace` family of functions to replace the patterns in a string with something else:

```
package main

import (
        "fmt"
        "regexp"
```

```
)

func main() {
    // Find numbers, capture the first digit
    re := regexp.MustCompile(`([0-9])[0-9]*`)
    fmt.Println(re.ReplaceAllString("This example replaces
    numbers  with 'x': 1, 100, 500.", "x"))
    // This example replaces numbers  with 'x': x, x, x.
    fmt.Println(re.ReplaceAllString("This example replaces all
    numbers with their first digits: 1, 100, 500.", "${1}"))
    // This example replaces all numbers with their first digits: 1,
    // 1, 5.

}
```

Templates

Templates are useful for generating data-driven textual output. The `text/template` package can be used in the following contexts:

- **Configuration files**: You can accept templates in configuration files, such as the following example that uses an `env` map variable to create environment-sensitive configurations

  ```
  logfile: {{.env.logDir}}/log.json
  ```

- **Reporting**: Use templates to generate output for command-line applications and reports

- **Web applications**: The `html/template` package provides HTML-safe templating functionality for template-based HTML generation to build web applications

Value substitution

The main use of templates is inserting data elements into structured text. This section describes how you can insert values computed in a program into a template.

How to do it...

Use the `{{.name}}` syntax to substitute a value in a template.

The following code segment executes a template using different inputs:

```
package main

import (
    "os"
```

```
        "text/template"
)

type Book struct {
    Title    string
    Author   string
    PubYear  int
}

const tp = `The book "{{.Title}}" by {{.Author}} was published in
{{.PubYear}}.
`

func main() {
    book1 := Book{
        Title:    "Pride and Prejudice",
        Author:   "Jane Austen",
        PubYear:  1813,
    }
    book2 := Book{
        Title:    "The Lord of the Rings",
        Author:   "J.R.R. Tolkien",
        PubYear:  1954,
    }
    tmpl, err := template.New("book").Parse(tp)
    if err != nil {
        panic(err)
    }
    tmpl.Execute(os.Stdout, book1)
    tmpl.Execute(os.Stdout, book2)
}
```

The preceding program outputs the following:

```
The book "Pride and Prejudice" by Jane Austen was published in 1813.
The book "The Lord of the Rings" by J.R.R. Tolkien was published in
1954.
```

The `template.New(name)` call creates an empty template with the given name (there'll be more on this later). The returned template object represents a template body (which is empty after the `New()` call). The Go template engine uses a template representing the body, as well as zero or more named templates that are associated with that body. The `tmpl.Parse(tp)` call parses the `tp` template as the body for the given `named` template. If there are other template definitions in `tp` that are defined using the `{{define}}` construct, those are kept within `tmpl` as well.

`tmpl.Execute(os.Stdout,book1)` executes the template, writing the output to `os.Stdout`. The second argument, `book1`, is the data used to evaluate the template. You access it by `"."`. So, for instance, when `{{.Author}}` is evaluated, the template engine reads `book1.Author`, using reflection, and outputs its value. In other words, `.` is `book1` for the first `tmpl.Execute` call, and `.` is `book2` for the second `tmpl.Execute` call in the preceding example.

Since this is done using reflection, the following produces the same output:

```
tmpl.Execute(os.Stdout,map[string]any {
    "Title":"Pride and Prejudice",
    "Author":   "Jane Austen",
    "PubYear": 1813,
    })
```

Iteration

A template can include tabular data or lists that are populated using slices or maps computed in a program. Templates provide an iteration mechanism to render such content.

How to do it...

- For slices/arrays, do the following:

  ```
  {{ range <slice> }}
    // Here, {{.}} refers the subsequent elements of the slice/
  array
  {{end}}
  ```

- For maps, do the following:

  ```
  {{ range <map> }}
    // Here, {{.}} refers to the subsequent values (not keys) of
  the map
    // The iteration order of the map is not guaranteed
  {{end}}
  ```

  Alternatively, do the following:

  ```
  {{ range $key, $value := <map> }}
    // Here, {{$key}} and {{$value}} are variables that are set to
    // subsequent key-value pairs of the map
  {{end}}
  ```

How it works...

Use `range` to loop through slices and maps.

Modify the preceding example with the following:

```
const tpIter = `{{range .}}
The book "{{.Title}}" by {{.Author}} was published in {{.PubYear}}.
{{end}}`
```

Then, modify it with the following too:

```
...
tmpl, err = template.New("bookIter").Parse(tpIter)
if err != nil {
    panic(err)
}
tmpl.Execute(os.Stdout, []Book{book1, book2})
```

Here is the output:

```
The book "Pride and Prejudice" by Jane Austen was published in 1813.

The book "The Lord of the Rings" by J.R.R. Tolkien was published in
1954.
```

Now, note that . is a slice of books, so we can range through the elements of it. When evaluating the section within `{{range .}}`, . is set to successive elements of the slice – during the first iteration, . is book1, and during the second iteration, . is book2.

We will deal with the empty lines shortly.

The same thing happens for maps:

```
tmpl.Execute(os.Stdout, map[int]Book{
    1: book1,
    2: book2,
})
```

Variables and scope

It is often necessary to define local variables within templates to keep computed values. The variables defined in templates follow similar scoping rules as variables defined in functions – the `{{range}}`, `{{if}}`, `{{with}}` and `{{define}}` blocks create a new scope.

A variable defined in a scope is accessible in all the scopes contained within that scope, but it is not accessible outside of it.

How to do it...

. (**dot**) refers to the "current object," as follows:

- At the top-level scope, . refers to the object passed as the data argument of the Execute method
- Inside a {{range}}, . refers to the current slice/array/map element
- Inside a {{with <expr>}}, . refers to the value of <expr>
- Inside a {{define}} block, . refers to the value of the object passed into {{template "name" <object>}}
- .X refers to the member named X in the current object:

  - If . is a map, then .X evaluates to the element with the X key
  - If . is a struct, then .X evaluates to the **exported** X member variable

> **Tip**
>
> Note the emphasis on **exported**. The template engine uses reflection to find the value of X in the current object. If the current object is a struct, reflection can only access the exported fields, so you cannot access unexported variables. However, if the current object is a map, this becomes a key lookup, and there is no such restriction. In other words, {{.name}} will only work if . is a map, but {{.Name}} will work for a . struct and a . map.

Define a new local variable that is visible in the current scope using the following:

```
$name := value
```

How it works...

Use the $name notation to assign a computed value to a variable instead of recomputing it every time:

```
{{ $disabled := false }}
{{ if eq .Selection "1"}}
  {{ $disabled = true }}
{{ end }}

<input type="text" value="{{.Value1}}" {{if $disabled}}
disabled{{end}}>
<input type="text" value="{{.Value2}}" {{if $disabled}}
disabled{{end}}>
```

The first section of this template is equivalent to the following:

```
disabled := false
if data.Selection == "1" {
  disabled=true
}
```

$ is necessary as the first character of the variable name. Without that, the template engine will think `name` is a function.

There's more – nested loops and conditionals

When you are dealing with nested loops or conditions, scoping can become a challenge. Every `{{range}}`, `{{if}}`, and `{{with}}` create a new scope. Variables defined within a scope are only accessible in that scope and all scopes enclosed in it. You can use this to create nested loops and still access variables defined in the enclosing scope:

```
type Book struct {
      Title    string
      Author   string
      Editions []Edition
}

type Edition struct {
      Edition int
      PubYear int
}

const tp = `{{range $bookIndex, $book := .}}
{{$book.Author}}
{{range $book.Editions}}
   {{$book.Title}} Edition: {{.Edition}} {{.PubYear}}
{{end}}
{{end}}`
```

In this template, the first `range` defines the loop index, `$bookIndex`, and the loop variable, `$book`, that can be used in the nested scopes. At this stage, . points to the slice of `Book` fields. The next `range` iterates the current `$book.Editions` – that is, . now points to the successive elements of the `Book.Editions` slice. The nested template accesses both the `Edition` fields and the `Book` fields from the enclosing scope.

Dealing with empty lines

Template actions (i.e., the code elements placed in a template) may result in unwanted empty spaces and lines. The Go template system offers some mechanisms to deal with these unwanted spaces.

How to do it...

Use - next to the template delimiter:

- `{{-`   will remove all spaces/tabs/newlines that were output before this template element
- `-}}` will remove all spaces/tabs/newlines that come after this template element

If a template directive produces output, such as the value of a variable, it will be written to the output stream. But if a template directive does not generate any output, such as a `{{range}}` or `{{if}}` statement, then it will be replaced with empty strings. And if those statements are on a line by themselves, those lines will be written to the output as well, like this:

```
{{range .}}
  {{if gt . 1}}
    {{.}}
  {{end}}
{{end}}
```

This template will produce an output every four lines. When there is nothing to output, it will print three empty lines.

Fix this by using "-" inside the `{{  }}` constructs. `{{  -}}` will remove all empty space (including lines) coming after, and `{{-  }}` will remove all empty spaces before, as follows:

```
{{range . -}}
  {{ if gt . 1 }}
    {{- . }}
  {{end -}}
{{end -}}
```

Here is the output:

```
2
  3
  4
  5
```

How can we get rid of the spaces at the beginning of each line? First, we have to find out why they are there, which is shown here:

```
    {{- . }}
__{{end -}}
```

The first "-" will remove all spaces before the value. We cannot put -}} in this line, or {{- end}}, as these solutions would remove line feeds as well. But we can do this:

```
{{range . -}}
{{ if gt . 1 }}
  {{- . }}
{{end -}}
{{end -}}
```

This will produce the following:

```
2
3
4
5
```

Template composition

As templates grow, they may become repetitive. To reduce such repetition, the Go template system offers named blocks (components) that can be reused within a template, just like functions in a program. Then, the final template can be composed of these components.

How to do it...

You can create template "components" that you can reuse in multiple contexts. To define a named template, use the {{define "name"}} construct:

```
{{define "template1"}}
  ...
{{end}}

{{define "template2"}}
  ...
{{end}}
```

Then, call that template using the `{{template "name" .}}` construct as if it is a function with a single argument:

```
{{template "template1" .}}
{{range .List}}
  {{template "template2" .}}
{{end}}
```

How it works...

The following example prints a book list using a named template:

```
package main

import (
    "os"
    "text/template"
)

const tp = `{{define "line"}}
{{.Title}} {{.Author}} {{.PubYear}}
{{end}}
Book list:
{{range . -}}
  {{template "line" .}}
{{end -}}
`

type Book struct {
    Title   string
    Author  string
    PubYear int
}

var books = []Book{
    {
        Title:   "Pride and Prejudice",
        Author:  "Jane Austen",
        PubYear: 1813,
    },
    {
        Title:   "To Kill a Mockingbird",
        Author:  "Harper Lee",
        PubYear: 1960,
```

```
        },
        {
                Title:    "The Great Gatsby",
                Author:   "F. Scott Fitzgerald",
                PubYear: 1925,
        },
        {
                Title:    "The Lord of the Rings",
                Author:   "J.R.R. Tolkien",
                PubYear: 1954,
        },
}

func main() {
        tmpl, err := template.New("body").Parse(tp)
        if err != nil {
                panic(err)
        }
        tmpl.Execute(os.Stdout, books)
}
```

The `tmpl` template contains two templates in this example – the template named `"body"` (because it is created with `template.New("body")`), and the template named `"line"` (because the template contains `{{define "line"}}`.) For each element of the slice, the `"body"` template instantiates `"line"` with successive elements of the `books` slice.

This is equivalent to the following:

```
const lineTemplate = `{{.Title}} {{.Author}} {{.PubYear}}`
const bodyTemplate = `Book list:
{{range . -}}
  {{template "line" .}}
{{end -}}`

func main() {
        tmpl, err := template.New("body").Parse(bodyTemplate)
        if err != nil {
                panic(err)
        }
        _, err = tmpl.New("line").Parse(lineTemplate)
        if err != nil {
                panic(err)
        }
        tmpl.Execute(os.Stdout, books)
}
```

Template composition – layout templates

When developing web applications, it is usually desirable to have a few templates specifying page layouts. Complete web pages are constructed by combining page components, developed as independent templates using this layout. Unfortunately, the Go template engine forces you to think of alternative solutions because Go template references are static. This means you would need a separate layout template for each page.

But there are alternatives.

I'll show you a basic idea that demonstrates how template composition can be used so that you can extend it, based on your use case, or how to use an available third-party library that does this. The crucial idea in composition using layout templates is that if you define a new template using an already-defined template name, the new definition overrides the older one.

How to do it...

- Create a layout template. Use empty templates or templates with default content for the sections you will redefine for each occasion.

- Create a configuration system where you define every possible composition. Each composition includes the layout template, as well as the templates defining the sections in the layout template.

- Compile each composition as a separate template.

How it works...

Create a layout template:

```
const layout=`
<!doctype html>
<html lang="en">
  <head>
  <title>{{template "pageTitle" .}}</title>
  </head>
  <body>
  {{template "pageHeader" .}}
  {{template "pageBody" .}}
  {{template "pageFooter" .}}
  </body>
</html>
{{define "pageTitle"}}{{end}}
{{define "pageHeader"}}{{end}}
{{define "pageBody"}}{{end}}
{{define "pageFooter"}}{{end}}`
```

This layout template defines four named templates with no content. For each new page, we can recreate these components:

```
const mainPage=`
{{define "pageTitle"}}Main Page{{end}}

{{define "pageHeader"}}
<h1>Main page</h1>
{{end}}

{{define "pageBody"}}
This is the page body.
{{end}}

{{define "pageFooter"}}
This is the page footer.
{{end}}`
```

We can define a second page, similar to the first one:

```
const secondPage=`
{{define "pageTitle"}}Second page{{end}}

{{define "pageHeader"}}
<h1>Second page</h1>
{{end}}

{{define "pageBody"}}
This is the page body for the second page.
{{end}}`
```

Now, we compose layout with mainPage to get the template for the main page, and then layout with secondPage to get the template for the second page:

```
import (
    "html/template"
)

func main() {
    mainPageTmpl := template.Must(template.New("body").Parse(layout))
    template.Must(mainPageTmpl.Parse(mainPage))

    secondPageTmpl := template.Must(template.New("body").
    Parse(layout))
```

```
      template.Must(secondPageTmpl.Parse(secondPage))
      mainPageTmpl.Execute(os.Stdout, nil)
      secondPageTmpl.Execute(os.Stdout, nil)
}
```

You can extend this pattern to build a sophisticated web application using layout templates, as well as a configuration file defining all the valid compositions of templates for each page. Such a YAML file looks like the following:

```
mainPage:
  - layouts/main.html
  - mainPage.html
  - fragments/status.html

detailPage:
  - layouts/2col.html
  - detailPage.html
  - fragments/status.html
...
```

When the application starts, you build each template for `mainPage` and `detailPage` by parsing its constituent templates in the given order, putting each template in a map. Then, you can look up the template name you want to generate and use the parsed template.

There's more...

The Go standard library documentation is always your best source for up-to-date information and great examples, such as the following:

- `https://pkg.go.dev/strings`
- `https://pkg.go.dev/text/template`
- `https://pkg.go.dev/html/template`
- `https://pkg.go.dev/fmt`
- `https://pkg.go.dev/bufio`

The following links are also useful:

- *Character Model for the World Wide Web: String Matching*: `https://www.w3.org/TR/charmod-norm/`
- *Character Properties, Case Mappings & Names FAQ*: `https://unicode.org/faq/casemap_charprop.html`

- RFC7564: PRECIS `https://www.rfc-editor.org/rfc/rfc7564`

- This is a great blog post about the Unicode normalization process: `https://go.dev/blog/normalization`

- For all encoding, internationalization, and Unicode-related problems that are not handled by the standard library, take a look at the packages here before searching for anything else: `https://pkg.go.dev/golang.org/x/text`

3

Working with Date and Time

Working with date and time can be difficult in any programming language. Go's standard library offers easy-to-use tools to work with date and time constructs. These may be somewhat different from what many people are used to. For example, there are libraries in different languages that make a distinction between a `time` type and a `date` type. Go's standard library only includes a `time.Time` type. That might make you feel disoriented when you're working with Go's time.

I'd like to think that Go's treatment of date/time reduces the chances of creating subtle bugs. You see, you have to be really careful and clear about what you mean when you talk about time: are you talking about a point in time or an interval? A date is actually an interval (for instance, 08/01/2024 starts at 08/01/2024T00:00:00 and continues until 08/01/2024T23:59:59) even though usually that is not the intent. A specific date/time value also depends on where you are measuring time. 2023-11-05T08:00 in Denver, Colorado is different from 2023-11-05T08:00 in Berlin, Germany. Time always moves forward, but date/time may skip or go backward: after 2023-11-05T02:59 in Denver, Colorado, time goes back to 2023-11-05T02:00 because that is when daylight savings time ends in Colorado. So there are actually two time instances for 2023-11-05T02:10:10, one in Mountain Daylight Time, and one in Mountain Standard Time.

There are many software bugs in production today that handle time incorrectly. For example, if you are computing when the subscription of a customer ends, you have to take into account the location of that customer and the time of day that subscription ends, otherwise, their subscriptions may terminate early (or late) on their last day.

This chapter contains the following recipes for working with date/time correctly:

- Working with Unix time
- Date/time components
- Date/time arithmetic
- Formatting and parsing date/time
- Working with time zones

- Timers

- Tickers

- Storing time information

Working with Unix time

Unix time is the number of seconds (or milliseconds, microseconds, or nanoseconds) passed since January 1, 1970 UTC (the epoch.) Go uses `int64` to represent these values, so Unix time as seconds can represent billions of years into the past or the future. Unix time as nanoseconds can represent date values between 1678 and 2262. Unix time is an absolute measure of an instance as the duration since (or until) the epoch. It is independent of the location, so with two Unix times, s and t, if s<t, then s happened before t, no matter the location. Because of these properties, Unix time is usually used as a timestamp that marks when an event happened (when a log is written, when a record is inserted, etc.).

How to do it...

- To get the current Unix time, use the following:

  - `time.Now().Unix()` `int64`: Unix time in seconds

  - `time.Now().UnixMilli()` `int64`: Unix time in milliseconds

  - `time.Now().UnixMicro()` `int64`: Unix time in microseconds

  - `time.Now().UnixNano()` `int64`: Unix time in nanoseconds

- Given a Unix time, convert it to a `time.Time` type using the following:

  - `time.Unix(sec, nanosec int64)` `time.Time`: Translate Unix time in seconds and/or nanoseconds to `time.Time`

  - `time.UnixMilli(int64)` `time.Time`: Translate Unix time in milliseconds to `time.Time`

  - `time.UnixMicro(int64)` `time.Time`: Translate Unix time in microseconds to `time.Time`

- To translate a Unix time to local time, use `localTime := time.Unix(unixTimeSeconds,0).In(location)`, where `location` is a `*time.Location` for the location in which to interpret the Unix time

Date/time components

When working with date values, you often have to compose a date/time from its components or need to access the components of a date/time value. This recipe shows how it can be done.

How to do it...

- To build a date/time value from parts, use the `time.Date` function

- To get the parts of a date/time value, use the `time.Time` methods:

  - `time.Day() int`

  - `time.Month() time.Month`

  - `time.Year() int`

  - `time.Date() (year, month, day int)`

  - `time.Hour() int`

  - `time.Minute() int`

  - `time.Second() int`

  - `time.Nanosecond() int`

  - `time.Zone() (name string, offset int)`

  - `time.Location() *time.Location`

`time.Date` will create a time value from its components:

```
d := time.Date(2020, 3, 31, 15, 30, 0, 0, time.UTC)
fmt.Println(d)
// 2020-03-31 15:30:00 +0000 UTC
```

The output will be normalized, as follows:

```
d := time.Date(2020, 3, 0, 15, 30, 0, 0, time.UTC)
fmt.Println(d)
// 2020-02-29 15:30:00 +0000 UTC
```

Since the day of the month starts from 1, creating a date with a 0 day will result in the last day of the previous month.

Once you have a `time.Time` value, you can get its components:

```
d := time.Date(2020, 3, 0, 15, 30, 0, 0, time.UTC)
fmt.Println(d.Day())
// 29
```

Again, `time.Date` normalizes the date value, so `d.Day()` will return 29.

Date/time arithmetic

Date/time arithmetic is necessary to answer questions such as the following:

- How long did it take to complete an operation?
- What time will it be after 5 minutes?
- How many days are there until next month?

This recipe shows how you can answer these questions using the `time` package.

How to do it...

- To find out how much time has passed between two instances in time, use the `Time.Sub` method to subtract them.
- To find the duration from now to a later time, use `time.Until(laterTime)`.
- To find how much time has passed since a given time, use `time.Since(beforeTime)`.
- To find out what time it will be after a certain duration, use the `Time.Add` method. Use negative duration to find the time before a certain duration.
- To add/subtract years, months, or days to/from a time, use the `Time.AddDate` method.
- To compare two `time.Time` values, use the following:

  - `Time.Equal` to check whether two time values represent the same instance
  - `Time.Before` or `Time.After` to check whether a time value is before or after a given time value

How it works...

A `time.Duration` type represents the time elapsed between two instances in nanoseconds as an `int64` value. In other words, if you subtract a `time.Time` value from another, you get a `time.Duration`:

```
dur := tm1.Sub(tm2)
```

Since `Duration` is an `int64` representing nanoseconds, you can do duration arithmetic:

```
// Add 1 day to duration
dur+=time.Hour*24
```

Note that the last operation in the preceding also involves multiplication since `time.Hour` is of the `time.Duration` type itself.

You can add a duration value to a `time.Time` value:

```
now := time.Now()
then := now.Add(dur)
```

> **Tip**
>
> Duration being an `int64` means that a `time.Duration` value is limited to around 290 years. This should be sufficient for most practical cases. However, if this is not the case for you, you need to build a solution for yourself or find a third-party library.

You can subtract the duration from a `time.Time` value by adding a negative duration value:

```
fmt.Println( then.Add(-dur).Equal(now) )
```

Note the use of the `Time.Equal` method. This compares two time instances taking into account their time zones, which can be different. For instance, `Time.Equal` will return `true` for `2024-01-09 09:00 MST` and `2024-01-09 08:00 PST`.

Use `Time.Before` and `Time.After` to compare time values. For instance, you can check whether an object with an expiration date has expired by using the following:

```
if object.Expiration.After(time.Now()) {
    // Object expired
}
```

You can also add years/months/days to a given date:

```
t:=time.Now()
// Subtract 1 year from now to get this moment in last year
lastYear := t.AddDate(-1,0,0)
// Add 1 day to get same time tomorrow
tomorrow := t.AddDate(0,0,1)
// Add 1 day to get the next month
nextMonth := t.AddDate(0,1,0)
```

The result of these operations will be normalized. For instance, if you subtract a year from `2020-02-29`, you will get `2019-03-01`. This causes problems when you are working with a date at the end of a month and you have to add/subtract month values. Adding a month to `2020-03-31` twice will yield `2020-06-01`, but adding two months will yield `2020-05-31`:

```
d := time.Date(2020, 3, 31, 0, 0, 0, 0, time.UTC)
fmt.Println(d.AddDate(0, 1, 0).AddDate(0, 1, 0))
// 2020-06-01 00:00:00 +0000 UTC
fmt.Println(d.AddDate(0, 2, 0))
// 2020-05-31 00:00:00 +0000 UTC
```

Formatting and parsing date/time

Go uses an interesting and somewhat controversial date/time formatting scheme. The date/time format is expressed using a specific point in time, adjusted such that every component of the date/time is a unique number:

- 1 is the month: "Jan" "January" "01" "1"

- 2 is the day of the month: "2" "_2" "02"

- 3 is the hour of the day in a 12-hour format: "15" "3" "03"

- 15 is the hour of the day in a 24-hour format,

- 4 is the minute: "4" "04"

- 5 is the second: "5" "05"

- 6 is the year: "2006" "06"

- MST is the timezone: "-0700" "-07:00" "-07" "-070000" "-07:00:00" "MST"

- 0 is the millisecond padded with 0s: "0" "000"

- 9 is the millisecond that is not padded: "9" "999"

How to do it...

- Use `time.Parse` with an appropriate format to parse date/time. Any parts of the date/time that are not specified in the format will be initialized to its zero value, which is January for months, 1 for the year, 1 for the day of the month, and 0 for everything else. If the time zone information is missing, the parsed date/time will be in UTC.

- Use `time.ParseInLocation` to parse date/time in a given location. The time zone will be determined based on the date value and the location.

- Use the `Format()` method to format a date/time value.

```go
func main() {
    t := time.Date(2024, 3, 8, 18, 2, 13, 500, time.UTC)

    fmt.Println("Date in yyyy/mm/dd format", t.Format("2006/01/02"))
    // Date in yyyy/mm/dd format 2024/03/08
    fmt.Println("Date in yyyy/m/d format", t.Format("2006/1/2"))
    // Date in yyyy/m/d format 2024/3/8
    fmt.Println("Date in yy/m/d format", t.Format("06/1/2"))
    // Date in yy/m/d format 24/3/8
    fmt.Println("Time in hh:mm format (12 hr)", t.Format("03:04"))
    // Time in hh:mm format (12 hr) 06:02
```

```
    fmt.Println("Time in hh:m format (24 hr)", t.Format("15:4"))
    // Time in hh:m format (24 hr) 18:2
    fmt.Println("Date-time with time zone", t.Format("2006-01-02
    13:04:05 -07:00"))
    // Date-time with time zone 2024-03-08 36:02:13 +00:00
}
```

Time zones change by location and by date. In the following example, even though the same location is used to parse the date, the time zone changes because July 9 is Mountain Daylight Time, but January 9 is Mountain Standard Time:

```
loc, _ := time.LoadLocation("America/Denver")
const format = "Jan 2, 2006 at 3:04pm"
str, _ := time.ParseInLocation(format, "Jul 9, 2012 at 5:02am", loc)
fmt.Println(str)
// 2012-07-09 05:02:00 -0600 MDT
str, _ = time.ParseInLocation(format, "Jan 9, 2012 at 5:02am", loc)
fmt.Println(str)
// 2012-01-09 05:02:00 -0700 MST
```

Working with time zones

The Go time.Time value includes time.Location, which can be one of two things:

- A real location, such as America/Denver. If this is the case, the actual time zone depends on the time value. For Denver, the time zone will be either MDT (Mountain Daylight Time) or MST (Mountain Standard Time) depending on the actual time value

- A fixed time zone that gives the offset.

Some applications work with **local time**. This is the date/time value captured at a particular location, and interpreted as the same value everywhere, as opposed to being interpreted as the same point in time. Birthdays (and thus, ages) are usually interpreted using local time. That is, if you are born on 2005-07-14, you will be considered 2 years old in New York (Eastern time zone) on 2007-07-14 at 00:00, but still be 1 year old at the same moment in time in Los Angeles, which is 2007-07-13 at 21:00 (Pacific time zone).

How to do it...

If you are working with moments in time, always capture date/time values with the associated location. Such date/time values can be translated into other time zones easily.

If you are working with local time in multiple time zones, recreate time.Time in a new location or time zone to translate.

How it works...

When you create a time.Time, it is always associated with a location:

```
// Create a new time using the local time zone
t := time.Date(2021,12,31,15,0,0,0, time.Local)
// 2021-12-31 15:00:00 -0700 MST
```

Once you have a time.Time, you can get the same moment in time in different time zones:

```
utcTime := t.In(time.UTC)
fmt.Println(utcTime)
// 2021-12-31 22:00:00 +0000 UTC

ny,err:=time.LoadLocation("America/New_York")
if err!=nil {
   panic(err)
}
nyTime := t.In(ny)
fmt.Println(nyTime)
// 2021-12-31 17:00:00 -0500 EST
```

These are different representations of the same moment in time in different time zones.

You can also create a custom time zone:

```
zone30 := time.FixedZone("30min", 30)
fmt.Println(t.In(zone30))
// 2021-12-31 22:00:30 +0000 30min
```

When you are dealing with local time, you discard the location and time zone information:

```
// Create a local time, UTC zone
t := time.Date(2021,12,31,15,0,0,0, time.UTC)
// 2021-12-31 15:00:00 +0000 UTC
```

To get the same time value in New York, use the following:

```
ny,err:=time.LoadLocation("America/New_York")
if err!=nil {
   panic(err)
}
nyTime := time.Date(t.Year(), t.Month(), t.Day(), t.Hour(),
t.Minute(), t.Second(), t.Nanosecond(), ny)
fmt.Println(nyTime)
// 2021-12-31 15:00:00 -0500 EST
```

Storing time information

A common problem is storing date/time information in databases, files, and so on in a portable manner, so that it can be interpreted correctly.

How to do it...

You should first identify the exact needs: do you need to store an instant of time or time of day?

- To store an instant of time, do one of the following:

  - Store Unix time at the needed granularity (that is, `time.Unix` for seconds, `time.UnixMilli` for milliseconds, etc.)

  - Store UTC time (`time.UTC()`)

- To store the time of day, store the `time.Duration` value that gives the instant in the day. The following function computes the instant within that day as `time.Duration`:

  ```
  func GetTimeOfDay(t time.Time) time.Duration {
    beginningOfDay:=time.Date(t.Year(),t.Month(),t.
    Day(),0,0,0,0,t.Location())
    return t.Sub(beginningOfDay)
  }
  ```

- To store a date value, you can clear the time portions of `time.Time`:

  ```
  date:=time.Date(t.Year(), t.Month(), t.Day(), 0,0,0,0,t.
  Location())
  ```

  Note that comparing dates stored in this manner can be problematic as each day will be interpreted to be a different instant in different time zones.

Timers

Use `time.Timer` to schedule some work to be done in the future. When the timer expires, you will receive a signal from a channel. You can use a timer to run a function later or to cancel a process that ran too long.

How to do it...

You can create a timer in one of two ways:

- Use `time.NewTimer` or `time.After`. The timer will send a signal through a channel when it expires. Use a `select` statement, or read from the channel to receive the timer expiration signal.

- Use `time.AfterFunc` to call a function when the timer expires.

How it works...

A `time.Timer` timer is created with `time.Duration`:

```
// Create a 10-second timer
timer := time.NewTimer(time.Second*10)
```

The timer contains a channel that will receive the current timestamp after 10 seconds pass. A timer is created with a channel capacity of 1, so the timer runtime will always be able to write to that channel and stop the timer. In other words, if you fail to read from a timer, it will not leak; it will eventually be garbage collected.

The timer can be used to stop a long-running process:

```
func longProcess() {
    timer := time.NewTimer(time.Second*10)
    for {
        processData()
        select {
          case <-timer.C:
              // 2 seconds passed
              return
          default:
        }
    }
}
```

The following example shows how a timer can be used to limit the time it takes to return from a function. If the computation completes within a second, the response is returned. If the computation takes longer, the function returns a channel that the caller can use to receive the result. This function also demonstrates how you can stop a timer:

```
func longComputation() (concurrent chan Result, result Result) {
    timer:=time.NewTimer(time.Second)
    concurrent=make(chan Result)
    // Start the concurrent computation. Its result will be received
    // from the channel
    go func() {
        concurrent <- processData()
    }()
    // Wait until result is available, or timer expires
    select {
        case result:=<-concurrent:
            // Result became available quickly. Stop the timer and return
```

```
        //the result.
        timer.Stop()
        return nil,result
    case <-timer.C:
        // Timer expired before result is computed. Return the channel
        return concurrent,Result{}
    }
}
```

Note that the timer can expire right before the `timer.Stop()` call. This is okay. Timers will eventually expire and be garbage collected. Calling `timer.Stop()` simply prevents the timer from being active longer than necessary.

> **Tip**
>
> You cannot call `Timer.Stop` concurrently while another goroutine is listening from the timer. So, if you have to call `Timer.Stop`, call it from the same goroutine that listens to the timer's channel.

The same thing can be achieved with `time.After`:

```
concurrent=make(chan Result)
// Start the concurrent computation. Its result will be received
// from the channel
go func() {
    concurrent <- processData()
}()
select {
    case result:=<-concurrent:
        return nil,result
    case <-time.After(time.Second):
        return concurrent,Result{}
}
```

Tickers

Use `time.Ticker` to perform a task periodically. You will periodically receive a signal through a channel. Unlike `time.Timer`, you have to be careful about how you dispose of tickers. If you forget to stop a ticker, it will not be garbage collected once it is out of scope, and it will leak.

How to do it...

1. Use time.Ticker to create a new ticker.

2. Read from the ticker's channel to receive the periodic ticks.

3. When you are done with the ticker, stop it. You don't have to drain the ticker's channel.

How it works...

Use a ticker for periodic events. A common pattern is the following:

```go
func poorMansClock(done chan struct{}) {
  // Create a new ticker with a 1 second period
  ticker:=time.NewTicker(time.Second)
  // Stop the ticker once we're done
  defer ticker.Stop()
  for {
    select {
      case <-done:
          return
      case <-ticker.C:
          fmt.Println(time.Now())
    }
  }
}
```

What happens if you miss ticks? This is possible if you run a long process that prevents you from listening to the ticker channel. Will the ticker send a flood of ticks when you start listening again?

Similar to time.Timer, time.Ticker uses a channel with a capacity of 1. Because of this, if you do not read from the channel, it can store, at most, one tick. When you start listening from the channel again, you will receive the tick that you missed immediately, and the next tick when its period expires. For example, consider the following program that calls a given function every second:

```go
func everySecond(f func(), done chan struct{}) {
  // Create a new ticker with a 1 second period
  ticker:=time.NewTicker(time.Second)
  start:=time.Now()
  // Stop the ticker once we're done
  defer ticker.Stop()
  for {
    select {
      case <-done:
          return
      case <-ticker.C:
```

```
        fmt.Println(time.Since(start).Milliseconds())
        // Call the function
        f()
      }
    }
}
```

Let's say the first call to f() runs for 10 milliseconds, but the second call runs for 1.5 seconds. While f() is running, there is nobody reading from the ticker's channel, so a tick will be missed. Once f() returns, the select statement will immediately read this missed tick, and after 500 milliseconds, it will receive the next tick. The output looks like this:

```
1000
2000
3500
4000
5000
. . .
```

> **Tip**
> Unlike time.Timer, you can stop a ticker concurrently while reading from its channel.

4

Working with Arrays, Slices, and Maps

Arrays, slices, and maps are the built-in container types defined by the Go language. They are essential parts of almost every program, and usually, the building blocks of other data structures. This section describes some of the common patterns of working with these basic data structures, as they have nuances that may not be obvious to a newcomer.

In this chapter, we will talk about the following:

- Working with arrays
- Working with slices
- Implementing a stack using slices
- Working with maps
- Implementing sets
- Using maps for thread-safe caching

Working with arrays

Arrays are fixed-size data structures. There is no way to resize an array or to create an array using a variable as its size (in other words, [n] int is valid only if n is a constant integer). Because of this, arrays are useful to represent an object with a fixed number of elements, such as a SHA256 hash, which is 32 bytes.

The zero-value for an array has zero-values for every element of the array. For instance, [5] int is initialized with five integers, all 0. A string array will have empty strings.

Creating arrays and passing them around

This recipe shows how you can create arrays and pass array values to functions and methods. We will also talk about the effects of passing arrays as values.

How to do it...

1. Create arrays using a fixed size:

   ```
   var arr [2]int // Array of 2 ints
   ```

   You can also declare an array using an array literal without specifying its size:

   ```
   x := [...]int{1,2} // Array of 2 ints
   ```

   You can specify array indexes similar to defining a map:

   ```
   y := [...]int{1, 4: 10} // Array of 5 ints,
   // [0]1, y[4]=10, all other elements are 0
   // [1 0 0 0 10]
   ```

2. Use arrays to define new types of fixed-size data:

   ```
   // SHA256 hash is 256 bits - 32 bytes
   type SHA256 [32]byte
   ```

3. Arrays are passed by value:

   ```
   func main() {
     var h SHA256
     h = getHash()
     // f will get a 32-byte array that is a copy of h
     f(h)
   ...
   }

   func f(hash SHA256) {
     hash[0]=0 // This changes the copy of `hash` passed to `f`.
               // It does not affect the `h` value declared in main
     ...
   }
   ```

> **Warning**
>
> Passing an array by value means that every time you use an array as an argument to a function, the array will be copied. If you pass an array `[1000] int64` to a function, the runtime will allocate and copy 8,000 bytes (int64 is 64 bits, which is 8 bytes, and 1,000 int64 values is 8,000 bytes.) The copy will be a shallow copy – that is, you pass an array containing pointers, or, if you pass an array containing structures containing pointers, the pointers will be copied, not the contents of those pointers.

See the following example:

```
func f(m [2]map[string]int) {
    m[0]["x"]=1
}

func main() {
  array := [2]map[string]int{}
  // A copy of array is passed to f
  // but array[0] and array[1] are maps
  // Contents of those maps are not copied.
  f(array)
  fmt.Println(array[0])
  // This will print [x:1]
}
```

Working with slices

A slice is a view over an array. You may be dealing with multiple slices that work with the same underlying data.

The zero-value for a slice is nil. Reading or writing a nil slice will `panic`; however, you can append to a nil slice, which will create a new slice.

Creating slices

There are several ways a slice can be created.

How to do it...

Use `make(sliceType,length[,capacity])`:

```
slice1 := make([]int,0)
// len(slice1)=0, cap(slice1)=0
slice2 := make([]int,0,10)
```

```
// len(slice2)=0, cap(slice2)=10
slice3 := make([]int,10)
// len(slice3)=10, cap(slice3)=10
```

In the previous code snippet, you see three different uses of make to create a slice:

- slice1:=make([]int,0) creates an empty slice, 0 being the length of the slice. The slice1 variable is initialized as a non-nil, 0-length slice.

- slice2 := make([]int,0,10) creates an empty slice with capacity 10. This is what you should prefer if you know the likely maximum size for this slice. This slice allocation avoids an allocate/copy operation up until the 11th element is appended.

- slice3 := make([]int,10) creates a slice with size 10 and capacity 10. The slice elements are initialized to 0. In general, with this form, the allocated slice will be initialized to the zero-value of its element type.

> **Tip**
>
> Be careful about allocating a slice with a non-zero length. I personally had to deal with really obscure bugs because I mistyped make([]int,10) instead of make([]int,0,10), and continued to append the 10 elements to the allocated slice, ending with 20 elements.

See the following example:

```
values:=make([]string,10)
for _,s:=range results {
   if someFunc(s) {
      values=append(values,s)
   }
}
```

The previous code snippet creates a string slice that has 10 empty strings, then the strings are appended by the for-loop.

You can also initialize a slice using a literal:

```
slice := []int{1,2,3,4,5}
// len(slice)=5 cap(slice)=5
```

Alternatively, you can leave a slice variable nil, and append to it. The append built-in will accept a nil slice, and create one:

```
// values slice is nil after declaration
var values []string
for _,x:=range results {
```

```
  if someFunc(s) {
    values=appennd(values, s)
  }
}
```

Creating a slice from an array

Many functions will accept slices and not arrays. If you have an array of values and need to pass it to a function that wants a slice, you need to create a slice from an array. This is easy and efficient. Creating a slice from an array is a constant-time operation.

How to do it...

Use the [:] notation to create a slice from the array. The slice will have the array as its underlying storage:

```
arr := [...]int{0, 1, 2, 3, 4, 5}
slice := arr[:] // slice has all elements of arr
slice[2]=10
// Here, arr = [...]int{0,1,10,3, 4,5}
// len(slice) = 6
// cap(slice) = 6
```

You can create a slice pointing to a section of the array:

```
slice2 := arr[1:3]
// Here, slice2 = {1,10}
// len(slice2) = 2
// cap(slice2) = 5
```

You can slice an existing slice. The bounds of the slicing operation are determined by the capacity of the original slice:

```
slice3 := slice2[0:4]
// len(slice3)=4
// cap(slice3)=5
// slice3 = {1,10,3,4}
```

How it works...

A slice is a data structure containing three values: slice length, capacity, and pointer to the underlying array. Slicing an array simply creates this data structure with a pointer initialized to the array. It is a constant-time operation.

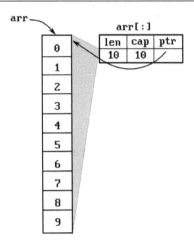

Figure 4.1 – Difference between an array arr and a slice arr[:]

Appending/inserting/deleting slice elements

Slices use arrays as their underlying storage, but it is not possible to grow arrays when you run out of space. Because of this, if an append operation exceeds the slice capacity, a new and larger array is allocated, and slice contents are copied to this new array.

How to do it...

To add new values to the end of the slice, use the append built-in function:

```
// Create an empty integer slice
islice := make([]int, 0)
// Append values 1, 2, 3 to islice, assign it to newSlice
newSlice := append(islice, 1, 2, 3)
// islice:   []
// newSlice: [1 2 3]

// Create an empty integer slice
islice = make([]int, 0)
// Another integer slice with 3 elements
otherSlice := []int{1, 2, 3}
// Append 'otherSlice' to 'islice'
newSlice = append(islice, otherSlice...)
newSlice = append(newSlice, otherSlice...)
// islice: []
// otherSlice: [1 2 3]
// newSlice: [1 2 3 1 2 3]
```

To remove elements from the beginning or the end of a slice, use slicing:

```
slice := []int{0, 1, 2, 3, 4, 5, 6, 7, 8, 9}
// Slice elements starting from index 1
suffix := slice[1:]
// suffix: [1 2 3 4 5 6 7 8 9]
// Slice elements starting from index 3
suffix2 := slice[3:]
// suffix2: [3 4 5 6 7 8 9]

// Slice elements up to index 5 (excluding 5)
prefix := slice[:5]
// prefix: [0 1 2 3 4]

// Slice elements from 3 up to index 6 (excluding 6)
mid := slice[3:6]
// [3 4 5]
```

Use the slices package to insert/delete elements from arbitrary locations in a slice:

- slices.Delete(slice,i,j) removes slice[i:j] elements from the slice and returns the modified slice
- slices.Insert(slice,i,value...) inserts the values starting at index i, shifting all elements starting from i to make space

```
slice := []int{0, 1, 2, 3, 4, 5, 6, 7, 8, 9}
// Remove the section slice[3:7]
edges := slices.Delete(slice, 3, 7)
// edges: [0 1 2 7 8 9]
// slice: [0 1 2 7 8 9 0 0 0 0]

inserted := slices.Insert(slice, 3, 3, 4)
// inserted: [0 1 2 3 4 7 8 9 0 0 0 0]
// edges: [0 1 2 7 8 9]
// slices: [0 1 2 7 8 9 0 0 0 0]
```

Alternatively, you can remove elements from a slice and truncate it using a for-loop, like in the following:

```
slice := []int{0, 1, 2, 3, 4, 5, 6, 7, 8, 9}
// Keep an index to write to
write:=0
for _, elem := range slice {
  if elem %2 == 0 { // Copy only even numbers
```

```
        slice[write]=elem
        write++
    }
}
// Truncate the slice
slice=slice[:write]
```

How it works...

A slice is a view over an array. It contains three pieces of information:

- `ptr`: A pointer to an element of an array, which is the starting location of the slice
- `len`: The number of elements in the slice
- `cap`: The capacity remaining in the underlying array for this slice

If you append elements to a slice beyond its capacity, a larger array is allocated by the runtime, and the contents of the slice are copied there. After this, the new slice points to a new array.

This is a source of confusion for many. A slice may share its elements with other slices. Thus, modifying one slice may modify others as well.

Figure 4.2 illustrates a case where the same underlying array is used for four different slices:

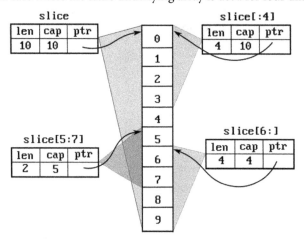

Figure 4.2 – Slices sharing the same underlying array

See the following example:

```
// Appends 1 to a slice, and returns the new slice
func Append1(input []int) []int {
    return append(input,1)
```

```
}

func main() {
    slice:= []int{0,1,2,3,4,5,6,7,8,9}
    shortSlice := slice[:4]
    // shortSlice: []int{0,1,2,3}
    newSlice:=Append1(slice[:4])
    // newSlice:= []int{0,1,2,3,1}
    // slice: []int{0,1,2,3,1,5,6,7,8,9}
}
```

Note that appending to newSlice also modified an element of slice, because newSlice has enough capacity to accommodate one more element, which overwrites slice[4].

Truncating a slice is simply creating a new slice that is shorter than the original. The underlying array does not change. See the following:

```
slice:= []int{0,1,2,3,4,5,6,7,8,9}
newSlice:=slice[:5]
// newSlice: []int{0,1,2,3,4}
```

Remember, newSlice is simply a data structure containing the same ptr and cap as slice, with a shorter len. Because of this, creating a new slice from an existing slice or an array is a constant-time operation (O(1)).

Implementing a stack using a slice

A surprisingly common use of a slice is to implement a stack. Here is how it is done.

How to do it...

A stack push is simply append:

```
// A generic stack of type T
type Stack[T any] []T

func (s *Stack[T]) Push(val T) {
    *s = append(*s, val)
}
```

To implement pop, truncate the slice:

```
func (s *Stack[T]) Pop() (val T) {
    val = (*s)[len(*s)-1]
```

```
    *s = (*s)[:len(*s)-1]
    return
}
```

Again, note the use of parentheses and indirections. We cannot write `*s[len(*s)-1]`, because that is interpreted as `*(s[len(*s)-1]`. To prevent that, we have `(*s)`.

Working with maps

You access the elements of an array or a slice using integer indexes. Maps provide a similar syntax to use index keys that are not only integers but also any type that is "comparable" (which means it can be compared using `==` or `!=`.) A map is an associative data type – that is, it stores key-value pairs. Each key appears once in a map. A Go map provides amortized constant-time access to its elements (that is, when measured over time, map element access should look like a constant-time operation.)

The Go map type provides convenient access to an underlying complicated data structure. It is one of the "reference" types – that is, assigning a map variable to another map simply assigns a pointer to the underlying structure and does not copy the elements of the map.

> **Warning**
>
> A map is an unordered collection. Do not rely on the ordering of elements in a map. The same order of insertion may result in different iteration orders in the same program at a different time.

Defining, initializing, and using maps

Similar to a slice, the zero-value for a map is nil. Reading from a nil map will have the same result as reading from a non-nil map that has no elements. Writing to a nil map will panic. This section shows different ways a map can be initialized and used.

How to do it...

Use `make` to create a new map, or use a literal. You cannot write to a nil map (but you can read from it!), so you must initialize all maps either with `make`, or by using a literal:

```
func main() {
    // Make a new empty map
    m1 := make(map[int]string)
    // Initilize a map using empty map literal
    m2 := map[int]string{}
    // Initialize a map using a map literal
    m3 := map[int]string {
        1: "a",
```

```
      2: "b",
  }
...
```

Unlike a slice, map values are not **addressable**:

```
type User struct {
  Name string
}

func main() {
    usersByID := make(map[int]User)
    usersByID[1]=User{Name:"John Doe"}
    fmt.Println(usersByID[1].Name)
    // Prints: John Doe

    // The following will give a compile error
    usersByID[1].Name="James"
...
}
```

In the previous example, you cannot set a member variable of a struct stored in a map. When you access that map element with usersByID[1], what you get back is a copy of User stored in the map, and the effect of setting its Name to something else will be lost, as that copy is not stored anywhere.

So, instead, you can read and assign the map value to an addressable variable, change it, and set it back:

```
user := usersByID[1]
user.Name="James"
usersByID[1]=user
```

Alternatively, you can store pointers in the map:

```
userPtrsByID := make(map[int]*User)
userPtrsByID[1]=&User {
  Name: "John Doe"
}
userPtrsByID[1].Name = "James" // This works.
```

If the map does not have an element for the given key, it will return the zero-value for the map value type:

```
user := usersByID[2]   // user is set to User{}
userPtr := userPtrsByID[2] // userPtr is set to nil
```

To distinguish whether the zero-value is returned because the map doesn't have the element from the situation where the zero-value is stored in the map, use the two-return value version of map lookup:

```
user, exists := usersByID[1] // exists = true
userPtr, exists := userPtrsByID[2] // exists = false
```

Use delete to delete an element from a map:

```
delete(usersByID, 1)
```

Implementing a set using a map

A set is useful to remove duplicates from a collection of values. Maps can be used as sets efficiently by utilizing a zero-size value structure.

How to do it...

Use a map whose key type is the element type of the set, and whose value type is struct{}:

```
stringSet := make(map[string]struct{})
```

Add values to the set with the struct{}{} value:

```
stringSet[value]=struct{}{}
```

Check for value existence using the two-value version of map lookup:

```
if _,exists:=stringSet[str]; exists {
  // String str exists in the set
}
```

A map is not ordered. If the ordering of elements is important, keep a slice with the map:

```
// Remove duplicate inputs from the input, preserving order
func DedupOrdered(input []string) []string {
    set:=make(map[string]struct{})
    output:=make([]string,0,len(input))
    for _,in:=range input {
      if _,exists:=set[in]; exists {
        continue
      }
      output=append(output,in)
      set[in]=struct{}{}
    }
    return output
}
```

How it works...

The `struct{}` structure is a zero-sized object. Such objects are handled separately by the compiler and the runtime. When used as a value in a map, the map will only allocate storage for its keys. So, it is an efficient way to implement sets.

> **Warning**
>
> Never rely on pointer equivalence for zero-sized structures. The compiler may choose to place two separate variables that have zero-size to the same memory location.
>
> The result of the following comparison is not defined:
>
> ```
> x:=&struct{}{}
> y:=&struct{}{}
> if x==y {
>     // Do something
> }
> ```
>
> The result of x==y may return `true` or `false`.

Composite keys

You need composite keys when you have multiple values that identify a particular object. For example, say you are dealing with a system where users may have multiple sessions. You can store this information in a map of maps, or you can create a composite key containing the user ID and session ID.

How to do it...

Use a comparable struct or an array as the map key. A comparable struct is, in general, a struct that does *not* contain the following:

- Slices
- Channels
- Functions
- Maps
- Other non-comparable structs

So, to use composite keys, perform the following steps:

1. Define a comparable struct:

```
type Key struct {
  UserID string
  SessionID string
}

type User struct {
  Name string

  ...
}

var compositeKeyMap = map[Key]User{}
```

2. Use an instance of the map key to access elements:

```
compositeKeyMap[Key{
  UserID: "123",
  SessionID: "1",
  }] = User {
    Name: "John Doe",
  }
```

3. You can use a literal map to initialize it:

```
var compositeKeyMap = map[Key]User {
   Key {
     UserID: "123",
     SessionID: "1",
   }: User {
     Name: "John Doe",
   },
}
```

How it works...

The map implementation generates hash values from its keys and then uses comparison operators to check for equivalence. Because of this, any data structure that is comparable can be used as a key value.

Be careful about pointer comparisons. A struct containing a pointer field will check for the equivalence of the pointer. Consider the following key:

```
type KeyWithPointer struct {
    UserID string
    SessionID *int
}

var sessionMap = map[KeyWithPointer]{}

func main() {
    session := 1
    key := KeyWithPointer{
        UserID: "John",
        SessionID: &session,
    }
    sessionMap[key]=User{ Name: "John Doe"}
```

In the previous code snippet, the composite map key contains a pointer to `session`, an integer. After you add an element to the map, changing the value of `session` will not affect the keys of the map pointing to that variable. The map key will still be pointing to the same variable. Another instance of `KeyWithPointer` can be used to locate the `User` object only if it is also pointing to the same `session` variable, as per the following:

```
fmt.Println( sessionMap[KeyWithPointer{
    UserID: "John",
    SessionID: &session,
    }].Name) // "John Doe"
```

But:

```
i:=1
fmt.Println( sessionMap[KeyWithPointer{
    UserID: "John",
    SessionID: &i,
    }].Name) // ""
```

Thread-safe caching with maps

Caching is sometimes necessary to attain an acceptable performance. The idea is to reuse values that have been computed or retrieved before. A map is a natural choice for caching such values but, due to their nature, caches are usually shared among multiple goroutines and you must be careful when using them.

Simple cache

This is a simple cache with a get/put method to retrieve objects from the cache and put elements into it.

How to do it...

To cache values that are accessible with a key, use a structure with a map and mutex:

```
type ObjectCache struct {
    mutex sync.RWMutex
    values map[string]*Object
}

// Initialize and return a new instance of the cache
func NewObjectCache() *ObjectCache {
    return &ObjectCache{
        values: make(map[string]*Object),
    }
}
```

Direct access to cache internals should be prevented to ensure the proper protocol is observed whenever the cache is used:

```
// Get an object from the cache
func (cache *ObjectCache) Get(key string) (*Object, bool) {
    cache.mutex.RLock()
    obj, exists := cache.values[key]
    cache.mutex.RUnlock()
    return obj, exists
}

// Put an object into the cache with the given key
func (cache *ObjectCache) Put(key string, value *Object) {
    cache.mutex.Lock()
    cache.values[key] = value
    cache.mutex.Unlock()
}
```

Cache with blocking behavior

If multiple goroutines ask for the same key from the simple cache in the previous example, they may all decide to retrieve the object and put it back into the cache. That is inefficient. Usually, you would want one of those goroutines to retrieve the object while the other waits. This can be done using sync.Once.

How to do it...

Cache elements are structures containing sync.Once to ensure one goroutine gets the object while others wait for it. Also, the cache contains a Get method that uses a getObjectFunc callback to retrieve an object if it is not in the cache:

```
type cacheItem struct {
    sync.Once
    object *Object
}

type ObjectCache struct {
    mutex sync.RWMutex
    values map[string]*cacheItem
    getObjectFunc func(string) (*Object, error)
}

func NewObjectCache(getObjectFunc func(string) (*Object,error))
*ObjectCache {
  return &ObjectCache{
      values: make(map[string]*cacheItem),
      getObjectFunc: getObjectFunc,
  }
}

func (item *cacheItem) get(key string, cache *ObjectCache) (err error)
{
  // Calling item.Once.Do
  item.Do(func() {
      item.object, err=cache.getObjectFunc(key)
  })
  return
}

func (cache *ObjectCache) Get(key string) (*Object, error) {
  cache.mutex.RLock()
  object, exists := cache.values[key]
  cache.mutex.RUnlock()
  if exists {
    return object.object, nil
  }
  cache.mutex.Lock()
  object, exists = cache.values[key]
  if !exists {
```

```
        object = &cacheItem{}
        cache.values[key] = object
    }
    cache.mutex.Unlock()
    err := object.get(key, cache)
    return object.object, err
}
```

How it works...

The Get method starts by read-locking the cache. Then it checks whether the key exists in the cache and unlocks it. If the value is cached, it is returned.

If the value is not in the cache, then the cache is write-locked, because this will be a concurrent modification to the values map. The values map is checked again to make sure another goroutine did not already put a value there. If not, this goroutine puts an uninitialized cacheItem in the cache and unlocks it.

The cacheItem contains a sync.Once, which will allow only one goroutine to call Once.Go while others are blocked waiting for the winning call to complete. This is when the getObjectFunc callback is invoked from the cacheItem.get method. At this point, there is no chance for a memory race, because only one goroutine can be executing the item.Do function. The result of the function will be stored in the cacheItem, so it will not cause any problems with the users of the values map. In fact, note that while getObjectFunc is running, the cache is not locked. There can be many other goroutines reading and/or writing to the cache.

5

Working with Types, Structs, and Interfaces

Go is a strongly typed language. That means every value in a program must be defined using a set of predefined basic types. The rules of the type system determine what can be done with those values, and how values of different types interact. The Go type system takes a simplistic approach; it only allows explicit conversions between values of different compatible types.

Go is also a statically typed language, which means that types of values are explicitly declared and checked at compile time, as opposed to being checked at runtime. This is different from scripting languages such as Python or JavaScript.

In this chapter, we will look at some of the properties of the Go type system, defining new types, structures, and interfaces, and considering how to make effective use of it to implement some common patterns.

This chapter contains the following recipes:

- Creating new types
- Using composition to extend types
- Initializing structures
- Working with interfaces
- Factory pattern
- Polymorphic containers

Creating new types

There are several reasons why you want to define new types. An important one is ensuring type safety. Type safety ensures that operations receive the correct type of data. A type-safe program is free of type errors, limiting possible errors in the program to logic errors only.

Other reasons for creating new types also include the following:

- You can share the methods and data fields of a type in multiple different types by *embedding* it.

- Later in this chapter, we will look at interfaces. You can define a set of methods for a new type to implement a given interface that lets you use that type in different contexts.

Creating a new type based on an existing type

Creating a new type allows you to enforce type-safety rules, and add type-specific methods.

How to do it...

Create a new type based on an existing type using the following syntax:

```
type <NewTypeName> <ExistingTypeName>
```

For example, the following declaration defines a new data type, Duration, as an unsigned 64-bit integer:

```
type Duration uint64
```

This is how the Go standard library defines time.Duration. To call the time.Sleep(d Duration) function, you now have to use a time.Duration value, or explicitly convert a numeric value to a time.Duration value.

> **Warning**
> When you create a new type from an existing type, the new type is created without any methods even if the existing type has methods defined.

Creating type-safe enumerations

In this recipe, we will define a set of constants (an enumeration) with a new type.

How to do it...

1. Define a new type:

   ```
   type Direction int
   ```

2. Create a sequence of constants representing the values of the enumeration using the new type. You can use iota for numeric constants to generate increasing numbers:

   ```
   const (
     DirectionLeft Direction = iota
   ```

```
    DirectionRight
)
```

3. Use the new type in functions or data elements expecting this new type:

```
func SetDirection(dir Direction) {...}

func main() {
   SetDirection(DirectionLeft)
   SetDirection(Direction(0))
   ...
}
```

> **Tip**
>
> This does not prevent someone from calling SetDirection(Direction(3)), which is an invalid value. This is usually only a problem for enumerated values read from user input or from third-party sources. You should validate the input at that point.

Creating struct types

A Go struct is a collection of fields. Define structs to group interrelated data fields to form a record. This recipe shows how to create new struct types in your program.

How to do it...

Create a struct type using the following syntax:

```
type NewTypeName struct {
    // List of fields
}
```

For instance:

```
type User struct {
   Username string
   Password string
}
```

Extending types

Go uses type composition through embedding, and structural typing through the use of interfaces. Let's start by examining what these mean.

When you embed an existing type into another, the methods and data fields defined for the embedded type become the methods and data fields of the embedding type. If you have worked with object-oriented languages, this may seem similar to class inheritance, but there is a crucial difference: if a class A is derived from a class B, then A is-a B, meaning wherever B is needed, you can substitute an instance of A. With composition, if A embeds B, A and B are distinct types, and you cannot use A where B is needed.

> **Tip**
> There is no type inheritance in Go. Go chooses composition over inheritance. The primary reason for this is the simplicity of combining components to build more complex ones. Most use cases of inheritance in object-oriented languages can be rearchitected using composition, interfaces, and structural typing. I used the word *"rearchitecting"* intentionally here: do *not* try to port existing object-oriented programs to Go by emulating inheritance. Instead, redesign and refactor them to be idiomatic Go programs using composition and interfaces.

The next recipes will look at how this can be done.

Extending a base type

First, we'll look at how we can extend a base type to share its data elements and methods in new types.

How to do it...

Let's say you have some data fields and functionality shared between multiple data types. Then you can create a base data type, and embed it into multiple other data types to share common parts:

```go
type Common struct {
  commonField int
}

func (a Common) CommonMethod() {}

type A struct {
  Common
  aField int
}

func (a A) AMethod() {}

type B struct {
  Common
  bField int
```

```
}

func (b B) BMethod() {}
```

In the preceding code snippet, the fields and methods of each struct are as follows:

Type	Fields	Methods
Common	commonField	CommonMethod
A	commonField, aField	CommonMethod, AMethod
B	commonField, bField	CommonMethod, BMethod

How it works...

We have used struct embedding to share common data elements and functionality in the previous section. The following example shows two structs, Customer and Product, that share the same Metadata structure. Metadata contains the unique identifier, creation date, and modification date of a record:

```
type Metadata struct {
  ID string
  CreatedAt time.Time
  ModifiedAt time.Time
}

// New initializes metadata fields
func (m *Metadata) New() {
  m.ID=uuid.New().String()
  m.CreatedAt=time.Now()
  m.ModifiedAt=m.CreatedAt
}

// Customer.New() uses the promoted Metadata.New() method.
// Calling Customer.New() will initialize Customer.Metadata, but
// will not modify Customer specific fields.
type Customer struct {
  Metadata
  Name string
}

// Product.New(string) shadows `Metadata.New() method. You cannot
// call `Product.New()`, but call `Product.New(string)` or
// `Product.Metadata.New()`
type Product struct {
```

```
    Metadata
    SKU string
}

func (p *Product) New(sku string) {
  // Initialize the metadata part of product
  p.Metadata.New()
  p.SKU=sku
}

func main() {
    c:=Customer{}
    c.New() // Initialize customer metadata

    p:=Product{}
    p.New("sku") // Initialize product metadata and sku
    // p.New() // Compile error: p.New() takes a string argument
}
```

Embedding is not inheritance. The receiver of an embedded struct method is *not* a copy of the defined struct. In the preceding snippet, when we call c.New(), the Metedata.New() method gets a receiver that is an instance of *Metadata, not an instance of *Customer.

Initializing structs

This recipe shows how you can use struct literals to initialize complex data structures containing embedded structures.

How to do it...

Go guarantees that all declared variables are initialized to their zero values. This is not very useful if you have a complicated data structure that should be initialized with default values or non-nil pointer components. For such cases, use constructor-like functions to create a new instance of a struct. The established convention is to write a NewX function for a type X that initializes an instance of X or *X and returns it.

Here, NewIndex creates a new initialized instance of the Index type:

```
type Index struct {
    index map[string]any
    name string
}

func NewIndex(name string) *Index {
```

```
  return &Index{
    index:make(map[string]any),
    name:name,
  }
}

func (index *Index) Name() string {return index.name}
func (index *Index) Add(key string, value any) {
  index.index[key]=value
}
```

Also, observe that the `Index.name` and `Index.index` fields are not exported. Thus, they can only be accessed using exported methods of `Index`. This pattern is useful for preventing unintentional modification of data fields.

Defining interfaces

Go uses "structural typing." If a type `T` defines all the methods of an interface `I`, then `T` implements `I`. This causes some confusion among developers who are well-versed in languages that use nominative typing, such as Java, where you explicitly have to *name* the constituent types.

Go interfaces are simply method sets. When a data type defines a set of methods, it also automatically implements all interfaces that contain a subset of its methods. For instance, if data type `A` defines a `func (A) F()` method, then `A` also implements the `interface { func F() }` and `interface{}` interfaces. If interface `A` is a subset of interface `B`, then a data type implementing interface `B` can be used wherever `A` is needed.

Interfaces as contracts

An interface can be used as a "specification," or like a "contract" that defines certain functions an implementation should satisfy.

How to do it...

Define an interface or a set of interfaces to specify the expected behavior of an object. This is suitable when multiple different implementations of the same interface are expected. For instance, the standard library `database/driver` SQL driver package defines a set of interfaces that should be implemented by different database drivers.

For example, the following code snippet defines a storage backend for storing files:

```
type Storage interface {
    Create(name string, reader io.Reader) error
    Read(name string) (io.ReadCloser,error)
```

```
    Update(name string, reader io.Reader) error
    Delete(name string) error
}
```

You can use the instances of objects that implement the `Storage` interface to store data in different backends, such as a filesystem or some network storage system.

In many cases, the data types used to declare the methods of such an interface are themselves dependent on the actual implementation. In that case, a system of interfaces is necessary. The standard library `database/driver` package uses this approach. As an example, consider the following authentication provider interface:

```
// Authenticator uses implementation-specific credentials to create an
// implementation-specific session
type Authenticator interface {
    Login(credentials Credentials) (Session,error)
}

// Credentials contains the credentials to authenticate a user to the
// backend
type Credentials interface {
    Serialize() []byte
    Type() string
}

// CredentialParse implementation parses backend-specific credentials
// from []byte input
type CredentialParser interface {
    Parse([]byte) (Credentials, error)
}

// A backend-specific session identifies the user and provides a way
// to close the session
type Session interface {
    UserID() string
    Close()
}
```

Factories

This section shows a recipe that is often used to support extendible structures, such as database drivers, where importing a particular database driver package automatically "registers" the driver to a factory.

How to do it...

1. Define an interface, or set of interfaces specifying how an implementation should behave.

2. Create a registry (a map), and a function to register implementations.

3. Every different implementation registers itself with the registry using `init()`.

4. Import the implementations that will be included in the program using the `main` package.

Let's implement an authentication framework using the `Authenticator` example from the last section. We will allow different implementations of the `Authenticator` framework.

First, define a factory interface and a map to keep all registered implementations:

```
package auth

type AuthenticatorFactory interface {
    NewInstance() Authenticator
}

var registry = map[string]AuthenticatorFactory{}
```

Then, declare an exported `Register` function:

```
func RegisterAuthenticator(name string, factory AuthenticatorFactory)
{
    registry[name]=factory
}
```

To dynamically create instances of authenticator, we'll need a function that looks like this:

```
func NewInstance(authType string) Authenticator {
    // Create a new instance using the selected factory.
    // If the given authType has not been registered, this will panic
    return registry[authType].NewInstance()
}
```

Implementations can register their own factories using the `init()` function:

```
type factory struct{}

func (factory) NewInstance() auth.Authenticator {
    // Create and return a new instance of db authenticator
}

func init() {
    auth.RegisterAuthenticator("dbauthenticator",factory{})
}
```

Finally, you have to stitch this together. The Go build system will only include packages that have been directly or indirectly used by the code accessible from `main()`, and the implementations are not directly referenced. We have to make sure those packages are imported, and thus, the implementations are registered. So, import them in `main`:

```
package main

import (
    _ "import/path/of/the/implementation"
    ...
)
```

The preceding `import` will include the implementation package in the program. Since the package is included in the program, its `init()` function will be called during program initialization, and the authenticator type it provides will be registered.

Defining interfaces where you use them

Structural typing allows you to define an interface when you need to use one, as opposed to pre-defining an exported interface. This is sometimes confused with "duck-typing" (if something walks like a duck and talks like a duck, it is a duck). The difference is that duck-typing refers to determining data type compatibility by looking at the subset of a type's structure at runtimes, whereas structural typing refers to looking at the structure of a type at compile time. This recipe shows how you can define interfaces as you need them.

How to do it...

Let's say you have code that looks like the following:

```
type A struct {
    ...
    options  map[string]any
}

func (a A) GetOptions() map[string]any {return a.options}

type B struct {
    ...
    options map[string]any
}

func (b B) GetOptions() map[string]any {return b.options}
```

If you want to write a function that will operate on the options of a variable of type A or B (or any type that has options), you can simply define an interface right there:

```
type withOptions interface {
  GetOptions() map[string]any
}

func ProcessOptions(item withOptions) {
  for key, value:=range item.GetOptions() {
    ...
  }
}
```

How it works...

Remember, Go uses structural typing. So, you can create an interface specifying a set of methods, and any data type declaring those methods will automatically implement that interface. Thus, you can create such interfaces ad hoc, and write functions that take instances of those interfaces to work with a potentially large number of data types.

If you used a nominative language, you would have had to specify that those types implement your interface. Not so in Go.

That also means that if you have an interface A and another interface B such that A declares the same methods as B, then any type that implements A also implements B. In other words, if you cannot import an interface because it is in a package that will cause a circular dependency if imported, or if that interface is not exported by that package, you can simply define an equivalent interface in your current package.

Using a function as an interface

Sometimes, you might encounter a situation where you have a function when an interface is needed. This recipe shows how you can define a new function data type that also implements an interface.

How to do it...

If you need to implement a single-method interface without any data elements, you can define a new type based on an empty struct and declare a method for that type to implement that interface. Alternatively, you can simply use the function itself as an implementation of that interface. The following excerpt is from the standard library net/http package:

```
// An interface with a single function
type Handler interface {
    ServeHTTP(ResponseWriter, *Request)
```

```
}

// Define a new function type matching the interface method signature
type HandlerFunc func(ResponseWriter, *Request)

// Implement the method for the function type
func (h HandlerFunc) ServeHTTP(w ResponseWriter, r *Request) {
    h(w.r) // Call the underlying function
}
```

Here, you can use functions of the HandlerFunc type whenever an implementation of the Handler interface is needed.

How it works...

The Go type system treats function types as any other defined type. Thus, you can declare methods for a function type. When you declare methods for a function type, the function type automatically implements all the interfaces that define all or some of those methods.

Let's examine this statement with an example. We can declare a new empty type as an implementation of the Handler interface:

```
type MyHandler struct{}

func (MyHandler) ServeHTTP(w ResponseWriter, r *Request) {...}
```

With this declaration, you can use instances of MyHandler wherever a Handler is required. However, observe that MyHandler has no data elements and only one method. So instead, we define a function type:

```
type MyHandler func(ResponseWriter,*Request)
```

Now MyHandler is a new named type. This is not that much different from declaring MyHandler as a struct, but in this case, MyHandler is a function with a fixed signature.

Since MyHandler is a named type, we can define methods for it:

```
func (h MyHandler) ServeHTTP(w ResponseWriter, r *Request) {
    h(w,r)
}
```

Since MyHandler now defined ServeHTTP method, it implements the Handler interface. However, MyHandler is a function type, so h is actually a function that has the same signature as ServeHTTP. Due to that, the h(w, r) call works, and MyHandler can be used in places where a Handler is required.

Discovering capabilities of data types at runtime – testing "implements" relationship

An interface provides a way to call the methods of an underlying data object. If the same interface is implemented by many different types, you can use a function to manipulate diverse data types by simply using their common interface. However, many times, you need to access the underlying object stored in an interface. Go provides several mechanisms to achieve that. We will look at `type-assertion` and `type-switch`.

How to do it...

Use interfaces and type assertions to discover different methods a type provides. Remember that an interface is a method set. A type that implements the methods given in an interface automatically implements that interface.

Use the following patterns to determine whether a data type has a method:

```go
func f(rd io.Reader) {
    // Is rd also an io.Writer?
    if wr, ok:= rd.(io.Writer); ok {
        // Yes, rd is an io.Writer, and wr is that writer.
        ...
    }

    // Does rd have a function ReadLine() (string,error)?
    // Define an interface here
    type hasReadLine interface {
        ReadLine() (string,error)
    }
    // And see if rd implements it:
    if readLine, ok:=rd.(hasReadLine); ok {
        // Yes, you can use readLine:
        line, err:=readLine.ReadLine()
        ...
    }

    // You can even define anonymous interfaces inline:
    if readLine, ok:=rd.(interface{ReadLine()(string,error)}); ok {
        line, err:=readLine.ReadLine()
    }
}
```

How it works...

Type assertions have two forms. The following form tests if an `intf` interface variable contains a concrete value of the `concreteValue` type:

```
value, ok:=intf.(concreteValue)
```

If the interface contains a value of that type, then `value` now has that value, and ok becomes `true`.

The second form tests whether the concrete value contained within the `intf` interface also implements the `otherIntf` interface:

```
value, ok:=intf.(otherIntf)
```

If the value contained in `intf` also has the methods declared by `otherIntf`, then `value` is now an interface value of the `otherIntf` type containing the same concrete value as `intf`, and ok is set to `true`.

Using this second form, you can test whether an interface variable implements the methods you need.

You may think you can do the same thing using reflection. Reflection is a method for discovering the names of fields and methods of types at runtime. It is not a performant or easy method to check such type equivalences.

Testing whether an interface value is one of the known types

A type-switch is used to test whether an interface value is a known concrete type, or whether it implements a certain interface. This recipe shows how it can be used.

How to do it...

Use a type-switch instead of a sequence of type assertions if you need to check an interface against multiple types.

The following example uses an `interface{}` to add two values. The values can either both be `int`, or both `float64`. The function also provides a way to override the addition behavior: if the value has a compatible `Add` method, it calls that instead:

```
// a and b must have the same types. They can be int, float64, or
// another type
// that has Add method.
func Add(a, b interface{}) interface{} {
    // type switch:
    // In this form, a matching case block will declare aValue
    // with the correct type
    switch aValue:=a.(type) {
```

```
    case int:
        // Here, aValue is an int
        // b must be an int!
        bValue:=b.(int)
        return aValue+bValue

    case float64:
        // Here, aValue is a float64
        // b must be a float64!
        bValue:=b.(float64)
        return aValue+bValue

    case interface { Add(interface{}) interface{} }:
        // Here, aValue is an interface {Add{interface{}) interface{}}
        return aValue.Add(b)

    default:
        // Here, aValue is not defined
        // This is an unhandled case
        return nil
    }
}
```

Note the way the type switch is used to extract the value contained in the interface if the case matches. This only works if the case lists a single type, and if the case is not the `default` case. For those cases, the variable is simply not defined and you work with the interface.

Ensuring a type implements an interface during development

During the development stages of a project, interface types may change quickly by adding new methods, or modifying existing method signatures by changing argument types or return types. How can developers make sure certain implementations of those interfaces are not broken by those changes?

How to do it...

Let's say your team defined the following interface:

```
type Car interface {
    Move(int,int)
}
```

We'll also say that you implemented that interface with the following struct:

```
type RaceCar struct {
    X, Y int
}

func (r *RaceCar) Move(dx, dy int) {
    r.X+=dx
    r.Y+=dy
}
```

However, later in the development, it turned out not all cars can move successfully, so the signature of the interface changes to the following:

```
type Car interface {
    Move(int,int) error
}
```

With this change, `RaceCar` no longer implements `Car`. Many times this error will be caught at compile time, but not always. For instance, if instances of `*RaceCar` are passed to functions that require any, the compilation will succeed, but a runtime panic will be raised if that argument is converted to a `Car` or `*RaceCar` via type assertion:

```
rc := item.(Car)
```

Let's say that you declare the following:

```
var _ Car = &RaceCar{}
```

Any modification to the `Car` interface that makes `*RaceCar` no longer implement the `Car` interface will be a compile error.

So, in general: declare a blank variable with the interface type, and assign it to the concrete type:

```
type I interface {...}

type Implem struct { ... }

// If something changes in Implem or I that causes Implem
// to no longer implement interface I, this will give a
// compile-time error
var _ I = Implem{}

// Same as above, but this ensures *Implem implements I
var _ I = &Implem{}
```

If there are changes that cause the type to no longer implement that interface, a compile error will be raised.

Deciding whether to use a pointer receiver or value receiver for methods

In this recipe, we'll explore how to choose between a pointer receiver and a value receiver for methods.

How to do it...

In general, use one kind, not both. There are two reasons for this:

- Consistency throughout the code.
- Mixing value and pointer receivers can result in data races.

If a method modifies the receiver object, use a pointer receiver. If a method does not modify the receiver object, or if the method relies on getting a copy of the receiver object, you can use a value receiver.

If you are implementing an immutable type, in most cases, you should use a value receiver.

If your structures are large, using a pointer receiver will reduce copy overhead. You can find different guidelines on whether or not a structure can be considered large. When in doubt, write a benchmark and measure.

How it works...

For a type T, if you declare a method using a value receiver, that method is declared for both T and *T. The method gets a copy of the receiver, not a pointer to it, so any modifications performed on the receiver will not be reflected to the object used for calling the method.

For example, the following method returns a copy of the original object while modifying one field:

```
type Action struct {
    Option string
}

// Returns a copy of a with the given option. The original a is not
// modified.
func (a Action) WithOption(option string) Action {
    a.Option=option
    return a
}

func main() {
```

```
    x:=Action{
        Option:"a",
    }
    y:=x.WithOption("b")
    fmt.Println(x.Option, y.Option) // Outputs: a b
}
```

A value receiver creates a shallow copy of the original. If the receiver struct has maps, slices, or pointers to other objects, only the map headers, slice headers, or pointers will be copied, not the contents of the pointed object. That means that even though the method gets a value receiver in the following example, changes to the map are reflected in both the original and the copy:

```
type T struct {
    m map[string]int
}

func (t T) add(k string, v int) {
    t.m[k]=v
}

func main() {
    t:=T{
        m:make(map[string]int,
    }
    t.add("a",1)
    fmt.Println(t) // [a:1]
}
```

Be careful about how this affects slice operations. A slice is a triple (`pointer, len, cap`), and that is what's copied when you pass a value receiver:

```
type T struct {
    s []string
}

func (t T) set(i int, s string) {
    t.s[i]=s
}

func (t T) add(s string) {
    t.s=append(t.s,s)
}

func main() {
```

```
t:=T{
   s: []string{"a","b"},
}
fmt.Println(t.s) // [a, b]

// Setting a slice element contained in the value receiver will be
// visible here
t.set(0,"x")
fmt.Println(t.s) // [x, b]

// Appending to the slice contained in the value receiver will not
// be visible here
// The appended slice header is set in the copy of t, the original
// never sees that update
t.add("y")
fmt.Println(t.s) // [x, b]
}
```

A pointer receiver is more straightforward to work with. The method always gets a pointer to the object it is called with. In the preceding example, declaring the add method with a pointer receiver behaves as expected:

```
func (t *T) add(s string) {
   t.s=append(t.s,s)
}


...
   t.add("y")
   fmt.Println(t.s) // [x, b, y]
```

At the beginning of this section, I also mentioned that mixing pointer and value receivers causes a data race. Here is how it happens.

Remember that a data race happens when a goroutine reads from a variable that is being concurrently modified by another. Consider the following example where the Version method uses a value receiver that causes a copy of T to be created:

```
type T struct {
   X int
}

func (t T) Version() int  {return 1}

func (t *T) SetValue(x int) {t.X=x}
```

```
func main() {
  t:=T{}

  go func () {
     t.SetValue(1) // Writes to t.X
  }()

  ver := t.Version() // Makes a copy of t, which reads t.X
  ...
}
```

The act of calling t.Version() creates a copy of the variable t, reading t.X concurrently as it is being modified, hence causing a race. This race is more obvious if t.Version reads from t.X explicitly. There is no guarantee that that read operation will see the effects of the write operation in the goroutine.

Polymorphic containers

In this context, a container is a data structure that holds many objects. The principles of this section can be applied to single objects as well. In other words, you can use the same idea when you have a single polymorphic variable or a struct field.

How to do it...

1. Define an interface containing the methods common to all data types that will be stored in the container.

2. Declare the container type using that interface.

3. Put instances of actual objects into the container.

4. When you retrieve objects from the container, you can either work with the object through the interface, or type-assert, get the actual type or another interface, and work with that.

How it works...

Here's a simple example that works with Shape objects. A Shape object is something that can be drawn on an image, and moved around:

```
type Shape interface {
  Draw(image.Image)
  Move(dx, dy int)
}
```

Shape has several implementations:

```
type Rectangle struct {
    rect image.Rectangle
    color color.Color
}

func (r *Rectangle) Draw(target image.Image) {...}
func (r *Rectangle) Move(dx, dy int) {...}

type Circle struct {
    center image.Point
    color color.Color
}

func (c *Circle) Draw(target image.Image) {...}
func (c *Circle) Move(dx, dy int) {...}
```

Both *Rectangle and *Circle implement the Shape interface (note that Rectangle and Circle do not.) Now we can work with a slice of Shapes:

```
func Draw(target image.Image, shapes []Shape) {
  for _,shape:=range shapes {
    shape.Draw(targeT)
  }
}
```

This is what the shapes slice looks like:

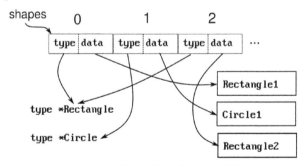

Figure 5.1 – Slice of interface variables

Since every interface contains a pointer to the actual shape, it is possible to use the interface to call methods that modify the object as well:

```
func Move(dx, dy int, shapes []Shape) {
  for _,shape:=range shapes {
```

```
    shape.Move(dx, dy)
  }
}
```

Accessing parts of an object not directly exposed via the interface

When working with interfaces, there are many occasions where you need to access the underlying object. This is achieved by type-assertion, that is, testing whether the value of an interface satisfies a given type, and if so, retrieving it.

How to do it...

Use type assertion or a type switch to test the type of the object contained in an interface:

```
func f(shape Shape) {

    if rect, ok := shape.(*Rectangle); ok {
        // shape contains a *Rectangle, and rect now points to it
    }

    switch actualShape := shape.(type) {
        case *Circle :
            // shape is a *Circle, and actualShape is a *Circle variable
        case *Rectangle:
            // shape is a *Rectangle, and actualShape is a *Rectangle
            // variable
        default:
            // shape is not a circle or rectangle. actualShape is not
            // defined here
    }
}
```

Accessing the embedding struct from the embedded struct

In object-oriented languages such as Java or C++, there is the concept of an abstract method or virtual method, together with type inheritance. One effect of this feature is that if you call a method M of a base class base, then the method that runs at runtime is the implementation of M that is declared for the actual object at runtime. In other words, you can invoke a method that will be overridden by other declarations, and you just don't know which method you are actually calling.

There are ways of doing the same thing in Go. This recipe shows how.

How to do it...

Let's say you need to write a circular linked list data structure whose elements will be structs embedding a base struct:

```
type ListNodeHeader struct {
    next Node
    prev Node
    list *List
}
```

The list itself is as follows:

```
type List struct {
    first Node
}
```

So, the list points to the `first` node, which is an arbitrary node in the list, and every node points to the next one, with the last node pointing back to the first.

We need a `Node` interface that defines the mechanics of maintaining a list. Of course, the `Node` interface will be implemented by `ListNodeHeader`, and thus, by all the nodes of the list:

```
type Node interface {
    ...
}
```

The users of the list are supposed to embed `ListHeader` to implement a `list` node:

```
type ByteSliceElement struct {
    ListNodeHeader
    Payload []byte
}

type StringElement struct {
    ListNodeHeader
    Payload string
}
```

Now the hard part is to implement the `Node` interface. Let's assume you would like to insert a `ByteSliceElement` in this list. Since `ByteSliceElement` embeds `ListNodeHeader`, it has all its methods and thus implements `Node`. However, we can't write, for instance, an `Insert` method for `ListNodeHeader` without knowing the actual object being inserted.

One way of doing this is by using the following pattern:

```
type Node interface {
    Insert(list *List, this Node)

    getHeader() *ListNodeHeader
}

func (header *ListNodeHeader) getHeader() *ListNodeHeader {return
header}

func (header *ListNodeHeader) Insert(list *List,this Node) {
    // If list is empty, this is the only node
    if list.first == nil {
        list.first = this
        header.next = this
        header.prev = this
        return
    }
    header.next=list.first
    header.prev=list.first.getHeader().prev
    header.prev.getHeader().next=this
    header.next.getHeader().prev=this
}
```

There are several things going on here. First, the `Insert` method gets two views of the node being inserted. If the node being inserted is a `*ByteSliceElement`, then it gets a Node version of this, and then it also gets the `*ListNodeHeader` embedded in `ByteSliceElement` as the receiver. Using this, it can adjust the members of the `ByteSliceElement` to point to the previous and next nodes.

However, it cannot access the `prev` and `next` members of a Node.

One option is what is shown: declare an unexported method in the Node interface that will return the `ListNodeHeader` from a given node. Another option is to add `getNext`/`setNext` and `getPrev`/`setPrev` methods to the interface.

Now you have achieved two things: first, any user of this list structure outside this package *must* embed `ListNodeHeader` to implement a list node. There is an unexported method in the interface. There is no way to implement such an interface in a different package. The only way is to embed a struct that already implements it.

Second, you have a polymorphic container data structure whose mechanics are managed by a base struct.

Checking whether an interface is nil

You may wonder why this is even a problem. After all, don't you just compare with nil? Not always.

An interface contains two values: the type of the value contained in the interface, and a pointer to that value. An interface is nil if both of those are nil. There are cases where an interface may point to a nil value of a type other than nil, which makes the interface non-nil.

You can't check for this case easily. You have to avoid creating interfaces with nil values.

How to do it...

Avoid converting a pointer to a variable that can be nil to an interface:

```
type myerror struct{}

func (myerror) Error() string { return "" }

func main() {
    var x *myerror
    var y error
    y = x // Avoid this
    if y!=nil {
        // y is not nil!
    }
}
```

Check for nil interface values explicitly instead, such as the following:

```
var y error
if x!=nil {
    y=x
}
```

Alternatively, use value errors instead of pointers. The following code avoids this problem altogether:

```
var x myerror
```

There is no chance of x being nil.

How it works...

As I explained earlier, an interface contains two values: type and value. What you are trying to avoid is creating an interface that contains a nil value with a non-nil type.

After the declaration that follows, the y interface is nil because both its type and its value are nil:

```
var y error
```

After the following assignment, the type stored in y is now the type of x, and the value is nil. Thus, y is no longer nil:

```
y=x
```

This also applies to return from a function:

```
func f() error {
    var x *myerror
    return x
}
```

The f function never returns nil.

6

Working with Generics

It happens often that you write a function that does some computation using values of a certain type (say, integers), but as the development progresses, you suddenly need to do the same thing but with another data type as well (say, float64). So you copy/paste the first function and modify it to have a different name and data types. Perhaps the most obvious and well-known examples of this situation are container data types such as maps and sets. You build a container type for integer values, then you do the same for it using strings, then for a struct, and so on.

Generics is a way of doing this code copy/paste at compile time using code templates. First, you create a function template (generic function) or a data type template (generic type). You instantiate a generic function or type by providing types. The compiler takes care of instantiating the template with the types you provided, and checks if the instantiated generic type or function is compilable with the types you provided.

In this chapter, you will learn how to use generic functions and data types for common scenarios:

- Generic functions

  - Writing a generic function that adds numbers

  - Declaring constraints as interfaces

  - Using generic functions as adapters and accessors

- Generic types

  - Writing a type-safe set

  - An ordered map -- using multiple type parameters

Generic functions

A generic function is a function template that takes types as parameters. The generic function must compile for all possible type assignments of its arguments. The types a generic function can accept are described by "type constraints." We will learn about these concepts in this section.

Writing a generic function that adds numbers

A good introductory example for illustrating generics is a function that adds numbers. These numbers can be various types of integers or floating-point numbers. Here, we will study several recipes with different capabilities.

How to do it...

A generic summation function that accepts `int` and `float64` numbers is as follows:

```
func Sum[T int | float64](values ...T) T {
    var result T
    for _, x := range values {
        result += x
    }
    return result
}
```

The construct `[T int | float64]` defines the type parameter for the `Sum` function:

- `T` is the type name. For instance, if you instantiate the `Sum` function for `int`, then `T` is `int`.

- The `int | float64` expression is the type constraint for `T`. In this case, it means "`T` is either `int` or `float64`." The constraint tells the compiler that the `Sum` function can only be instantiated for `int` or `float64` values.

As I explained before, a generic function is only a template. For instance, you cannot declare a function variable and assign it to `Sum`, because `Sum` is not a real function. The following statement instantiates the `Sum` generic function for `int`:

```
fmt.Println(Sum[int](1,2,3))
```

For many cases, the compiler can infer the type parameter, so the following is also valid. Since all the arguments are `int` values, the compiler infers that what is meant here is `Sum[int]`:

```
fmt.Println(Sum(1,2,3))
```

But in the following case, the instantiated function is `Sum[float64]`, and the arguments are interpreted as `float64` values:

```
fmt.Println(Sum[float64](1,2,3))
```

The generic function must compile successfully for all possible `T`. In this case, `T` can be an `int` or a `float64`, so the function body must be valid for `T` being an `int` and `T` being a `float64`. The type constraints allow the compiler to produce meaningful compile-time errors. For example, the `[T int | float64 | big.Int]` constraint does not compile, because `result+=x` does not compile for `big.Int`.

The Sum function will not work for types derived from `int` or `float64`, for instance:

```
type ID int
```

Even though `ID` is an `int`, `Sum[ID]` will result in a compile error, because `ID` is a new type. To include all types derived from an `int`, use `~int` in the constraint – for example:

```
func Sum[T ~int | ~float64](values ...T) T{...}
```

This declaration will handle all types derived from `int` and `float64`.

Declaring constraints as interfaces

It is not practical to keep repeating constraints when you declare new functions. Instead, you can define them in an interface as a type list or as a method list.

How to do it...

A Go interface specifies a method set. Go generics implementation extends this definition so that interfaces define type sets when used as constraints. This requires some changes to accommodate basic types because basic types (such as `int`) do not have methods. So there are two types of syntax when it comes to interfaces as constraints:

1. Type lists specify the list of types acceptable in place of a type parameter. For example, the following `UnsignedInteger` constraint accepts all unsigned integer types and all types derived from unsigned integers:

    ```
    type UnsignedInteger interface {
      ~uint8 | ~uint16 | ~uint32 | ~uint64
    }
    ```

2. Method sets specify the methods that must be implemented by types that are acceptable. The following `Stringer` constraint accepts all types that have the `String()` `string` method:

    ```
    type Stringer interface {
      String() string
    }
    ```

These constraints can be combined. For instance, the following `UnsignedIntegerStringer` constraint accepts types that are derived from an unsigned integer type, and that have the `String()` `string` method:

```
type UnsignedIntegerString interface {
  UnsignedInteger
  Stringer
}
```

The `Stringer` interface can both be used as a constraint and as an interface. The `UnsignedInteger` and `UnsignedIntegerString` interfaces can only be used as constraints.

Using generic functions as accessors and adapters

Generic functions offer practical solutions for type-safe accessors and type adapters. For instance, initializing an `*int` variable with a constant value requires declaring a temporary value, which can be simplified by a generic function. This recipe includes several such accessors and adapters.

How to do it...

This generic function makes a pointer from arbitrary values:

```go
func ToPtr[T any](value T) *T {
    return &value
}
```

This can be used to initialize pointers without a temporary variable:

```go
type UpdateRequest struct {
  Name *string
  . . .
}
. . .
request:=UpdateRequest {
  Name:ToPtr("test"),
}
```

Similarly, this generic function makes a slice from arbitrary values:

```go
func ToSlice[T any](value T) []T {
        return []T{value}
}


func main() {
  fmt.Println(ToSlice(1))
  // Prints an int slice: [1]
}
```

The following generic function returns the last element of a slice:

```go
func Last[T any](slice []T) (T, bool) {
    if len(slice) == 0 {
      var zero T
```

```
        return zero, false
    }
    return slice[len(slice)-1], true
}
```

It returns `false` if the slice is empty.

The following generic function can be used to adapt functions that return a value and an error to be used in contexts that accept only the value. The function panics if there is an error:

```
func Must[T any](value T, err error) T {
    if err != nil {
        panic(err)
    }
    return value
}
```

This adapts the `f() (T, error)` function into `Must(f()) T`.

Returning a zero value from a generic function

As I said before, a generic function must compile for all possible types allowed by the type constraints. This may cause trouble when creating a zero value.

How to do it...

To create a zero value of a parameterized type, simply declare a variable:

```
func Search[T []E, E comparable](slice T,value E) (E, bool) {
    for _,v:=range slice {
        if v==value {
            return v,true
        }
    }
    // Declare a zero value like this
    var zero E
    return zero, false
}
```

Using type assertion on generic arguments

Sometimes you need to do something different based on the type of a value in a generic function. That requires a type assertion or a type switch – both work for interfaces. However, there is no guarantee that the function will be instantiated for an interface. This recipe shows how you can achieve this.

How to do it...

Let's say you have a generic function that treats integers differently:

```
func Print[T any](value T) {
    // The following does not work because value is not necessarily an
    // interface{}.
    if intValue, ok:=value.(int); ok {
        ...
    } else {
        ...
    }
}
```

To make this work, you have to make sure the value is an interface:

```
func Print[T any](value T) {
    // Convert value to an interface
    valueIntf := any{value)
    if intValue, ok:=valueIntf.(int); ok {
        // Value is an integer
    } else {
        // Value is not an integer
    }
}
```

The same idea works for a type switch:

```
func Print[T any](value T) {
    switch v:=any(value).(type) {
    case int:
        // Value is an integer
    default;
        // Value is not an integer
    }
}
```

Generic types

The generic function syntax extends naturally to generic types. A generic type also has the same type parameters and constraints, and every method of that type also implicitly has the same parameters as the type itself.

Writing a type-safe set

A type-safe set can be implemented using a map [T] struct { }. One thing to be careful about is that T cannot be any type. Only comparable types can be map keys, and there is a predefined constraint to address this need.

How to do it...

1. Declare a parameterized set type using map:

```
type Set[T comparable] map[T]struct{}
```

2. Declare the methods of the type using the same type parameter(s). When declaring methods, you have to refer to the type parameters by name only:

```
// Has returns if the set has the given value
func (s Set[T]) Has(value T) bool {
    _, exists := s[value]
    return exists
}

// Add adds values to s
func (s Set[T]) Add(values ...T) {
    for _, v := range values {
        s[v] = struct{}{}
    }
}

// Remove removes values from s
func (s Set[T]) Remove(values ...T) {
    for _, v := range values {
        delete(s, v)
    }
}
```

3. If necessary, create a generic constructor for the new type:

```
// NewSet creates a new set
func NewSet[T comparable]() Set[T] {
    return make(Set[T])
}
```

4. Instantiate the type to use it:

```
stringSet := NewSet[string]()
```

Note the explicit instantiation of the NewSet function with the string type parameter. The compiler cannot infer what type you mean, so you have to spell out NewSet [string] (). Then the compiler instantiates the Set [string] type, which also instantiates all methods of that type.

An ordered map – using multiple type parameters

This implementation of an ordered map allows you to keep the order of elements added to a map using a slice combined with a map.

How to do it...

1. Define a struct with two type parameters:

```
type OrderedMap [Key comparable, Value any] struct {
    m       map [Key] Value
    slice [] Key
}
```

Since Key will be used as the map key, it has to be comparable. There are no constraints on the value type.

Define the methods for the type. The methods are now declared using both Key and Value:

```
// Add key:value to the map
func (m *OrderedMap [Key, Value]) Add (key Key, value Value) {
    _, exists := m.m [key]
    if exists {
        m.m [key] = value
    } else {
        m.slice = append (m.slice, key)
        m.m [key] = value
    }
}


// ValueAt returns the value at the given index
func (m *OrderedMap [Key, Value]) ValueAt (index int) Value {
    return m.m [m.slice [index]]
}


// KeyAt returns the key at the given index
func (m *OrderedMap [Key, Value]) KeyAt (index int) Key {
    return m.slice [index]
}


// Get returns the value corresponding to the key, and whether or not
```

```
// key exists
func (m *OrderedMap[Key, Value]) Get(key Key) (Value, bool) {
    v, bool := m.m[key]
    return v, bool
}
```

> **Tip**
>
> The type parameters for the receiver are matched by position, not name. In other words, you can define a method as follows:
>
> ```
> func (m *OrderedMap[K, V]) ValueAt(index int) V {
>
>     return m.m[m.slice[index]]
>
> }
> ```

Here, K is for Key, and V is for Value.

1. Define a constructor generic function if necessary:

```
func NewOrderedMap[Key comparable, Value any]() *OrderedMap[Key,
Value] {
    return &OrderedMap[Key, Value]{
        m:      make(map[Key]Value),
        slice: make([]Key, 0),
    }
}
```

> **Tip**
>
> A constructor is necessary in this case because we want to initialize the map in the generic struct. It is tempting to check for a nil map every time you want to add something to the container. You have to choose between the convenience of having a container type whose zero value is ready to use versus the performance penalty you pay checking a nil map every time something is added.

7

Concurrency

Concurrency is a core part of the Go language. Unlike many other languages that support concurrency via rich multi-threading libraries, Go provides relatively few language primitives to write concurrent programs.

Let's start by emphasizing that concurrency is **not** parallelism. Concurrency is about how you write programs; parallelism is about how programs run. A concurrent program specifies what parts of the program can run in parallel. Depending on the actual execution, concurrent parts of a program may run sequentially, concurrently using time-sharing, or in parallel. A correct concurrent program yields the same result regardless of how it is run.

This chapter introduces some of the Go concurrency primitives using recipes. In this chapter, you will learn about the following:

- Creating goroutines
- Running multiple independent functions concurrently and waiting for them to end
- Sending and receiving data using channels
- Sending data to a channel from multiple goroutines
- Collecting the results of concurrent computations using channels
- Working with multiple channels using the `select` statement
- Canceling a goroutine
- Detecting cancelation using nonblocking `select`
- Updating shared variables concurrently

Doing things concurrently using goroutines

A goroutine is a function that runs concurrently with other goroutines. When a program starts, the Go runtime creates several goroutines. One of these goroutines runs the garbage collector. Another goroutine runs the `main` function. As the program executes, it creates more goroutines as necessary.

A typical go program may have thousands of goroutines all running concurrently. The Go runtime schedules these goroutines to operating system threads. Each operating system thread is assigned a number of goroutines that it runs using time sharing. At any given moment, there can be as many active goroutines as the number of logical processors:

```
Number of threads per core * Number of cores per CPU * Number of CPUs
```

Creating goroutines

Goroutines are an integral part of the Go language. You create goroutines using the go keyword.

How to do it...

Create goroutines using the go keyword followed by a function call:

```
func f() {
  // Do some work
}

func main() {
  go f()
  ...
}
```

When go f() is evaluated, the runtime creates a new goroutine and calls the f function. The goroutine running main also continues running. In other words, when the go keyword is evaluated, the program execution splits into two concurrent execution streams – one is the original execution stream (in the preceding example, the stream that is running main) and the other runs the function that comes after the go keyword.

The function can take arguments if necessary:

```
func f(i int) {
  // Do some work
}

func main() {
  var x int
  go f(x)
  ...
}
```

The arguments to the function are evaluated before the goroutine starts. That is, the main goroutine first evaluates the argument of f (which is, in this case, the x value) and then creates a new goroutine and runs f.

It is common practice to use a closure to run goroutines. They provide the context necessary for understanding code. They also prevent passing many variables as arguments to goroutines:

```
func main() {
  var x int
  var y int
  ...
  go func(i int) {
    if y > 0 {
      // Do some work
    }
  }(x)
  ...
}
```

Here, x is passed as an argument to the goroutine, but y is captured.

When the function run by the go keyword ends, the goroutine terminates.

Running multiple independent functions concurrently and waiting for them to complete

When you have multiple independent functions that do not share data, you can use this recipe to run them concurrently. We will also use sync.WaitGroup to wait for the goroutines to finish.

How to do it...

1. Create an instance of sync.WaitGroup to wait for goroutines:

    ```
    wg := sync.WaitGroup{}
    ```

    A sync.WaitGroup is simply a thread-safe counter. We will use wg.Add(1) for each goroutine we create, and use wg.Done() to subtract 1 whenever a goroutine ends. Then we can wait for the waitgroup to reach zero, signaling the termination of all goroutines.

2. For each function that will run concurrently, do the following:

    - Add 1 to the wait group

    - Start a new goroutine

    - Call defer wg.Done() to make sure you signal goroutine termination

    ```
    wg.Add(1)
    go func() {
      defer wg.Done()
      // Do work
    }()
    ```

> **Tip**
>
> Instead of adding 1 to the wait group for every goroutine, you can simply add the number of goroutines. For instance, if you know that you will create 5 goroutines, you can simply do `wg.Add(5)` before creating the first goroutine.

3. Wait for the goroutines to end:

    ```
    wg.Wait()
    ```

    This call will block until wg reaches zero, that is, until all goroutines call `wg.Done()`.

4. Now, you can use the results of all the goroutines.

    The crucial detail of this recipe is that all goroutines are independent, which means the following:

    All variables written by each goroutine are used exclusively by that goroutine until `wg.Done()`. Goroutines may read shared variables, but they cannot write to them. After `wg.Done()`, all goroutines are terminated and the variables they wrote can be used.

5. No goroutine depends on the result of another goroutine.

You should not attempt to read the results of a goroutine before `wg.Wait`. That is a memory race with undefined behavior.

A **memory race** happens when you write to a shared variable concurrently with other writes or reads. The result of a program containing a memory race is undefined.

Communicating between goroutines using channels

More often than not, multiple goroutines have to communicate and coordinate to distribute work, manage state, and collate results of computations. Channels are the preferred mechanism for this. A channel is a synchronization mechanism with an optional fixed-size buffer.

> **Tip:**
>
> The following recipes show channels that are closed. Closing a channel is a method for communicating end of data. If you do not close a channel, it will be garbage collected when it is no longer referenced. In other words, you don't need to close a channel if you don't need to signal end of data to the receivers.

Sending and receiving data using channels

A goroutine can send to a channel if there is another goroutine waiting to receive from it, or in the case of a buffered channel, there is space available in the channel buffer. Otherwise, the goroutine is blocked until it can send.

A goroutine can receive from a channel if there is another goroutine waiting to send to it, or in the case of a buffered channel, there is data in the channel buffer. Otherwise, the receiver is blocked until it can receive.

How to do it...

1. Create a channel with the type of data it will pass. The following example creates a channel that can pass strings.

    ```
    ch := make(chan string)
    ```

2. In a goroutine, send data elements to the channel. When all data elements are sent, close the channel:

    ```
    go func() {
      for _, str := range stringData {
          // Send the string to the channel. This will block until
          // another goroutine can receive from the channel.
          ch <- str
      }
      // Close the channel when done. This is the way to signal the
      // receiver goroutine that there is no more data available.
      close(ch)
    }()
    ```

3. Receive data from the channel in another goroutine. In the following example, the main goroutine receives strings from the channel and prints them. The `for` loop ends when the channel is closed:

    ```
    for str := range ch {
      fmt.Println(str)
    }
    ```

Sending data to a channel from multiple goroutines

There are cases where you have many goroutines working on a piece of a problem, and when they are done, they send the result using a channel. A problem with this situation is deciding when to close the channel. This recipe shows how it is done.

How to do It...

1. Create the result channel with the data type it will pass:

    ```
    ch := make(chan string)
    ```

2. Create the listener goroutine and a wait group to wait for its completion later. This goroutine will be blocked until the other goroutines start sending data:

```go
// Allocate results
results := make([]string, 0)
// WaitGroup will be used later to wait for the listener
// goroutine to end
listenerWg := sync.WaitGroup{}
listenerWg.Add(1)
go func() {
  defer listenerWg.Done()
  // Collect results and store in a slice
  for str:=range ch {
    results=append(results,str)
  }
}()
```

3. Create a wait group to keep track of the goroutines that will write to the result channel. Then, create goroutines that send to the channel:

```go
wg := sync.WaitGroup{}
for _,input := range inputs {
  wg.Add(1)
  go func(data string) {
    defer wg.Done()
    ch <- processInput(data)
  }(input)
}
```

4. Wait for the processing goroutines to end and close the result channel:

```go
// Wait for all goroutines to end
wg.Wait()
// Close the channel to signal end of data
// This will signal the listener goroutine that no more data
// will be arriving via the channel
close(ch)
```

5. Wait for the listener goroutine to end:

```go
listenerWg.Wait()
```

Now you can use the results slice.

Collecting the results of concurrent computations using channels

Often, you have multiple goroutines working on parts of a problem and you have to collect the result of each goroutine to compile a single result object. Channels are the perfect mechanism for this.

How to do it...

1. Create a channel to collect the results of the computation:

    ```
    resultCh := make(chan int)
    ```

    In this example, the resultCh channel is a channel of int values. That is, the results of the computations will be integers.

2. Create a sync.WaitGroup instance to wait for the goroutines:

    ```
    wg := sync.WaitGroup{}
    ```

3. Distribute work among goroutines. Each goroutine should have access to the resultCh. Add each goroutine to the wait group, and make sure to call defer wg.Done() in the goroutine.

4. Perform the computation in the goroutine, and send the result to the resultCh:

    ```
    var inputs [][]int=[]int{...}

    ...
    for i:=range inputs {
      wg.Add(1)
      go func(data []int) {
        defer wg.Done()
        // Perform the computation
        // computeResult takes a []int, and returns int
        // Send the result to resultCh
        resultCh <- computeResult(data)
      }(inputs[i])
    }
    ```

5. Here, you have to do two things: wait for all goroutines to complete and collect the results from the resultCh. There are two ways you can do this:

    *   Collect the results while waiting for the goroutines to end concurrently. That is, create a goroutine and wait for the goroutines to end. When all goroutines are done, close the channel:

    ```
    go func() {
      // Wait for the goroutines to end
      wg.Wait()
      // When all goroutines are done, close the channel
    ```

```
    close(resultCh)
}()
```

```
// Create a slice to contain results of the computations
results:=make([]int,0)
// Collect the results from the `resultCh`
// The for-loop will terminate when resultCh is closed
for result:=range resultCh {
   results=append(results,result)
}
```

- Collect the results asynchronously while waiting for the goroutines to end. When all goroutines are completed, close the channel. However, when you close the channel, the goroutine that collects the results may still be running. We have to wait for that goroutine to end as well. We can use another wait group for that purpose:

```
results:=make([]int,0)
// Create a new wait group just for the result collection
// goroutine
collectWg := sync.WaitGroup{}
// Add the collection goroutine to the waitgroup
collectWg.Add(1)
go func() {
   // Announce the completion of this goroutine
   defer collectWg.Done()
   // Collect results. The for-loop will terminate when resultCh
   // is closed.
   for result:= range resultCh {
      results=append(results,result)
   }
}()
```

```
// Wait for the goroutines to end.
wg.Wait()
// Close the channel so the result collection goroutine can
// finish
close(resultCh)
// Now wait for the result collection goroutine to finish
collectWg.Wait()
// results slice is ready
```

Working with multiple channels using the select statement

You can only send data or receive data from a channel at any given time. If you are interacting with multiple goroutines (and thus, multiple concurrent events), you need a language construct that will let you interact with multiple channels at once. That construct is the `select` statement.

This section shows how `select` is used.

How to do it...

A blocking `select` statement chooses an active case from zero or more cases. Each case is a channel send or channel receive event. If there are no active cases (that is, none of the channels can be sent to or received from), `select` is blocked.

In the following example, the `select` statement waits to receive from one of two channels. The program receives from only one of the channels. If both channels are ready, one of the channels will be picked randomly. The other channel will be left unread:

```
ch1:=make(chan int)
ch2:=make(chan int)
go func() {
   ch1<-1
}()
go func() {
   ch2<-2
}()

select {
case data1:= <- ch1:
   fmt.Println("Read from channel 1: %v", data1)
case data2:= <- ch2:
   fmt.Println("Read from channel 2: %v", data2)
}
```

Canceling goroutines

Creating goroutines is easy and efficient in Go, but you also have to make sure your goroutines end eventually. If a goroutine is left running unintentionally, it is called a "leaked" goroutine. If a program keeps leaking goroutines, eventually it crashes with an out-of-memory error.

Some goroutines perform a limited number of operations and terminate naturally, but some run indefinitely until an external stimulus is received. A common pattern for long-running goroutines to receive such stimulus is to use a `done` channel.

How to do it...

1. Create a done channel with an empty data type:

    ```
    done:=make(chan struct{})
    ```

2. Create a channel to provide input to goroutines:

    ```
    input := make(chan int)
    ```

3. Create goroutines that look like this:

    ```
    go func() {
      for {
        select {
          case data:= <- input:
            // Process data
          case <-done:
            // Done signal. Terminate
            return
        }
      }
    }()
    ```

To cancel the goroutine(s), simply close the done channel:

```
close(done)
```

This will enable the case <-done branch in all the goroutines that are listening to the done channel, and they will terminate.

Detecting cancelation using nonblocking select

A non-blocking select has a default case. When the select statement runs, it checks all the available cases, and if none of them are available, the default case is selected. This allows a select to continue without blocking.

How to do it...

1. Create a done channel with an empty data type:

    ```
    done:=make(chan struct{})
    ```

2. Create goroutines that look like this:

    ```
    go func() {
      for {
        select {
    ```

```
      case <-done:
         // Done signal. Terminate
         return
       default:
         // Done signal is not sent. Continue
     }
     // Do work
   }
 }()
```

To cancel the goroutine(s), simply close the done channel.

```
close(done)
```

Sharing memory

One of the most famous Go idioms is: "Do not communicate by sharing memory, share memory by communicating." Channels are for sharing memory by communicating. Communicating by sharing memory is done using shared variables in multiple goroutines. Even though it is discouraged, there are many use cases where shared memory makes more sense than a channel. If at least one of the goroutines updates a shared variable that is read by other goroutines, you have to ensure that there are no memory races.

A memory race happens when a goroutine updates a variable concurrently while another goroutine reads from it or writes to it. When this happens, there is no guarantee that the update to that variable will be seen by other goroutines. A famous example of this situation is the busy-wait loop:

```
func main() {
  done:=false
  go func() {
    // Wait while done==false
    for !done {}
    fmt.Println("Done is true now")
  }()
  done=true
  // Wait indefinitely
  select{}
}
```

This program has a memory race. The done=true assignment is concurrent with the for !done loop. That means, even though the main goroutine runs done=true, the goroutine reading done may never see that update, staying in the for loop indefinitely.

Updating shared variables concurrently

The Go memory model guarantees that the effect of a variable write is visible to instructions that come after that write within that goroutine only. That is, if you update a shared variable, you have to use special tools to make that update visible to other goroutines. A simple way to ensure this is to use a mutex. Mutex stands for "mutual exclusion." A mutex is a tool you can use to ensure the following:

- Only one goroutine updates a variable at any given time

- Once that update is done and the mutex is released, all goroutines can see that update

In this recipe, we show how this is done.

How to do it...

The section of a program that updates shared variables is a "critical section." You use a mutex to ensure that only a single goroutine can enter its critical section.

Declare a mutex to protect a critical section:

```
// cacheMutex will be used to protect access to cache
var cacheMutex sync.Mutex
var cache map[string]any = map[string]any{}
```

A mutex protects a set of shared variables. For instance, if you have goroutines that update a single integer, you declare a mutex for the critical sections that update that integer. You must use the same mutex every time you read or write that integer value.

When updating the shared variable(s), first lock the mutex. Then perform the update and unlock the mutex:

```
cacheMutex.Lock()
cache[key]=value
cacheMutex.Unlock()
```

With this pattern, if multiple goroutines attempt to update cache, they will queue at cacheMutex.Lock() and only one will be allowed. When that goroutine performs the update, it will call cacheMutex.Unlock(), which will enable one of the waiting goroutines to acquire the lock and update the cache again.

When reading the shared variable, first lock the mutex. Then perform the read, and then unlock the mutex:

```
cacheMutex.Lock()
cachedValue, cached := cache[key]
cacheMutex.Unlock()
if cached {
  // Value found in cache
}
```

8

Errors and Panics

Go error handling has been nothing but polarizing. Those who came from a background in languages with exception handling (such as Java) tend to hate it, and those who came from a background in languages where errors are values returned from functions (such as C) feel comfortable with it.

Having a background in both, I am of the opinion that the explicit nature of error handling forces you to think about exceptional situations at every step of the development. Error generation, error passing, and error handling require the same type of discipline and scrutiny as the "happy path" (which is when no errors happen).

If you noticed, I make a distinction between three phases of dealing with errors:

- Detection and generation of errors deal with detecting an exceptional situation and capturing diagnostic information

- Passing of errors deals with allowing errors to be propagated up the stack, optionally decorating them with contextual information

- Handling of errors deals with actually resolving the error, which may include terminating the program

In this chapter, you will learn about the following:

- How to generate errors

- How to pass them by annotating them using contextual information

- How to handle errors

- Organizing errors in a project

- Dealing with panics

Returning and handling errors

This recipe shows how to detect errors and how to wrap errors with additional contextual information.

How to do it...

Use the last return value of a function or method for errors:

```
func DoesNotReturnError() {...}

func MayReturnError() error {...}

func MayReturnStringAndError() (string,error) {...}
```

If the function or method is successful, it will return `nil` error. If an error condition is detected within the function or method, either return that error verbatim or wrap the error with another one containing contextual information:

```
func LoadConfig(f string) (*Config, error) {
    file, err:=os.Open(f)
    if err!=nil {
        return nil, fmt.Errorf("file %s: %w", f,err)
    }
    defer file.Close()
    var cfg Config
    err = json.NewDecoder(file).Decode(&cfg)
    if err!=nil {
        return nil, fmt.Errorf("While unmarshaling %s: %w",f,err)
    }
    return &cfg, nil
}
```

> **Tip**
> Do not use `panic` as a replacement for error. `panic` should be used to signal a potential bug or unrecoverable situation. An error is used to signal a context-dependent situation, such as a missing file or invalid input.

How it works...

Go uses explicit error detection and handling. That means there is no implicit or hidden execution path for errors (such as throwing an exception). Go errors are simply interface values and an error being `nil` is interpreted as the absence of an error. The above function calls some file management functions that can return an error. When that happens (that is, when the function returns a non-`nil` error), this function simply wraps that error with additional information and returns it. The additional information allows the caller, and sometimes the user of the program to determine the correct course of action.

Wrapping errors to add contextual information

Using the standard library `errors` package, you can wrap an error with another error that contains additional contextual information. This package also provides facilities and conventions that will let you check if an error tree contains a particular error or extract a particular error from an error tree.

How to do it...

Add contextual information to an error using `fmt.Errorf`. In the following example, the returned error will contain the error returned from `os.Open`, and it will also include the file name:

```
file, err := os.Open(fileName)
if err!=nil {
    return fmt.Errorf("%w: While opening %s",err,fileName)
}
```

Note the use of `%w` verb in `fmt.Errorf` above. The %w verb is used to create an error wrapping the one given as its argument. If we used %v or %s, the returned error would contain the text of the original error, but it would not wrap it.

Comparing errors

When you wrap an error with additional information, the new error value is not of the same type or value as the original error. For instance, `os.Open` may return `os.ErrNotExist` if the file is not found, and if you wrap this error with additional information, such as the file name, the caller of this function will need a way to get to the original error to handle it properly. This recipe shows how to deal with such wrapped error values.

How to do it...

Checking if there is an error or not is simple: check if an error value is `nil` or not:

```
file, err := os.Open(fileName)
if err!=nil {
  // File could not be opened
}
```

Checking if an error is what you expect should be done using `errors.Is`:

```
file, err := os.Open(fileName)
if errors.Is(err,os.ErrNotExist) {
  // File does not exist
}
```

How it works...

`errors.Is(err,target error)` compares if `err` is equal to `target` by doing the following:

1. It checks if `err==target`.
2. If that fails, it checks if `err` has an `Is(error) bool` method by calling `err.Is(target)`.
3. If that fails, it checks if `err` has an `Unwrap() error` method and `err.Unwrap()` is not `nil` by checking if `err.Unwrap()` is equal to `target`.
4. If that fails, it checks if `err` has an `Unwrap() []error` method, and if `target` is equal to any one of those slice elements.

The meaning of this is that if you wrap an error, the caller can still check if the wrapped error happened and behave accordingly.

If you define an error using `errors.New()` or `fmt.Errorf()`, then the returned error interface contains a pointer to an object. In this case, the fact that two errors have the same string representation doesn't mean that they are equal. The following program shows this situation:

```
var e1 = errors.New("test")
var e2 = errors.New("test")
if e1 != e2 {
    fmt.Println("Errors are different!")
}
```

Above, even though the error strings are the same, `e1` and `e2` are pointers pointing to different objects. The program will print `Errors are different`. Thus, declaring errors like the following works:

```
var (
  ErrNotFound = errors.New("Not found")
)
```

A comparison to `ErrNotFound` will compare if an error value is a pointer to the same object as `ErrNotFound`.

Structured errors

A **structured error** provides contextual information that can be crucial in handling the errors before they reach the user of a program. This recipe shows how such errors can be used.

How to do it...

1. Define a struct containing metadata that captures the error situation.
2. Implement the `Error() string` method to make it an `error`.

3. If the error can wrap other errors, include an error or [] error to store those.

4. Optionally, implement the Is(error) bool method to control how to compare this error.

5. Optionally, implement Unwrap() error or Unwrap() [] error to return wrapped errors.

How it works...

Any data type implementing the error interface (containing only one method, Error() string) can be used as an error. This means that you can create data structures containing detailed error information that can be later acted upon. So, if you need several data fields to describe an error, instead of building an elaborate string and returning it via fmt.Errorf, you can use a struct.

As an example, let's assume you are parsing a multi-line formatted text input. Returning accurate and useful information to your users is important; nobody will enjoy receiving a Syntax error message without showing where the error is. So, you declare this error structure:

```
type ErrSyntax struct {
    Line int
    Col int
    Diag string
}

func (err ErrSyntax) Error() string {
    return fmt.Sprintf("Syntax error line: %d col: %d, %s", err.Line,
    err.Col, err.Diag)
}
```

You can now generate useful error information:

```
func ParseInput(input string) error {
    ...
    if nextRune != ',' {
      return ErrSyntax {
          Line: line,
          Col: col,
          Diag: "Expected comma",
      }
    }
    ...
}
```

You can use this error information to display useful messages to your users or control an interactive response, such as positioning the cursor to where the error is or highlighting text near the error location.

Wrapping structured errors

A structured error can be used to decorate another error with additional information by wrapping it. This recipe shows how to do that.

How to do it...

1. Keep an error member variable (or a slice of errors) to store the root cause in the structure.
2. Implement `Unwrap() error` (or `Unwrap() []error`) method.

How it works...

You can wrap the root cause error in a structured error. This allows you to add structured contextual information about the error:

```go
type ErrFile struct {
    Name string
    When string
    Err error
}

func (err ErrFile) Error() string {
    return fmt.Sprintf("%s: file %s, when %s", err.Err, err.Name, err.
    When)
}

func (err ErrFile) Unwrap() error { return err.Err }

func ReadConfigFile(name string) error {
  f, err:=os.Open(name)
  if err!=nil {
     return ErrFile {
        Name: name,
        Err:err,
        When: "opening configuration file",
     }
  }
  ...
}
```

Note that Unwrap is necessary. Without that, the following code will fail to detect that the error is derived from os.ErrNotFound:

```
err:=ReadConfig("config.json")
if errors.Is(err,os.ErrNotFound) {
    // file not found
}
```

With the Unwrap method, the errors.Is function can descend the enclosed errors, and determine if at least one of them is os.ErrNotFound.

Comparing structured errors by type

In languages that support try-catch blocks, you usually catch errors based on their type. You can emulate the same functionality relying on errors.Is.

How to do it...

Implement the Is(error) bool method in your error type to define what type of equivalence you care about.

How it works...

You may remember that the errors.Is(err,target) function first tests if err = target, and if that fails, it tests if err.Is(target), provided err implements the Is(error) bool method. So, you can use the Is(error) bool method to tune how to compare your custom error types. Without the Is(error) bool method, errors.Is will compare using ==, which will fail if the contents of two errors are different even if they are the same type. The following example allows you to check if the given error contains ErrSyntax somewhere in the error tree:

```
type ErrSyntax struct {
    Line int
    Col int
    Err error
}

func (err ErrSyntax) Error() string {...}

func (err ErrSyntax) Is(e error) bool {
    _,ok:=e.(ErrSyntax)
    return ok
}
```

Now, you can test if an error is a syntax error:

```
err:=Parse(input)
if errors.Is(err,ErrSyntax{}) {
    // err is a syntax error
}
```

Extracting a specific error from the error tree

How to do it...

Use the `errors.As` function to descend an error tree, find a particular error, and extract it.

How it works...

Similar to the `errors.Is` function, `errors.As(err error, target any) bool` descends the error tree of `err` until an error that is assignable to `target` is found. That is done by the following:

1. It checks if the value pointed to by `target` is assignable to the value pointed to by `err`.

2. If that fails, it checks if `err` has an `As(error) bool` method by calling `err.As(target)`. If it returns `true`, then an error is found.

3. If not, it checks if `err` has an `Unwrap() error` method and `err.Unwrap()` is not `nil`, descending the tree.

4. Otherwise, it checks if `err` has an `Unwrap() []error` method, and if it returns a non-empty slice, it descends the tree for each of those until a match is found.

In other words, `errors.As` copies the error that can be assigned to `target` into `target`.

The following example can be used to extract an instance of `ErrSyntax` from an error tree:

```
func (err ErrSyntax) As(target any) bool {
    if tgt, ok:=target.(*ErrSyntax); ok {
        *tgt=err
        return true
    }
    return false
}

func main() {
    ...
    err:=Parse(in)
    var syntaxError ErrSyntax
    if errors.As(err,&syntaxError) {
```

```
        // syntaxError has a copy of the ErrSyntax
    }
    ...
}
```

Note the use of pointers here. The error struct is used as a value, and you want a copy of that error struct, so you pass a pointer to it: an instance of `ErrSyntax` can be copied into an instance of `*ErrSyntax`. If your program used `*ErrSyntax` as the error value, you need to send `**ErrSyntax` by declaring `var syntaxError *ErrSyntax` and passing `&syntaxError` to copy the pointer into the memory location pointed to by the double-pointer.

Dealing with panics

In general, a **panic** is an unrecoverable situation, such as resource exhaustion or a violation of an invariant (that is, a bug). Some panics, such as out of memory or divide by zero, will be raised by the runtime (or raised by the hardware and transferred to the program as a panic). You should generate a panic in your program when you detect a bug. But how do you decide if a situation is a bug and you should panic or an error?

In general, an external input (user input, data submitted by an API, or data read from a file) should not cause a panic. Such situations should be detected and returned as meaningful errors to the user. A panic in this situation would be, for instance, a failed compilation of a regular expression that is declared as a constant string in your program. The input is not something that can be fixed by re-running the program with different inputs; it is simply a bug.

If a panic is not handled with `recover`, the program will terminate by printing diagnostic output, including the reason for panic and the stacks of active goroutines.

Panicking when necessary

Most of the time, deciding whether to panic or to return an error is not an easy decision. This recipe offers some guidelines to make that decision easier.

How to do it...

There are two situations where you can panic. Panic if either of the following is the case:

- An invariant is violated
- The program cannot continue in the current state

An invariant is a condition that cannot be violated in a program. Thus, if you detect that it is violated, instead of returning an error, panic.

The following example is from a graph library I wrote. A graph contains nodes and edges, managed by a *Graph structure. The Graph.NewEdge method creates a new edge between two nodes. Those two nodes must belong to the same graph as the receiver of the NewEdge method so it is appropriate to panic if that is not the case, as follows:

```go
func (g *Graph) NewEdge(from,to *Node) *Edge {
   if from.graph!=g {
      panic("from node is not in graph")
   }
   if to.graph!=g {
      panic("to node is not in graph")
   }
   ...
}
```

Above, there is nothing that can be gained by returning an error from this method. This is clearly a bug the caller did not realize, and if the program is allowed to continue, the integrity of the Graph object will be violated, creating hard-to-find bugs. The best course of action is to panic.

The second situation is a broad case where continuation is not possible. As an example, consider you are writing a web application and you load HTML templates from the file system. If the compilation of such a template fails, the program cannot continue. You should panic.

Recovering from panics

An unhandled panic will terminate the program. Often, this is the only correct course of action. However, there are cases where you want to fail whatever caused the error, log it, and continue. For example, a server handling many requests concurrently does not terminate just because one of the requests panicked. This recipe shows how you can recover from a panic.

How to do it...

Use a recover statement in a defer function:

```go
func main() {
   defer func() {
      if r:=recover(); r != nil {
         // deal with the panic
      }
   }()

   ...
}
```

How it works...

When a program panics, the panicking function will return after all deferred blocks are executed. The stack of that goroutine will unroll one function after the other, cleaning up by running their `deferred` statements, until the beginning of the goroutine is reached, or one of the deferred functions invokes `recover`. If the panic is not recovered, the program will crash by printing out diagnostic and stack information. If the panic is recovered, the `recover()` function will return whatever parameter was given to `panic`, which can be any value.

So, if you recover from a panic, you should check if the recovered value is an error that you can use to give more useful information.

Changing return value in recover

When you recover from a panic, you usually want to return some sort of error describing what happened. This recipe shows you how to do that.

How to do it...

To change the return value of a function when recovered from a panic, use named return values.

How it works...

A **named return value** allows you to access and set the return values of a function. As shown below, you can change the return value of a function using named return values:

```
func process() (err error) {
    defer func() {
        r:=recover()
        if e, ok:=r.(error); ok {
            err = e
        }
    }
```

Capturing the stack trace of a panic

Printing or logging a stack trace when a panic is detected is a critical tool in identifying problems at runtime. This recipe shows how you can add a stack trace to your logging messages.

How to do it...

Use the `debug.Stack` function with `recover`:

```go
import "runtime/debug"
import "fmt"

func main() {
    defer func() {
        if r := recover(); r != nil {
            stackTrace := string(debug.Stack())
            // Work with stackTrace
            fmt.Println(stackTrace)
        }
    }()
    f()
}

func f() {
    var i *int
    *i=0
}
```

When inside the recovery function, the `debug.Stack` function will return the stack of the panic that is being recovered, not the stack where it is called. Thus, if you can log this information or print it, it will show you the exact location of the source of the panic.

> **Warning**
>
> Getting the stack this way is an expensive operation. Use it carefully and only when necessary.

The preceding program will print the following:

```
goroutine 1 [running]:
runtime/debug.Stack()
        /usr/local/go-faketime/src/runtime/debug/stack.go:24 +0x5e
main.main.func1()
        /tmp/sandbox381445105/prog.go:13 +0x25
panic({0x48bbc0?, 0x5287c0?})
        /usr/local/go-faketime/src/runtime/panic.go:770 +0x132
```

```
main.f(...)
      /tmp/sandbox381445105/prog.go:23
main.main()
      /tmp/sandbox381445105/prog.go:18 +0x2e
```

Here:

- `prog.go:13` is where `debug.Stack()` is called
- `prog.go:23` is where `*i=0` is executed
- `prog.go:18` is where `f()` is called

As you can see, the stack pinpoints the exact location of the error (`prog.go:23`).

9
The Context Package

Context is the circumstances in which something happens. When we are talking about a program, the context is the program environment, settings, and so on. For a server program (an HTTP server responding to a client request, an RPC server responding to function calls, etc.) or a program that responds to user requests (an interactive program, a command-line application, etc.), you can talk about a request-specific context. A request-specific context is created when the server or program starts processing a particular request and terminates when the processing ends. The request context contains information such as a request identifier that helps you identify log messages generated while processing a request, or the identity of the caller so you can determine the access rights of the caller. One of the uses of the context package is to provide an abstraction of such a request context, that is, an object that keeps request-specific data.

You may also have concerns about the running time of a request. You usually want to limit the amount of time a request is processed, or you may want to detect that the client is no longer interested in the results of the request (such as a WebSocket peer disconnecting). The context package is designed to handle these use cases as well.

The context package defines the context.Context interface. It has two uses:

- Add a timeout and/or cancellation to request processing
- Pass request-specific metadata down the stack

The use of context.Context is not limited to server programs. The term "request processing" should be taken in a broad sense: the request can be a network request through a TCP connection, an HTTP request, a command read from a command line, running a program with a certain flag, and so on. So, the uses for context.Context are much more diverse.

This chapter shows common uses of the context package. In this chapter, you will learn about the following:

- Passing request-scoped data using context
- Using contexts for cancellation and timeouts

Using context for passing request-scoped data

Request-scoped objects are those that are created when request processing starts and discarded when request processing ends. These are usually lightweight objects, such as a request identifier, authentication information identifying the caller, or loggers. In this section, you will see how these objects can be passed around using a context.

How to do it...

The idiomatic way of adding data values to a context is as follows:

1. Define a context key type. This avoids accidental name collisions. The use of an unexported type name such as the following is common. This pattern limits the ability to put or get context values of this particular type to the current package:

    ```
    type requestIDKeyType int
    ```

> **Warning**
>
> You might be tempted to use `struct{}` instead of `int` here. After all, `struct{}` does not consume any additional memory. You have to be very careful when working with 0-size structures as the Go language specification does not offer any guarantees about the equivalence of two 0-size structures. That is, if you create multiple variables of a 0-size type, they may sometimes be equal and sometimes not. In short, do not use `struct{}` for this.

2. Define the key value, or values, using the key type. In the following code line, `requestIDKey` is defined to be of type `requestIDKeyType` with the value 0 (`requestIDKey` is initialized to its 0 value when declared):

    ```
    var requestIDKey requestIDKeyType
    ```

3. Use `context.WithValue` to add the new value to the context. You can define a couple of helper functions to set and get values to and from the context:

    ```
    func WithRequestID(ctx context.Context, requestID string)
    context.Context {
      return context.WithValue(ctx, requestIDKey, requestID)
    }

    func GetRequestID(ctx context.Context) string {
      id,_:=ctx.Value(requestIDKey).(string)
      return id
    }
    ```

4. Pass the new context to the functions called from the current function:

```
newCtx:=WithRequestID(ctx,requestID)
handleRequest(newCtx)
```

How it works...

You may have noticed that `context.Context` does not exactly look like a key-value map (there is no `SetValue` method; in fact, `context.Context` is immutable) even though you can use it to store key-value pairs. In fact, you cannot add a key value to a context, but you can get a new context containing that key value while keeping the old context. Contexts have layers like an onion; every addition to a context creates a new context that is linked to the old one, but with more features:

```
// ctx: An empty context
ctx := context.Background()
// ctx1: ctx + {key1:value1}
ctx1 := context.WithValue(ctx, "key1", "value1")
// ctx2: ctx1 + {key2:value2}
ctx2 := context.WithValue(ctx, "key2", "value2")
```

In the preceding code, ctx, ctx1, and ctx2 are three different contexts. The ctx context is empty. ctx1 contains ctx and the key1: value1 key-value pair. ctx2 contains ctx1 and the key2: value2 key-value pair . So, say you do the following:

```
val1,_ := ctx2.Value("key1")
val2,_ := ctx2.Value("key2")
fmt.Println(val1, val2)
```

This will print the following:

```
value1 value2
```

Say you do the same with ctx1:

```
val1,_ = ctx1.Value("key1")
val2,_ = ctx1.Value("key2")
fmt.Println(val1, val2)
```

This will print the following:

```
value1 <nil>
```

The following is used for ctx:

```
val1,_ = ctx.Value("key1")
val2,_ = ctx.Value("key2")
fmt.Println(val1, val2)
```

This will print the following:

```
<nil> <nil>
```

> **Tip**
> Even though you cannot set the values in a context (that is, a context is immutable), you can set a pointer to a struct and set the values in that struct.

That is:

```
type ctxData struct {
  value int
}

...
ctx:=context.WithValue(context.Background(),dataKey, &ctxData{})
...
if data,exists:=ctx.Value(dataKey); exists {
  data.(*ctxData).value=1
}
```

The standard library provides a couple of predefined context values:

- `context.Background()` returns a context that has no values and that cannot be canceled. This is usually the base context for most operations.

- `context.TODO()` is similar to `context.Background()` with a name that says wherever it is used should eventually be refactored to accept a real context.

There's more...

A context is usually shared among multiple goroutines. You have to be careful about concurrency issues especially if you put pointers to objects in a context. Take a look at the following example, which shows an authentication middleware for an HTTP service:

```
type AuthInfo struct {
  // Set when AuthInfo is created
  UserID string
  // Lazy-initialized
  privileges map[string]Privilege
}

type authInfoKeyType int
var authInfoKey authInfoKeyType
```

```
// Set the privileges if is it not initialized.
// Do not do this!!
func (auth *AuthInfo) GetPrivileges() map[string]Privilege {
   if auth.privileges==nil {
      auth.privileges=GetPrivileges(auth.UserID)
   }
   return auth.privileges
}

// Authentication middleware
func AuthMiddleware(next http.Handler) func(http.Handler) http.Handler
{
    return func(next http.Handler) http.Handler {
        return http.HandlerFunc(func(w http.ResponseWriter, r *http.
        Request) {
            // Authenticate the caller
            var authInfo *AuthInfo
            var err error
            authInfo, err = authenticate(r)
            if err != nil {
                http.Error(w, err.Error(), http.StatusUnauthorized)
                return
            }
            // Create a new context with the authentication info
            newCtx := context.WithValue(r.Context(), authInfoKey,
            authInfo)
            // Pass the new context to the next handler
            next.ServeHTTP(w, r.WithContext(newCtx))
        })
    }
}
```

The authentication middleware creates an *AuthInfo instance and calls the next handler in the chain using a context with the authentication info. The problem in this code is that *AuthInfo contains a privileges field that is initialized when AuthInfo.GetPrivileges is called. Since the context can be passed to multiple goroutines by the handlers, this lazy initialization scheme is prone to data races; several goroutines calling AuthInfo.GetPrivileges may attempt to initialize the map multiple times, one overwriting the other.

This can be corrected using a mutex:

```
type AuthInfo struct {
  sync.Mutex
  UserID string
```

```
    privileges map[string]Privilege
}

func (auth *AuthInfo) GetPrivileges() map[string]Privilege {
    // Use mutex to initialize the privileges in a thread-safe way
    auth.Lock()
    defer auth.Unlock()
    if auth.privileges==nil {
        auth.privileges=GetPrivileges(auth.UserID)
    }
    return auth.privileges
}
```

It can also be corrected by initializing the privileges once in the middleware:

```
authInfo, err=authenticate(r)
if err!=nil {
    http.Error(w,err.Error(),http.StatusUnauthorized)
    return
}
// Initialize the privileges here when the structure is created
authInfo.GetPrivileges()
```

Using context for cancellations

There are several reasons why you might want to cancel a computation: the client may have disconnected, or you may have multiple goroutines working on a computation and one of them failed, so you no longer want the others to continue. You can use other methods, such as a done channel that you close to signal cancellation, but a context can be more convenient depending on the use case. A context can be canceled many times (only the first call will actually cancel; the remaining ones will be ignored), whereas you cannot close an already closed channel as it will panic. Also, you can create a tree of contexts where canceling one context only cancels goroutines controlled by it, without affecting others.

How to do it...

These are the steps to create a cancelable context and to detect a cancellation:

1. Use context.WithCancel to create a new cancelable context based on an existing context, and a cancellation function:

    ```
    ctx:=context.Background()
    cancelable, cancel:=context.WithCancel(ctx)
    defer cancel()
    ```

    Make sure the cancel function is eventually called. Canceling releases the resources associated with the context.

2. Pass the cancelable context to computations or goroutines that can be canceled:

```
go cancelableGoroutine1(cancelable)
go cancelableGoroutine2(cancelable)
cancelableFunc(cancelable)
```

3. In the cancelable function, check whether the context is canceled using the `ctx.Done()` channel, or `ctx.Err()`:

```
func cancelableFunc(ctx context.Context) {
    // Process some data
    // Check context cancelation
    select {
        case <-ctx.Done():
            // Context canceled
            return
        default:
    }
    // Continue computation
}
```

Or, use the following:

```
func cancelableFunc(ctx context.Context) {
    // Process some data
    // Check context cancelation
    if ctx.Err()!=nil {
        // Context canceled
        return
    }
    // Continue computation
}
```

4. To cancel a function manually, call the cancellation function:

```
ctx:=context.Background()
cancelable, cancel:=context.WithCancel(ctx)
defer cancel()
wg:=sync.WaitGroup{}
wg.Add(1)
go cancelableGoroutine1(cancelable,&wg)
if err:=process(ctx); err!=nil {
    // Cancel the context
    cancel()
    // Do other things
}
wg.Wait()
```

5. Ensure the `cancel` function is called eventually (use `defer cancel()`):

```
cancelable, cancel := context.WithCancel(ctx)
defer cancel()
...
```

> **Warning**
>
> Ensuring `cancel` is called is important. If you do not cancel a cancelable context, goroutines associated with that context will leak (i.e., there will be no way to terminate the goroutines and they will consume memory).

> **Tip**
>
> The `cancel` function can be called multiple times. Subsequent calls will be ignored.

How it works...

`context.WithCancel` returns a new context and the `cancel` closure. The returned context is a cancelable context based on the original context:

```
// Empty context, no cancelation
originalContext := context.Background()
// Cancelable context based on originalContext
cancelableContext1, cancel1 := context.WithCancel(originalContext)
```

You can use this context to control several goroutines:

```
go f1(cancelableContext1)
go f2(cancelableContext1)
```

You can also create other cancelable contexts based on a cancelable context:

```
cancelableContext2, cancel2 := context.WithCancel(cancelableContext)
go g1(cancelableContext2)
go g2(cancelableContext2)
```

Now, we have two cancelable contexts. Calling `cancel2` will only cancel `cancelableContext2`:

```
cancal2() // canceling g1 and g2 only
```

Calling `cancel1` will cancel both `cancelableContext1` and `cancelableContext2`:

```
cancel1() // canceling f1, f2, g1, g2
```

Context cancellation is not an automated way to cancel goroutines. You have to check for context cancellation and cleanup accordingly:

```go
func f1(cancelableContext context.Context) {
    for {
        if cancelableContext.Err()!=nil {
            // Context is canceled
            // Cleanup and return
            return
        }
        // Process
    }
}
```

Using context for timeouts

A timeout is simply an automated cancellation. The context will cancel after a timer expires. This is useful in limiting resource consumption for computations that are not likely to finish.

How to do it...

These are the steps to create a context with timeout and to detect when a timeout event happens:

1. Use context.WithTimeout to create a new cancelable context that will auto-cancel after a given duration based on an existing context and a cancellation function:

    ```go
    ctx:=context.Background()
    timeoutable, cancel:=context.WithTimeout(ctx,5*time.Second)
    defer cancel()
    ```

    Alternatively, you can use WithDeadline to cancel the context at a given moment.

    Make sure the cancel function is eventually called.

2. Pass the timeout context to computations or goroutines that can time out:

    ```go
    go longRunningGoroutine1(timeoutable)
    go longRunningGoroutine2(timeoutable)
    ```

3. In the goroutine, check whether the context is canceled using the ctx.Done() channel or ctx.Err():

    ```go
    func longRunningGoroutine(ctx context.Context) {
        // Process some data
        // Check context cancelation
        select {
    ```

```
        case <-ctx.Done():
            // Context canceled
            return
        default:
    }
    // Continue computation
}
```

Alternatively, use the following:

```
func cancelableFunc(ctx context.Context) {
    // Process some data
    // Check context cancelation
    if ctx.Err()!=nil {
        // Context canceled
        return
    }
    // Continue computation
}
```

4. To cancel a function manually, call the cancellation function:

```
ctx:=context.Background()
timeoutable, cancel:=context.WithTimeout(ctx, 5*time.Second)
defer cancel()
wg:=sync.WaitGroup{}
wg.Add(1)
go longRunningGoroutine(timeoutable,&wg)
if err:=process(ctx); err!=nil {
    // Cancel the context
    cancel()
    // Do other things
}
wg.Wait()
```

5. Ensure the cancel function is called eventually (use defer cancel()):

```
timeoutable, cancel := context.WithTimeout(ctx,5*time.Second)
defer cancel()
...
```

How it works...

The timeout feature is simply cancellation with an attached timer. When the timer expires, the context is canceled.

There's more...

There may be situations where a goroutine blocks without any obvious way to cancel it. For instance, you may block waiting to read from a network connection:

```go
func readData(conn net.Conn) {
  // Read a block of data from the connection
  msg:=make([]byte,1024)
  n, err:=conn.Read(msg)
  ...
}
```

This operation cannot be canceled, because Read does not take Context. If you want to cancel such an operation, you can close the underlying connection (or file) asynchronously. The following code snippet demonstrates a use case where all data from a connection must be read within one second, or a goroutine will close the connection asynchronously:

```go
timeout, cancel := context.WithTimeout(context.Background(),1*time.
Second)
defer cancel()

// Close the connection when context times out
go func() {
    // Wait for cancelation signal
    <-cancelable.Done()
    // Close the connection
    conn.Close()
} ()

wg:=sync.WaitGroup()
wg.Add(1)
// This goroutine must complete within a second, or the connection
// will be closed
go func() {
    defer wg.Done()
     // Read a block of data from the connetion
    msg:=make([]byte,1024)
    // This call may block
    n, err:=conn.Read(msg)
    if err!=nil {
       return
    }
    // Process data
} ()
```

```
wg.Wait() // Wait for the processing of connection to complete
...
```

Using cancellations and timeouts in servers

Network servers usually start a new context when a new request is received. Usually, the server cancels the context when the requester closes the connection. Most HTTP frameworks, including the standard library, follow this basic pattern. If you are writing your own TCP server, you have to implement it yourself.

How to do it...

These are the steps to handle network connections with a timeout or cancellation:

1. When you accept a network connection, create a new context with a cancellation or timeout:

2. Ensure the context is canceled eventually.

3. Pass the context to the handler:

```
ln, err:=net.Listen("tcp",":8080")
if err!=nil {
  return err
}
for {
  conn, err:=ln.Accept()
  if err!=nil {
    return err
  }
  go func(c net.Conn) {
    // Step 1:
    // Request times out after duration: RequestTimeout
    ctx, cancel:=context.WithTimeout(context.
    Background(),RequestTimeout)

    // Step 2:
    // Make sure cancel is called
    defer cancel()

    // Step 3:
    // Pass the context to handler
    handleRequest(ctx,c)
  }(conn)
}
```

10

Working with Large Data

There are several ways you can utilize Go concurrency primitives to process large amounts of data efficiently. Unlike threads, goroutines can be created without much overhead. Having thousands of goroutines in a program is common. With that in mind, we will look at some common patterns of dealing with large amounts of data concurrently.

This chapter includes the following recipes:

- Worker pools
- Connection pools
- Pipelines
- Working with large result sets

Worker pools

Let's say you have large amounts of data elements (for instance, image files) and you want to apply the same logic to each of them. You can write a function that processes one instance of the input, and then call this function in a `for` loop. Such a program will process the input elements sequentially, and if each element takes t seconds to process, all inputs will be completed at last at $n.t$ seconds, n being the number of inputs.

If you want to increase throughput by using concurrent programming, you can create a pool of worker goroutines. You can feed the next input to an idle member of the worker pool, and while that is being processed, you can assign the subsequent input to another member. If you have p logical processors (which can be cores of physical processors) running in parallel, the result can be available in as fast as $n.t/p$ seconds (this is a theoretical upper limit because the distribution of load among parallel processes is not always perfect, and there is also synchronization and communication overhead).

We will look at two different ways of implementing worker pools next.

Capped worker pools

If there is not an expensive initialization (for instance, loading a file or establishing a network connection can be expensive) for each worker, it is best to create workers as necessary with a given limit on the number of workers.

How to do it...

Create a new goroutine for each input. Use a channel as a synchronized counter to limit the maximum number of workers (here, the channel is used as a *semaphore*). Use an output channel to collect the results, if any:

```go
// Establish a maximum pool size
const maxPoolSize = 100

func main() {
    // 1. Initialization
    // Receive outputs from the pool via outputCh
    outputCh := make(chan Output)
    // A semaphore to limit the pool size
    sem := make(chan struct{}, maxPoolSize)

    // 2. Read outputs
    // Reader goroutine reads results until outputCh is closed
    readerWg := sync.WaitGroup{}
    readerWg.Add(1)
    go func() {
        defer readerWg.Done()
        for result := range outputCh {
            // process result
            fmt.Println(result)
        }
    }()

    // 3. Processing loop
    // Create the workers as needed, but the number of active workers
    // are limited by the capacity of sem
    wg := sync.WaitGroup{}
    // This loop sends the inputs to workers, creating them as
    // necessary
    for {
        nextInput, done := getNextInput()
        if done {
            break
```

```
        }
        wg.Add(1)
        // This will block if there are too many goroutines
        sem <- struct{}{}
        go func(inp Input) {
            defer wg.Done()
            defer func() {
                <-sem
            }()
            outputCh <- doWork(inp)
        }(nextInput)
    }

    // 4. Wait until processing is complete
    // This goroutine waits until all worker pool goroutines are done,
    // then closes the output channel
    go func() {
        // Wait until processing is complete
        wg.Wait()
        // Close the output channel so the reader goroutine can
        // terminate
        close(outputCh)
    }()

    // Wait until the output channel is closed
    readerWg.Wait()
    // If we are here, all goroutines are done
}
```

How it works...

1. First is initialization. We create two channels:

    - outputCh: The output of the worker pool. Each worker will write the result to this channel.

    - sem: The semaphore channel that will be used to limit the number of active workers. It is created with a maxPoolSize capacity. When we start a new worker goroutines, we send one element to this channel. Send operations will not block as long as the sem channel has fewer than maxPoolSize elements in it. When a worker goroutine is done, it receives one element from the channel, freeing capacity. Since this channel has maxPoolSize capacity, a send operation will block until a goroutine ends and receives from the channel if maxPoolSize workers are running.

2. **Read outputs**: We start a goroutine to read from the `outputCh` before starting the process, so the results can be read before all the input is sent to workers. Since the number of workers is limited, the workers will block after creating `maxPoolSize` of them, so we have to start listening for the outputs before creating the worker pool.

3. **Processing loop**: We read the next input and create a new worker to work on it. Active workers are tracked with the wg WaitGroup, which will later be used to wait for the workers to finish. Before creating a new worker, we send an element to the semaphore channel. If there are already `maxPoolSize` workers running, this will block until one of them terminates. The worker processes the input, writes the output to the `outputCh` and terminates, receiving one element from the semaphore.

4. This goroutine waits for the WaitGroup that keeps track of the workers. When all workers are done, the output channel is closed. That also signals the reader WaitGroup created at *Step 2*.

5. Wait until output processing is complete. The program has to wait until all outputs are generated. This only happens after the closing of the `outputCh` (which happens at #4), and then releasing of the `readerWg`.

Fixed-size worker pools

A fixed-size worker pool makes sense if creating a worker is an expensive operation. Simply create the maximum number of workers that read from a common input channel. This input channel deals with distributing work among the available workers.

How to do it...

There are several ways this can be achieved. We will look at two.

In the following function, a fixed-size worker pool is created with `poolSize` workers. All workers read from the same input channel and write the output to the same output channel. This program uses a reader goroutine to collect the results from the worker pool while providing the inputs in the same goroutine as the caller:

```
const poolSize = 50

func workerPoolWithConcurrentReader() {
    // 1. Initialization
    // Send inputs to the pool via inputCh
    inputCh := make(chan Input)
    // Receive outputs from the pool via outputCh
    outputCh := make(chan Output)

    // 2. Create the pool of workers
    wg := sync.WaitGroup{}
    for i := 0; i < poolSize; i++ {
```

```
        wg.Add(1)
        go func() {
            defer wg.Done()
            for work := range inputCh {
                outputCh <- doWork(work)
            }
        }()
    }
    // 3.a Reader goroutine
    // Reader goroutine reads results until outputCh is closed
    readerWg := sync.WaitGroup{}
    readerWg.Add(1)
    go func() {
        defer readerWg.Done()
        for result := range outputCh {
            // process result
            fmt.Println(result)
        }
    }()

    // 4. Wait workers
    // This goroutine waits until all worker pool goroutines are done,
    // then closes the output channel
    go func() {
        // Wait until processing is complete
        wg.Wait()
        // Close the output channel so the reader goroutine can
        // terminate
        close(outputCh)
    }()

    // 5.a Send inputs
    // This loop sends the inputs to the worker pool
    for {
        nextInput, done := getNextInput()
        if done {
            break
        }
        inputCh <- nextInput
    }
    // Close the input channel, so worker pool goroutines terminate
    close(inputCh)
    // Wait until the output channel is closed
    readerWg.Wait()
```

```
    // If we are here, all goroutines are done
}
```

The following version uses a goroutine to submit the work to the worker pool, while reading the results in the same goroutine as the caller:

```
func workerPoolWithConcurrentWriter() {
    // 1. Initialization
    // Send inputs to the pool via inputCh
    inputCh := make(chan Input)
    // Receive outputs from the pool via outputCh
    outputCh := make(chan Output)

    // 2. Create the pool of workers
    wg := sync.WaitGroup{}
    for i := 0; i < poolSize; i++ {
        wg.Add(1)
        go func() {
            defer wg.Done()
            for work := range inputCh {
                outputCh <- doWork(work)
            }
        }()
    }

    // 3.b Writer goroutine
    // Writer goroutine submits work to the worker pool
    go func() {
        for {
            nextInput, done := getNextInput()
            if done {
                break
            }
            inputCh <- nextInput
        }
        // Close the input channel, so worker pool goroutines
        // terminate
        close(inputCh)
    }()

    // 4. Wait workers
    // This goroutine waits until all worker pool goroutines are done,
    // then closes the output channel
```

```
go func() {
    // Wait until processing is complete
    wg.Wait()
    // Close the output channel so the reader goroutine can
    // terminate
    close(outputCh)
}()

// 5.b Read results
// Read results until outputCh is closed
for result := range outputCh {
    // process result
    fmt.Println(result)
}
}
```

How it works...

1.   First is initialization. We create two channels:

   - inputCh: This is the input to the worker pool. Each worker in the pool reads from the same inputCh in a for-range loop, so when a worker receives an input, it stops listening from the channel, allowing another worker to pick up the next input.

   - outputCh: This is the output of the worker pool. All workers write the output to this channel when they are done.

2.   Create the pool of workers: Since this is a fixed-size pool, we can create the workers in a simple for-loop. A WaitGroup is necessary so that we can wait for the processing to complete. Each worker reads from the inputCh until it is closed, processes the input, and writes to the outputCh.

The rest of the algorithm is different for the two examples. Let's start by looking at the first case:

1.   **Reader goroutine**: The output of the worker pool is read in this separate goroutine until the outputCh is closed. When the outputCh is closed, the readerWg is signaled.

2.   **Wait workers**: This is a separate goroutine that waits for the completion of all workers. When all workers terminate (which happens because the inputCh is closed), it closes the outputCh.

3.   This for loop sends inputs to the inputCh, and then closes the inputCh. This causes all the workers to terminate when they complete their work. When all the workers terminate, the outputCh is closed by the goroutine created at #4. When the output processing is complete, readerWg is signaled, terminating computation.

Next, let's look at the second case:

1. **Writer goroutine**: The inputs to the worker pool are generated by this goroutine. It sends all inputs to the inputCh one by one, and when all inputs are sent, it closes the inputCh, causing the worker pool to terminate.

2. **Wait workers**: These work the same as in the preceding case.

3. **Read results**: This for loop reads the results from the outputCh until it is closed. The outputCh will be closed when all workers are completed.

Connection pools

A connection pool is useful when dealing with multiple users of a scarce resource where establishing an instance of that resource can be expensive, such as a network connection, or database connection. Using a pair of channels, you can implement an efficient thread-safe connection pool.

How to do it...

Create a connection pool type with two channels with PoolSize capacity :

- available keeps the connections that are already established, but returned to the pool

- total keeps the total number of connections, that is, the number of available plus the number of connections that are actively in use

To get a connection from the pool, check the available channel. If one is available, return that. Otherwise, check the total connection pool , and create a new one if the limit is not exceeded.

Users of this pool should return the connections to the pool after they are done by sending the connection to the available channel.

The following code snippet illustrates such a connection pool:

```
type ConnectionPool struct {
    // This channel keeps connections returned to the pool
    available chan net.Conn
    // This channel counts the total number of connection active
    total     chan struct{}
}

func NewConnectionPool(poolSize int) *ConnectionPool {
  return &ConnectionPool {
    available: make(chan net.Conn,poolSize),
    total: make(chan struct{}, poolSize),
  }
}
```

```go
func (pool *ConnectionPool) GetConnection() (net.Conn, error) {
    select {
    // If there are connections available in the pool, return one
    case conn := <-pool.available:
        fmt.Printf("Returning an idle connection.\n")
        return conn, nil

    default:
        // No connections are available
        select {
        case conn := <-pool.available:
            fmt.Printf("Returning an idle connection.\n")
            return conn, nil

        case pool.total <- struct{}{}: // Wait until pool is not full
            fmt.Println("Creating a new connection")
            // Create a new connection
            conn, err := net.Dial("tcp", "localhost:2000")
            if err != nil {
                return nil, err
            }
            return conn, nil
        }
    }
}

func (pool *ConnectionPool) Release(conn net.Conn) {
    pool.available <- conn
    fmt.Printf("Releasing a connection. \n")
}

func (pool *ConnectionPool) Close(conn net.Conn) {
    fmt.Println("Closing connection")
    conn.Close()
    <-pool.total
}
```

How it works...

1. Initialize the connection pool with a PoolSize:

    ```go
    pool := NewConnectionPool(PoolSize)
    ```

2. This will create two channels, both with `PoolSize` capacity. The `available` channel will hold all connections that are returned to the pool while `total` will keep the number of established connections.

3. To get a new connection, use the following:

    ```
    conn, err := pool.GetConnection()
    ```

    This implementation of `GetConnection` illustrates how channel priorities can be established. `GetConnection` will return an idle connection if one is available in the `available` channel. Otherwise, it will enter the `default` case where it will either create a new connection or use one that is returned to the `available` channel.

    Note the pattern of nested `select` statements in `GetConnection`. This is a common pattern for implementing priority among channels. If there is a connection available, then `case conn := <-pool.available` will be chosen and the connection will be removed from the available connections channel. However, if there are no connections available when the first `select` statement is run, the `default` case will execute, which will execute a `select` between the `conn:=<-pool.available` and `pool.total<-struct{}{}` cases. If the first case becomes available (which happens when some other goroutine returns a connection to the pool), that connection will be returned to the caller. If the second case becomes available (which happens when a connection is closed, thus removing an element from `pool.total`), a new connection is created and returned to the caller.

4. When the client of the pool is done with the connection, it should call the following:

    ```
    pool.Release(conn)
    ```

5. This will add the connection to the `available` channel.

    If a connection becomes unresponsive, it can be closed by the client. When this happens, the pool should be notified, and `total` should be decremented but the connection should not be added to `available`. This is done by the following:

    ```
    pool.Close(conn)
    ```

Pipelines

Whenever you have several stages of operations performed on an input, you can construct a pipeline. Goroutines and channels can be used to construct high-throughput processing pipelines with different structures.

Simple pipeline without fan-out/fan-in

A simple pipeline can be constructed by connecting each stage running in its own goroutine using channels. The structure of the pipeline looks like *Figure 10.1*.

Figure 10.1: Simple asynchronous pipeline

How to do it...

This pipeline uses a separate error channel to report processing errors. We use a custom error type to capture diagnostic information:

```
type PipelineError struct {
    // The stage in which error happened
    Stage    int
    // The payload
    Payload any
    // The actual error
    Err      error
}
```

Every stage is implemented as a function that creates a new goroutine. The goroutine reads input data from an input channel, and writes the output to an output channel:

```
func Stage1(input <-chan InputPayload, errCh chan<- error) <-chan
Stage2Payload {
    // 1. Create the output channel for this stage.
    // This will be the input for the next stage
    output := make(chan Stage2Payload)
    // 2. Create processing goroutine
    go func() {
        // 3. Close the output channel when done
        defer close(output)
        // 4. Process all inputs until input channel is closed
        for in := range input {
            // 5. Process data
            err := processData(in.Id)
            // 6. Send errors to the error channel
            if err != nil {
                errCh <- PipelineError{
                    Stage:   1,
                    Payload: in,
                    Err:     err,
                }
                continue
            }
            // 7. Send the output to the next stage
```

```
                output <- Stage2Payload{
                    Id: in.Id,
                }
            }
        }()
        return output
    }
```

Stages 2 and 3 are implemented using the same pattern.

The pipeline is put together as follows:

```
func main() {
    // 1. Create the input and error channels
    errCh := make(chan error)
    inputCh := make(chan InputPayload)

    // 2. Prepare the pipeline by attaching stages
    outputCh := Stage3(Stage2(Stage1(inputCh, errCh), errCh), errCh)

    // 3. Feed input asynchronously
    go func() {
        defer close(inputCh)
        for i := 0; i < 1000; i++ {
            inputCh <- InputPayload{
                Id: i,
            }
        }
    }()

    // 4. Listen to the error channel asynchronously
    go func() {
        for err := range errCh {
            fmt.Println(err)
        }
    }()

    // 5. Read outputs
    for out := range outputCh {
        fmt.Println(out)
    }
    // 6. Close the error channel
    close(errCh)
}
```

For each stage, follow these steps:

1. Create the output channel for the stage. This will be passed into the next stage as the input channel.

2. The processing goroutine continues running after the stage function returns.

3. Make sure the output channel of this stage is closed when the processing goroutine terminates.

4. Read inputs from the previous stage until the input channel is closed.

5. Process the input.

6. If there is an error, send the error to the error channel. No output will be generated.

7. Send the output to the next stage.

> **Warning**
>
> Each stage runs in its own goroutine. That means that once you pass the payload to the next stage, you should not access that payload in the current stage. If the payload contains pointers, or if the payload itself is a pointer, data races may occur.

The pipeline setup is done as follows:

1. Create the input channel and the error channel.

    Attach stages to form the pipeline. The output of stage n becomes the input of stage n+1. The output of the last stage becomes the output channel.

2. Send the inputs to the input channel asynchronously. When all inputs are sent, close the input channel. This will terminate the first stage, closing its output channel, which is also the input channel for stage 2. This goes on until all stages exit.

3. Start a goroutine to listen and record errors.

4. Collect the outputs.

5. Close the error channel so that the error collecting goroutine terminates.

Pipeline with worker pools as stages

The previous example used a single worker for each stage. You can increase the throughput of a pipeline by replacing each stage with worker pools. The resulting pipeline is depicted in *Figure 10.2*.

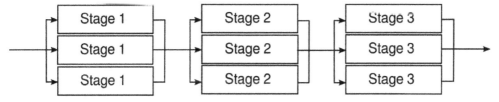

Figure 10.2: Pipeline with worker pools as stages

How to do it...

Each stage now creates multiple goroutines, all reading from the same input channel (fan-out). The output of each worker is written to a common output channel (fan-in), which becomes the input for the next stage. We can no longer close the stage output channel whenever the input channel is closed because there are now multiple goroutines writing to that output channel. Instead, we use a wait group and a second goroutine to close the output when all of the processing goroutines terminate:

```go
func Stage1(input <-chan InputPayload, errCh chan<- error, nInstances
int) <-chan Stage2Payload {
    // 1. Create the common output channel
    output := make(chan Stage2Payload)
    // 2. Close the output channel when all the processing is done
    wg := sync.WaitGroup{}
    // 3. Create nInstances goroutines
    for i := 0; i < nInstances; i++ {
        wg.Add(1)
        go func() {
            defer wg.Done()
            // Process all inputs
            for in := range input {
                // Process data
                err := processData(in.Id)
                if err != nil {
                    errCh <- PipelineError{
                        Stage:    1,
                        Payload: in,
                        Err:      err,
                    }
                    continue
                }
                //Send output to the common output channel
                output <- Stage2Payload{
                    Id: in.Id,
                }
            }
        }()
    }
    // 4. Another goroutine waits until all workers are done, and
    //closes the output channel
```

```go
    go func() {
        wg.Wait()
        close(output)
    }()
    return output
}
```

The pipeline is constructed as in the previous case:

```go
func main() {
    errCh := make(chan error)
    inputCh := make(chan InputPayload)
    nInstances := 5
    // Prepare the pipeline by attaching stages
    outputCh := Stage3(Stage2(Stage1(inputCh, errCh, nInstances),
    errCh, nInstances), errCh, nInstances)

    // Feed input asynchronously
    go func() {
        defer close(inputCh)
        for i := 0; i < 1000; i++ {
            inputCh <- InputPayload{
                Id: i,
            }
        }
    }()

    // Listen to the error channel asynchronously
    go func() {
        for err := range errCh {
            fmt.Println(err)
        }
    }()

    // Read outputs
    for out := range outputCh {
        fmt.Println(out)
    }
    // Close the error channel
    close(errCh)
}
```

How it works...

For each stage, follow these steps:

1. Create the output channel, which will become the input channel for the next stage.

    There are multiple goroutines reading from the same input channel in a for-range loop, so when the input channel is closed, all those goroutines will terminate. However, we cannot `defer close` the output channel, because that will result in closing the output channel multiple times (which will panic). So instead, we use a `WaitGroup` to keep track of the worker goroutines. A separate goroutine waits on that wait group, and when all goroutines terminate, it closes the output channel.

2. Create `nInstances` goroutines that all read from the same input channel, and write to the output channel. In case of an error, the workers send the error to the error channel.

3. This is the goroutine that waits for the worker goroutines to finish. When they do, it closes the output channel.

The pipeline setup is identical to the previous section, except that the initialization also sends the worker pool size to stage functions.

Pipeline with fan-out and fan-in

In this setup, stages are wired one after the other using dedicated channels, as shown in *Figure 10.3*:

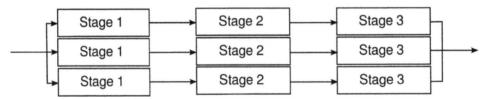

Figure 10.3: Pipeline with fan-out and fan-in

How to do it...

Each pipeline stage reads from a given input channel, and writes to an output channel, as follows:

```
func Stage1(input <-chan InputPayload, errCh chan<- error) <-chan
Stage2Payload {
    output := make(chan Stage2Payload)
    go func() {
        defer close(output)
        // Process all inputs
        for in := range input {
            // Process data
```

```
                err := processData(in.Id)
                if err != nil {
                    errCh <- PipelineError{
                        Stage:    1,
                        Payload: in,
                        Err:      err,
                    }
                    continue
                }
                output <- Stage2Payload{
                    Id: in.Id,
                }
            }
        }()
        return output
}
```

A separate `fanIn` function takes a list of output channels, and combines them using a goroutine listening to each channel:

```
func fanIn(inputs []<-chan OutputPayload) <-chan OutputPayload {
    result := make(chan OutputPayload)

    // Listen to input channels in separate goroutines
    inputWg := sync.WaitGroup{}
    for inputIndex := range inputs {
        inputWg.Add(1)
        go func(index int) {
            defer inputWg.Done()
            for data := range inputs[index] {
                // Send the data to the output
                result <- data
            }
        }(inputIndex)
    }

    // When all input channels are closed, close the fan in ch
    go func() {
        inputWg.Wait()
        close(result)
    }()

    return result
}
```

The pipeline is setup in a for-loop by combining the output of each stage to the input of the next stage. The resulting output channels are all directed to the `fanIn` function:

```go
func main() {
    errCh := make(chan error)
    inputCh := make(chan InputPayload)

    poolSize := 5
    outputs := make([]<-chan OutputPayload, 0)
    // All Stage1 goroutines listen to a single input channel
    for i := 0; i < poolSize; i++ {
        outputCh1 := Stage1(inputCh, errCh)
        outputCh2 := Stage2(outputCh1, errCh)
        outputCh3 := Stage3(outputCh2, errCh)
        outputs = append(outputs, outputCh3)
    }

    outputCh := fanIn(outputs)

    // Feed input asynchronously
    go func() {
        defer close(inputCh)
        for i := 0; i < 1000; i++ {
            inputCh <- InputPayload{
                Id: i,
            }
        }
    }()

    // Listen to the error channel asynchronously
    go func() {
        for err := range errCh {
            fmt.Println(err)
        }
    }()

    // Read outputs
    for out := range outputCh {
        fmt.Println(out)
    }
    // Close the error channel
    close(errCh)

}
```

How it works...

The worker stages are identical to the simple pipeline case. The fan-in stage works as follows.

For every output channel, the fan-in function creates a goroutine that reads data from that output channel and writes to a common channel. This common channel becomes the combined output channel of the pipeline. The fan-in function creates another goroutine that waits on a `wait` group that keeps track of all the goroutines. When they are all complete, this goroutine closes the output channel.

The `main` constructs the pipeline by connecting the output of each stage to the input of the next. The output channels of the last stage are stored in a slice and passed to the fan-in function. The output channel of the fan-in function becomes the combined output of the pipeline.

Note that all these pipeline variations use a separate error channel. An alternative approach is to store any error in the payload and pass it to the next stage. If the incoming payload has a non-nil error, all stages pass it to the next one, so the payload can be recorded as an error at the end of the pipeline:

```
type Stage2Paylaod struct {
    // Payload data
    Err error
}

func Stage2(input <-chan Stage2Payload) <-chan Stage3Payload {
    output := make(chan Stage2Payload)
    go func() {
        defer close(output)
        // Process all inputs
        for in := range input {
            // If there is error, pass it
            if in.Err!=nil {
                output <- StagerPayload {
                    Err: in.Err,
                }
                continue
            }
            ...
```

Also note that except for the simple pipeline case, they also return results out of order because multiple inputs go through the pipeline at any given moment, and there is no guarantee on the order they arrive at the output.

Working with large result sets

When working with potentially large result sets, it may not always be feasible to load all data to memory and work on it. You may need to stream data elements in a controlled manner. This section shows how to deal with such situations using concurrency primitives.

Streaming results using a goroutine

In this use case, a goroutine sends the results of a query via a channel. A context can be used to cancel the streaming goroutine.

How to do it...

Create a data structure that holds the data elements and error information:

```
type Result struct {
  Err error
  // Other data elements
}
```

The `StreamResults` function runs the database query and creates a goroutine that iterates the query results. The goroutine sends each result via a channel:

```
func StreamResults(
    ctx context.Context,
    db *sql.DB,
    query string,
    args ...any,
) (<-chan Result, error) {
    rows, err := db.QueryContext(ctx, query, args...)
    if err != nil {
        return nil, err
    }
    output := make(chan Result)
    go func() {
        defer rows.Close()
        defer close(output)
        var result Result
        for rows.Next() {
            // Check context cancellation
            if result.Err = ctx.Err(); result.Err != nil {
                // Context canceled. return
                output <- result
                return
```

```
            }
            // Set result fields
            result.Err = buildResult(rows, &result)
            output <- result
        }
        // If there was an error, return it
        if result.Err = rows.Err(); result.Err != nil {
            output <- result
        }
    }()
    return output, nil
}
```

Use the streaming results as follows:

```
// Setup a cancelable context
cancelableCtx, cancel := context.WithCancel(ctx)
defer cancel()

// Call the streaming API
results, err := StreamResults(cancelableCtx,db,"SELECT EMAIL FROM
USERS")
if err!=nil {
  return err
}
// Collect and process results
for result:=range results {
    if result.Err!=nil {
        // Handle error in the result
        continue
    }
    // Process the result
    if err:=ProcessResult(result); err!=nil {
        // Processing error. Cancel streaming results
        cancel()
        // Expect to receive at least one more message from the channel,
        // because the streaming gorutine sends the error
        for range results {}
    }
}
```

How it works...

Even though we looked at a database query example, this pattern is useful any time you are dealing with a function that generates potentially large amounts of data. Instead of loading all data into memory, this pattern loads and processes data items one by one.

The `StreamResults` generator function starts a goroutine closure that captures the context and additional information necessary to produce results (in this case, a `sql.Rows` instance). The generator function creates a channel and returns immediately. The goroutine collects results and sends them to the channel. When all results are processed or an error is detected, the channel is closed.

It is now up to the caller to communicate with the goroutine. The caller collects the results from the channel until the channel is closed, and processes them one by one. The caller also checks the error field in the received message to handle any errors detected by the goroutine.

This scheme uses a cancelable context. When the context is canceled, the goroutine sends another message through the channel before closing it, so the caller must drain the channel if context cancellation happens.

11
Working with JSON

JSON is an acronym for JavaScript Object Notation. It is a popular format for data interchange because JSON objects closely resemble structured types (`structs` in Go), and it is text-based encoding, making the encoded data human-readable. It supports arrays, objects (name-value pairs), and relatively few basic types (strings, numbers, booleans, and `null`). These properties make JSON a fairly easy format to work with.

Encoding refers to the process of transforming data elements into a sequence of bytes. When you encode (or marshal) data elements in JSON, you create a textual representation of those data elements while following JSON syntax rules. The reverse process, decoding (or unmarshaling) assigns JSON values to Go objects. The encoding process is lossy: you have to describe data values as text, and that is not always obvious for complex data types. When you decode such data, you have to know how to interpret the textual representation so you can parse the JSON representation correctly.

In this chapter, we will first look at the encoding and decoding of basic data types. Then we will look at some recipes that deal with more complicated data types and use cases. You should use these recipes as a guide when implementing your own solutions. These recipes demonstrate solutions to particular use cases, and you may need to adopt them for your specific needs.

This chapter includes the following recipes:

- Encoding structs
- Dealing with embedded structs
- Encoding without defining structs
- Decoding structs
- Decoding with interfaces, maps, and slices
- Other ways of decoding numbers
- Marshaling/unmarshaling custom data types
- Custom marshaling/unmarshaling of object keys

- Dynamic field names
- Polymorphic data structures
- Streaming JSON data

Marshaling/unmarshaling basics

The `encoding/json` package of the standard library provides convenient functions and conventions to encode/decode JSON data.

Encoding structs

Go struct types are usually encoded as JSON objects. This section shows the standard library tools that deal with the encoding of data types.

How to do it...

1. Use `json` tags to annotate struct fields with their JSON keys:

```
type Config struct {
  Version   string `json:"ver"`   // Encoded as "ver"
  Name      string                // Encoded as "Name"
  Type      string `json:"type,omitempty"` // Encoded as "type",
                                   // and will be omitted if
                                   // empty
  Style     string `json:"-"`     // Not encoded
  value     string                // Unexported field, not encoded
  kind      string `json:"kind"`  // Unexported field, not encoded
}
```

2. Use the `json.Marshal` function to encode Go data objects in JSON. The standard library uses the following conventions for basic types:

Go Declaration	Value	JSON output
`NumberValue int json:"num"`	0	"num" : 0
`NumberValue *int json:"num"`	nil	"num" : null
`NumberValue *int json:"num,omitempty"`	nil	omitted
`BoolValue bool json:"bvalue"`	true	"bvalue" : true
`BoolValue *bool json:"bvalue"`	nil	"bvalue" : null
`BoolValue *bool json:"bvalue,omitempty"`	nil	omitted

Go Declaration	Value	JSON output
`StringValue string json:"svalue"`	"str"	`"svalue":"str"`
`StringValue string json:"svalue"`	" "	`"svalue":""`
`StringValue string` `json:"svalue,omitempty"`	"str"	`"svalue":"str"`
`StringValue string` `json:"svalue,omitempty"`	" "	omitted
``StringValue *string `json:"svalue"``	nil	`"svalue": null`
`StringValue *string` ``json:"svalue,omitempty"``	nil	omitted

- The `struct` and `map` types are marshaled as JSON objects

- Slice and array types are marshaled as JSON arrays

- If a type implements the `json.Marshaler` interface, then the `json.Marshaler.MarshalJSON` method of the variable instance is called to encode data

- If a type implements the `encoding.TextMarshaler` interface, then the value is encoded as a JSON string, and the string value is obtained from the `encoding.TextMarshaler.MarshalText` method of the value

- Anything else will fail with `UnsupportedValueError`

> **Tip**
> Only exported fields of struct types can be marshaled.

> **Tip**
> If there are no JSON tags for a struct field, its JSON object key will be the same as the field name.

Consider the following code segment:

```go
type Config struct {
    Version   string `json:"ver"`  // Encoded as "ver"
    Name      string                // Encoded as "Name"
    Type      string `json:"type,omitempty"` // Encoded as "type",
                                             // and will be omitted if
                                             // empty
    Style     string `json:"-"`    // Not encoded
    value     string                // Unexported field, not encoded
    kind      string `json:"kind"` // Unexported field, not encoded
}
```

```
...
cfg := Config{
     Version: "1.1",
     Name:     "name",
     Type:     "example",
     Style:    "json",
     value:    "example config value",
     kind:     "test",
}
data, err := json.Marshal(cfg)
fmt.Println(string(err))
```

This prints the following:

```
{"ver":"1.1","Name":"name","type":"example"}
```

> **Tip**
> The order of fields in the encoded JSON object is the same as the order in which fields are declared.

Dealing with embedded structs

Fields of a struct type will be encoded as JSON objects. If there are embedded structs, then the encoder has two options: encode the embedded struct at the same level as the enclosing struct or as a new JSON object.

How to do it...

1. Use JSON tags to name enclosing struct fields and the embedded struct fields:

   ```
   type Enclosing struct {
        Field string `json:"field"`
        Embedded
   }

   type Embedded struct {
        Field string `json:"embeddedField"`
   }
   ```

2. Use json.Marshal to encode the struct as a JSON object:

   ```
   enc := Enclosing{
        Field: "enclosing",
        Embedded: Embedded{
   ```

```
                    Field: "embedded",
            },
    }
    data, err = json.Marshal(enc)
    // {"field":"enclosing","embeddedField":"embedded"}
```

3. Adding a json tag to the embedded struct will create a nested JSON object:

```
    type Enclosing struct {
        Field string `json:"field"`
        Embedded `json:"embedded"`
    }

    type Embedded struct {
        Field string `json:"embeddedField"`
    }
    ...
    enc := Enclosing{
        Field: "enclosing",
        Embedded: Embedded{
            Field: "embedded",
        },
    }
    data, err = json.Marshal(enc)
    // {"field":"enclosing","embedded":{"embeddedField":"embedded"}}
```

Encoding without defining structs

Basic data types, slices, and maps can be used to encode JSON data.

How to do it...

*   Use a map to represent JSON objects:

```
    config:=map[string]any{
      "ver": "1.0",
      "Name": "config",
      "type": "example",
      }
    data, err:=json.Marshal(config)
    // `{"ver":"1.0","Name":"config","type":"example"}`
```

- Use a slice to represent JSON arrays:

```
numbersWithNil:=[]any{ 1, 2, nil, 3 }
data, err:=json.Marshal(numbersWithNil)
// `[1,2,null,3]`
```

- Match the desired JSON structure to Go equivalents:

```
configurations:=map[string]map[string]any {
  "cfg1": {
     "ver": "1.0",
     "Name": "config1",
  },
  "cfg2": {
     "ver": "1.1",
     "Name" : "config2",
  },
}
data, err:=json.Marshal(configurations)
// {"cfg1":{"Name":"config1","ver":"1.0"},
"cfg2":{"Name":"config2","ver":"1.1"}}`
```

Decoding structs

Encoding Go data objects in JSON is a relatively easy task: well-defined data types and semantics are translated into a less expressive representation, usually resulting in some information loss. For instance, an integer variable and a `float64` variable may be encoded to give identical output. Because of this, decoding JSON data is usually more difficult.

How to do it...

1. Use JSON tags to map JSON keys to struct fields.

2. Use the `json.Unmarshal` function to decode JSON data into Go data objects. The standard library uses the following conventions for basic types:

JSON Input	Go type	Result
`"strValue"`	`string`	`"strValue"`
`1 (number)`	`int`	`1`
`1.2 (number)`	`int`	`error`
`1.2 (number)`	`float64, float32`	`1.2`
`true`	`bool`	`true`
`null`	`string`	Variable left unmodified

JSON Input	Go type	Result
`null`	`int`	Variable left unmodified
`"strValue"`	`*string`	`"strValue"`
`null`	`*string`	`nil`
`1`	`*int`	`1`
`null`	`*int`	`nil`
`true`	`*bool`	`true`
`null`	`*bool`	`nil`

If the Go type is `interface{}`, the standard library creates objects using the following convention:

JSON Input	Result
`"strValue"`	`"strValue"`
`1`	`float64(1)`
`1.2`	`float64(1.2)`
`true`	`true`
`null`	`nil`
JSON Object	`map[string]any`
JSON array	`[]any`

- If the target Go type implements the `json.Unmarshaler` interface, then `json.Unmarshal`. `UnmarshalJSON` is called to decode data. This operation may involve creating a new instance of the target type if necessary.

- If the target Go type implements the `encoding.TextUnmarshaler` interface and the input is a quoted JSON string, then `encoding.TextUnmarshaler.UnmarshalText` is called to decode the value.

- Anything else will fail with `UnsupportedValueError`.

> **Tip**
> Numeric values may cause confusion if the JSON input includes values of various numeric types. For instance, if a JSON numeric value is unmarshaled to an `int` value, it will work if the JSON data is representable as an integer, but fail if the JSON data has a floating-point value.

> **Tip**
> The JSON decoder will never change the unexported fields of a struct. The decoder uses reflection, and only the exported fields are accessible via reflection.

> **Tip**
> JSON fields that do not have matching Go fields will be ignored.

Decoding with interfaces, maps, and slices

When decoding Go values to JSON, the Go value types dictate how JSON encoding will be done. JSON does not have a rich type system like Go. Valid JSON types are string, number, boolean, object, array, and null. When you decode JSON data into a Go struct, it is still the Go type system that dictates how JSON data should be interpreted. But when you decode JSON into an `interface{}`, things change. Now it is the JSON data that dictates how Go values should be constructed, and this sometimes causes unexpected results.

How to do it...

To unmarshal JSON data into an interface, use the following:

```
var output interface{}
err:=json.Unmarshal(jsonData,&output)
```

This creates an object tree based on the following translation rules:

JSON	Go
Object	`map[string]interface{}`
Array	`[]interface{}`
number	`float64`
boolean	`bool`
string	`string`
null	`nil`

Other ways of decoding numbers

When decoded into an `interface{}`, JSON numbers are converted to `float64`. This is not always the desired result. You can use `json.Number` instead.

How to do it...

Use `json.Decoder` with `UseNumber`:

```
var output interface{}
decoder:=json.NewDecoder(strings.NewReader(`[1.1,2,3,4.4]`))
```

```
// Tell the decoder to use json.Number instead of float64
decoder.UseNumber()
err:=decoder.Decode(&output)
// [1.1 2 3 4.4]
```

Every element of `output` in the preceding example is an instance of `json.Number`. You can translate it to an `int`, `float64`, or `big.Int` as necessary.

Dealing with missing and optional values

You usually have to deal with JSON input with missing fields and have to generate JSON where empty fields are omitted. This section provides recipes showing how to deal with these scenarios.

Omitting empty fields when encoding

Omitting empty fields from JSON encoding usually saves space and makes the JSON more reader-friendly. However, what is meant by "empty" should be clear.

How to do it...

Use the `,omitempty` JSON tag to omit empty string values, zero integer/floating-point values, zero `time.Duration` values, and `nil` pointer values.

The `,omitempty` tag does not work for `time.Time` values. Use `*time.Time` and set it to `nil` to omit empty time values:

```
type Config struct {
    . . .
    Type       string `json:"type,omitempty"`
    IntValue   int    `json:"intValue,omitempty"`
    FloatValue float64 `json:"floatValue,omitempty"`
    When       *time.Time  `json:"when,omitempty"`
    HowLong    time.Duration `json:"howLong,omitempty"`
}
```

Sometimes it is important to distinguish between an empty string and a null string. In JavaScript and JSON, `null` is a valid value for strings. If that is the case, use `*string`:

```
type Config struct {
  Value  *string `json:"value,omitempty"`
  . . .
}
```

. . .

```go
emptyString := ""
emptyValue := Config {
    Value: &emptyString,
}
// JSON output: { "value": "" }

nullValue := Config {
    Value: nil,
}
// JSON output: {}
```

Dealing with missing fields when decoding

There are several use cases where developers have to deal with sparse JSON data that does not include all data fields. For instance, a partial update API call may accept a JSON object that contains only those fields that should be updated, without modifying any unspecified data field. In such cases, it becomes important to identify which fields were provided. Then there are use cases where it is appropriate to assume default values for missing fields.

How to do it...

If you want to determine which fields are specified in a JSON input, use pointer fields. Any fields missing in the input will remain as nil.

To provide default values for missing fields, initialize those fields to their default values before unmarshaling:

```go
type APIRequest struct {
    // If type is not specified, it will be nil
    Type    *string `json:"type"`
    // There will be a default value for seq
    Seq     int     `json:"seq"`
    ...
}

func handler(w http.ResponseWriter,r *http.Request) {
  data, err:=io.ReadAll(r.Body)
  if err!=nil {
     http.Error(w, "Bad request",http.StatusBadRequest)
     return
  }
  req:=APIRequest{
     Seq: 1,  // Set the default value
  }
  if err:=json.Unmarshal(data, &req); err!=nil {
```

```
        http.Error(w, "Bad request", http.StatusBadRequest)
        return
    }
    // Check which fields are provided
    if req.Type!=nil {
        ...
    }
    // If seq is provided in the input, req.Seq will be set to that
    // value. Otherwise, it will be 1.
    if req.Seq==1 {
        ...
    }
}
```

Customizing JSON encoding/decoding

Sometimes JSON encoding of certain data structures does not match their representations in the program. When this happens, you have to customize how a certain data element is encoded to JSON or decoded from JSON.

Marshaling/unmarshaling custom data types

Use these recipes when you have data elements whose JSON representation needs to be generated programmatically.

How to do it...

To control how a data object is encoded in JSON, implement the `json.Marshaler` interface:

```
// TypeAndID is encoded to JSON as type:id
type TypeAndID struct {
  Type string
  ID int
}

// Implementation of json.Marshaler
func (t TypeAndID) MarshalJSON() (out []byte, err error) {
  s := fmt.Sprintf(`"%s:%d"`,t.Type,t.ID)
  out=[]byte(s)
  return
}
```

To control how a data object is decoded from JSON, implement the `json.Unmarshaler` interface:

> **Tip**
>
> An unmarshaler must have a pointer receiver.

```go
// Implementation of json.Unmarshaler. Note the pointer receiver
func (t *TypeAndID) UnmarshalJSON(in []byte) (err error) {
    if len(in)<2 || in[0] != '"' || in[len(in)-1] != '"' {
        err = ErrInvalidTypeAndID
        return
    }
    in = in[1 : len(in)-1]
    parts := strings.Split(string(in), ":")
    if len(parts) != 2 {
        err = ErrInvalidTypeAndID
        return
    }
    // The second part must be a valid integer
    t.ID, err = strconv.Atoi(parts[1])
    if err != nil {
        return
    }
    t.Type = parts[0]
    return
}
```

Custom marshaling/unmarshaling of object keys

Maps are marshaled/unmarshaled as JSON objects. But if you have a map that has keys other than a string type, how can you marshal/unmarshal it to JSON?

How to do it...

The solution depends on the exact type of the key:

1. Maps with key types derived from string or integer types can be marshaled/unmarshaled using the standard library methods:

    ```go
    type Key int64

    func main() {
        var m map[Key]int
        err := json.Unmarshal([]byte(`{"123":123}`), &m)
        if err!=nil {
            panic(err)
    ```

```
    }
        fmt.Println(m[123]) // Prints 123
    }
```

2. If map keys require additional processing for marshaling/unmarshaling, implement the encoding.TextMarshaler and encoding.TextUnmarshaler interfaces:

```
// Key is an uint that is encoded as an hex strings for JSON key
type Key uint

func (k *Key) UnmarshalText(data []byte) error {
    v, err := strconv.ParseInt(string(data), 16, 64)
    if err != nil {
        return err
    }
    *k = Key(v)
    return nil
}

func (k Key) MarshalText() ([]byte, error) {
    s := strconv.FormatUint(uint64(k), 16)
    return []byte(s), nil
}

func main() {
    input := `{
    "13AD": "5037",
    "3E22": "15906",
    "90A3": "37027"
}`

    var data map[Key]string
    if err := json.Unmarshal([]byte(input), &data); err != nil
{
        panic(err)
    }
    fmt.Println(data)
    d, err := json.Marshal(map[Key]any{
        Key(123): "123",
        Key(255): "255",
    })
    if err != nil {
        panic(err)
```

```
        }
        fmt.Println(string(d))
    }
}
```

Dynamic field names

There are cases where the field names (object keys) are not constant. For example, an API may prefer to return a list of objects as a JSON object where unique identifiers of each object are the key. In such cases, it is not possible to use json tags in a struct.

How to do it...

Use a map[string]ValueType to represent an object with dynamic field names:

```
type User struct {
    Name string `json:"name"`
    Type string `json:"type"`
}

type Users struct {
    Users map[string]User `json:"users"`
}

func main() {
    input := `{
  "users": {
      "abb64dfe-d4a8-47a5-b7b0-7613fe3fd11f": {
          "name": "John",
          "type": "admin"
      },
      "b158161c-0588-4c67-8e4b-c07a8978f711": {
          "name": "Amy",
          "type": "editor"
      }
    }
  }`
    var users Users
    if err := json.Unmarshal([]byte(input), &users); err != nil {
        panic(err)
    }
}
```

Polymorphic data structures

A polymorphic data structure can be one of several different types that share a common interface. The actual type is determined at runtime. For runtime objects, the Go type system ensures type-safe operations using such fields. With the use of interfaces, polymorphic objects can be marshaled as JSON easily. A problem arises when you need to unmarshal a polymorphic JSON object. In this recipe, we will look at one way of achieving this.

Custom unmarshaling with two passes

The first pass unmarshals discriminator fields while leaving the rest of the input unprocessed. Based on the discriminator, the concrete instance of the object is constructed and unmarshaled.

How to do it...

1. We will work with an example `Key` structure in this section. The `Key` structure holds different types of cryptographic public keys, whose type is given in a `Type` field:

    ```
    type KeyType string

    const (
        KeyTypeRSA      = "rsa"
        KeyTypeED25519 = "ed25519"
    )

    type Key struct {
        Type KeyType            `json:"type"`
        Key  crypto.PublicKey `json:"key"`
    }
    ```

2. Define the JSON tags for the data structure as usual. Most polymorphic structures can be marshaled without a custom marshaler because the runtime type of objects is known during marshaling.

    Define another struct that is a copy of the original, with dynamically typed parts replaced with a `json.RawMessage` type field:

    ```
    type keyUnmarshal struct {
        Type KeyType           `json:"type"`
        Key  json.RawMessage `json:"key"`
    }
    ```

3. Create an unmarshaler for the original struct. In this unmarshaler, first unmarshal the input to an instance of the struct created in step 2:

    ```
    func (k *Key) UnmarshalJSON(in []byte) error {
        var key keyUnmarshal
    ```

```
        err := json.Unmarshal(in, &key)
        if err != nil {
            return err
        }
```

4. Using the type discriminator fields, decide how to decode the dynamic part. The following example uses a factory to obtain a type-specific unmarshaler:

```
        k.Type = key.Type
        unmarshaler := KeyUnmarshalers[key.Type]
        if unmarshaler == nil {
            return ErrInvalidKeyType
        }
```

5. Unmarshal the dynamically typed part (which is a json.RawMessage) into an instance of the correctly typed variable:

```
        k.Key, err = unmarshaler(key.Key)
        if err != nil {
            return err
        }
        return nil
    }
```

The factory is a simple map that knows the unmarshalers for different types of keys:

```
var (
        KeyUnmarshalers = map[KeyType]func(json.RawMessage)
        (crypto.PublicKey, error){}
)

func RegisterKeyUnmarshaler(keyType KeyType, unmarshaler
func(json.RawMessage) (crypto.PublicKey, error)) {
        KeyUnmarshalers[keyType] = unmarshaler
}

...
RegisterKeyUnmarshaler(KeyTypeRSA, func(in json.RawMessage)
(crypto.PublicKey, error) {
        var key rsa.PublicKey
        if err := json.Unmarshal(in, &key); err != nil {
            return nil, err
        }
        return &key, nil
})
```

```
RegisterKeyUnmarshaler(KeyTypeED25519, func(in json.RawMessage)
(crypto.PublicKey, error) {
    var key ed25519.PublicKey
    if err := json.Unmarshal(in, &key); err != nil {
        return nil, err
    }
    return &key, nil
})
```

This is an extensible factory framework that can be initialized with additional unmarshalers determined at build time. Simply create an unmarshaler function for a type of object, and register it using the preceding `RegisterKeyUnmarshaler` function to support new key types.

> **Tip**
> A common way to register such features is to use the `init()` function of packages. When you import that package, unmarshaler types supported by the package will be registered.

Streaming JSON data

When you have to deal with large amounts of data efficiently, you should consider streaming data instead of working on the whole dataset at once. This section describes some methods for streaming JSON data.

Streaming an array of objects

This recipe is useful if you have a generator (a goroutine, a database cursor, etc.) that produces data elements, and you want to stream these as a JSON array instead of storing everything before marshaling it.

How to do it...

1. Create a generator. This can be

    * a goroutine that sends data elements through a channel,

    * a cursor-like object containing a `Next()` method,

    * or some other data generator.

2. Create an instance of `json.Encoder` with `io.Writer` representing the target. The target can be a file, standard output, a buffer, a network connection, and so on.

3. Write the array beginning delimiter for the array, that is, `[`.

4. Encode each data element, preceded by a comma if necessary.

5. Write the array closing delimiter, that is, `]`.

The following example assumes there is a generator goroutine writing Data instances to the input channel. The generator closes the channel when there are no more Data instances. Here, we assume Data is JSON marshalable:

```
func stream(out io.Writer, input <-chan Data) error {
    enc := json.NewEncoder(out)
    if _, err := out.Write([]byte{'['}); err != nil {
        return err
    }
    first := true
    for obj := range input {
        if first {
            first = false
        } else {
            if _, err := out.Write([]byte{','}); err != nil {
                return err
            }
        }
        if err := enc.Encode(obj); err != nil {
            return err
        }
    }

    if _, err := out.Write([]byte{']'}); err != nil {
        return err
    }
    return nil
}
```

Parsing an array of objects

If you have a JSON data source providing an array of objects, you can parse these elements and process them using json.Decoder.

How to do it...

1. Create json.Decoder reading from the input stream.

2. Parse the array beginning delimiter ([) using json.Decoder.Token().

3. Decode each element of the array until decoding fails.

4. When decoding fails, you have to determine whether the stream ended, or whether there is really an error. To check for that, read the next token using json.Decoder.Token(). If the next token is read successfully and if it is an array end delimiter,], then the stream parsing ended successfully. Otherwise, there is an error in the input data.

The following example assumes that json.Decoder is already constructed to read from an input stream. The output is stored in a slice. Alternatively, the output can be processed as elements are parsed, or each element can be sent to a processing goroutine through a channel:

```go
func parse(input *json.Decoder) (output []Data, err error) {
    // Parse the array beginning delimiter
    var tok json.Token
    tok, err = input.Token()
    if err != nil {
        return
    }
    if tok != json.Delim('[') {
        err = fmt.Errorf("Array begin delimiter expected")
        return
    }
    // Parse array elements using Decode
    for {
        var data Data
        err = input.Decode(&data)
        if err != nil {
            // Decode failed. Either there is an input error, or
            // we are at the end of the stream
            tok, err = input.Token()
            if err != nil {
                // Data error
                return
            }
            // Are we at the end?
            if tok == json.Delim(']') {
                // Yes, there is no error
                err = nil
                break
            }
        }
        output = append(output, data)
    }
    return
}
```

Other ways of streaming JSON

There are other ways of streaming JSON:

- Concatenated JSON simply writes JSON objects one after the other

- Newline-delimited JSON writes every JSON object as a separate line

- Record separator-delimited JSON uses a special record separator character, 0x1E, and optionally a newline between each JSON object

- Length-prefixed JSON prefixes the string length of every JSON object as a decimal number

All these can be read and written using `json.Decoder` and `json.Encoder`. A simple package for JSON streaming can be found here: `https://github.com/bserdar/jsonstream`.

Security considerations

Whenever you accept data from outside your application (user-entered data, API calls, reading a file, etc.), you have to be concerned about malicious input. JSON input is relatively safe because JSON parsers do not perform data expansions like YAML or XML parsers do. Nevertheless, there are still things you need to consider when dealing with JSON data.

How to do it...

- Limit the amount of data when accepting third-party JSON input. Do not blindly use `io.ReadAll` or `json.Decode`:

```
const MessageSizeLimit = 10240

func handler(w http.ResponseWriter, r *http.Request) {
  reader:=http.MaxBytesReader(w,r.Body,MessageSizeLimit)
  data, err := io.ReadAll(reader)
  if errors.Is(err,&http.MaxBytesError{}) {
    // If this happens, error is already sent.
    return
  }
  ...
}
```

- Always provide an upper limit for resource allocations based on data you read from third-party input. For instance, if you are reading a length-prefixed JSON stream where each JSON object is prefixed by its length, do not allocate a `[]byte` to store the next object. Reject the input if the length is too large.

12

Processes

This chapter has recipes that show how to run external programs, how to interact with them, and how to terminate a process gracefully. There are some key points to keep in mind when dealing with external processes:

- When you start an external process, it runs concurrently with your program.
- If you need to communicate with a child process, you have to use an interprocess communication mechanism, such as pipes.
- When you run a child process, its standard input and standard output streams appear to the parent process as independent concurrent streams. You cannot rely on the ordering of data you receive from these streams.

This section covers the following main recipes:

- Running external programs
- Passing arguments to a process
- Processing output from a child process using a pipe
- Providing input to a child process
- Changing environment variables of a child process
- Graceful termination using signals

Running external programs

There are many use cases where you want to execute an external program to perform a task. Usually, this is because performing the same task within your own program is not possible or not easy. For example, you may choose to execute several instances of an external image processing program to modify a group of images. Another use case is when you want to configure some device using programs provided by its manufacturer. This recipe includes several ways to execute external programs.

How to do it...

Use exec.Command or exec.CommandContext to run another program from your program. exec.Command is appropriate if you do not need to cancel (kill) the child process or impose a timeout. Otherwise, use exec.CommandContext, and cancel or time out the context to kill the child process:

1. Create the exec.Command (or exec.CommandContext) object using the name of the program and its arguments:

    - If you need to search the program in the platform's executable commands path, do not include any path separators

    - If you use path separators in the program name, it must be a path relative to exec.Command.Dir, or if exec.Command.Dir is empty, it must be a path relative to the current working directory

    - Use an absolute path if you know where the executable is

2. Prepare the input and output streams to capture program output, or to send input via the standard input stream.

3. Start the program.

4. Wait for the program to end.

The following example builds a Go program using the go command under the sub/ directory:

```go
// Run "go build" to build the subprocess in the "sub" directory
func buildProgram() {
    // Create a Command with the executable and its arguments
    cmd := exec.Command(
        "go", "build", "-o", "subprocess", ".")

    // Set the working directory
    cmd.Dir = "sub"

    // Collect the stdout and stderr as a combined output from the
    // process
    // This will run the process, and wait for it to end
    output, err := cmd.CombinedOutput()
    if err != nil {
        panic(err)
    }

    // The build command will not print anything if successful. So if
    // there is any output, it is a failure.
```

```
    if len(output) > 0 {
        panic(string(output))
    }
}
```

The above example will collect the process output as a combined string. The standard output and standard error from the program will be returned as a single string, so you have no way of identifying what parts of the output string came from standard output and what parts from standard error. Make sure you can parse the output correctly.

> **Warning**
>
> The standard output and standard error streams of a process are independent concurrent streams. In general, there is no portable way to determine which stream produced output first. This may have serious implications. For example, suppose you executed a program that produces a stream of lines on stdout, but whenever it detects an error, it prints a message to standard error that is something like "last printed line has problems." But when you read the error in your program, the last printed line may not have arrived in your program yet.

The following program demonstrates the use of exec.CommandContext and pipes:

```
// Run the program built by buildProgram function for 10ms, reading
// from the output
// and error pipes concurrently
func runSubProcessStreamingOutputs() {
    // Create a context with timeout
    ctx, cancel := context.WithTimeout(context.Background(), 10*time.
    Millisecond)
    defer cancel()

    // Create the command that will timeout in 10ms
    cmd := exec.CommandContext(ctx, "sub/subprocess")

    // Pipe the output and error streams
    stdout, err := cmd.StdoutPipe()
    if err != nil {
        panic(err)
    }
    stderr, err := cmd.StderrPipe()
    if err != nil {
        panic(err)
    }

    // Read from stderr from a separate goroutine
```

```go
    go func() {
        io.Copy(os.Stderr, stderr)
    }()

    // Start running the program
    err = cmd.Start()
    if err != nil {
        panic(err)
    }

    // Copy the stdout of the child program to our stdout
    io.Copy(os.Stdout, stdout)

    // Wait for the program to end
    err = cmd.Wait()
    if err != nil {
        fmt.Println(err)
    }
}
```

The previous example taps into the standard output and standard error outputs of the child process. Note that the program starts reading from the `stderr` stream before the program starts. That goroutine will block until the child process outputs an error or until the child process terminates, at which point, the `stderr` pipe will be closed and the goroutine will terminate. The part that reads from the standard output runs in the main goroutine, before `cmd.Wait`. This ordering is important. If the child process starts producing output on `stdout` but the parent program is not listening, the child process will block. Calling `cmd.Wait` at this point would create a deadlock, but the runtime cannot detect this as such because the parent program is reliant on the behavior of the child.

You can assign the same stream to `stdout` and `stderr` of the child process, as shown here:

```go
// Run the build subprocess for 10 ms with combined output
func runSubProcessCombinedOutput() {
    // Create a context with timeout
    ctx, cancel := context.WithTimeout(context.Background(), 10*time.
    Millisecond)
    defer cancel()

    // Define the command with the context
    cmd := exec.CommandContext(ctx, "sub/subprocess")

    // Assign both stdout and stderr to the same stream. This is
    // equivalent to calling CombinedOutput
    cmd.Stdout = os.Stdout
```

```
        cmd.Stderr = os.Stdout

    // Start the process
    err := cmd.Start()
    if err != nil {
        panic(err)
    }

    // Wait until it ends. The output will be printed to our stdout
    err = cmd.Wait()
    if err != nil {
        fmt.Println(err)
    }
}
```

The preceding approach is similar to running the child process with CombinedOutput. Assigning cmd.Stdout and cmd.Stderr to the same stream has the same effect as combining both outputs of the child process.

Passing arguments to a process

The mechanics of passing arguments to a child process can be confusing. Shell environments parse and expand process arguments. For example, a *.txt argument is replaced by a list of filenames matching that pattern, and each of those filenames becomes a separate argument. This recipe talks about how to pass such arguments to child processes correctly.

There are two options to pass arguments to a child process.

Expanding arguments

The first option is to perform the shell argument processing manually.

How to do it...

To manually perform shell processing, follow these steps:

1. Remove shell-specific quoting from arguments, such as the shell command:

    - The ./prog "test directory" shell command becomes cmd:=exec.Command("./prog","test directory").

    - The ./prog dir1 "long dir name" '"quoted name"' Bash command becomes cmd:=exec.Command("./prog", "long dir name", "'\"quoted name\"'"). Note the Bash-specific treatment of quotes.

2. Expand the patterns. ./prog *.txt becomes cmd:=exec.Command("./prog",listFiles("*.txt")...), where listFiles is a function that returns a slice of filenames.

Tip

Passing a list of files separated by a space will pass them as a single argument. That is, cmd:=exec.Command("./prog","file1.txt file2.txt") will pass a single argument to the process, which is file1.txt file2.txt.

---

3. Substitute the environment variables. /.prog $HOME becomes cmd:=exec.Command("./prog", os.Getenv("HOME")). Running cmd:=exec.Command("./prog", "$HOME") will pass the string $HOME to the program, not its value from the environment.

4. Finally, you have to manually process pipelines. That is, for a ./prog >output.txt shell command, you have to run cmd:=exec.Command("./prog"), create an output.txt file, and set cmd.Stdout=outputFile.

Running the command via the shell

The second option is to run the program via a shell.

How to do it...

Use the platform-specific shell and its syntax to run a command:

```
var cmd *exec.Cmd
switch runtime.GOOS {
case "windows":
    cmd = exec.Command("cmd", "/C", "echo test>test.txt")
case "darwin": // Mac OS
    cmd = exec.Command("/bin/sh", "-c", "echo test>test.txt")
case "linux": // Linux system, assuming there is bash
    cmd = exec.Command("/bin/bash", "-c", "echo test>test.txt")
default: // Some other OS. Assume it has `sh`
    cmd = exec.Command("/bin/sh", "-c", "echo test>test.txt")
}
out, err := cmd.Output()
```

This example selects cmd for Windows platforms, /bin/sh for Darwin (Mac), /bin/bash for Linux, and /bin/sh for anything else. The command passed to the shell contains a redirection, which is handled by the shell. The output of the command will be written to test.txt.

Processing output from a child process using a pipe

Remember that the standard output and standard error streams of a process are concurrent streams. If the output generated by the child process is potentially unbounded, you can work with it in a separate goroutine. This recipe shows how.

How to do it...

A few words about pipes. A pipe is a stream-based analog of a Go channel. It is a **first-in, first-out** (**FIFO**) communication mechanism with two ends: a writer and a reader. The reader side blocks until the writer writes something, and the writer side blocks until the reader reads from it. When you are done with a pipe, you close the writer side, which also closes the reader side of the pipe. This happens when a child process terminates. If you close the reader side of a pipe and then write to it, the program will receive a signal and possibly terminate. This happens if the parent program terminates before the child does.

1. Create the command, and get its `StdoutPipe`:

   ```
   ctx, cancel := context.WithTimeout(context.Background(),
   10*time.Millisecond)
   defer cancel()
   cmd := exec.CommandContext(ctx, "sub/subprocess")
   pipe, err := cmd.StdoutPipe()
   if err != nil {
     panic(err)
   }
   ```

2. Create a new goroutine and read from the stdout of the child process. Work with the output of the child process in this goroutine:

   ```
   // Read from the pipe in a separate goroutine
   go func() {
     // Filter lines that contain "0"
     scanner := bufio.NewScanner(pipe)
     for scanner.Scan() {
       line := scanner.Text()
       if strings.Contains(line, "0")  {
         fmt.Printf("Filtered line: %s\n", line)
       }
     }
     if err := scanner.Err(); err != nil {
       fmt.Println("Scanner error: %v", err)
     }
   }()
   ```

3. Start the process:

```
err = cmd.Start()
if err != nil {
  panic(err)
}
```

4. Wait for the process to end:

```
err = cmd.Wait()
if err != nil {
  fmt.Println(err)
}
```

Providing input to a child process

There are two methods you can use to provide input to a child process: set cmd.Stdin to a stream or use cmd.StdinPipe to obtain a writer to send the input to the child process.

How to do it...

1. Create the command:

```
// Run grep and search for a word
cmd := exec.Command("grep", word)
```

2. Provide the input to the process by setting the Stdin stream:

```
// Open a file
input, err := os.Open("input.txt")
if err != nil {
  panic(err)
}
cmd.Stdin = input
```

3. Run the program and wait for it to end:

```
if err = cmd.Start(); err != nil {
  panic(err)
}
if err = cmd.Wait(); err != nil {
  panic(err)
}
```

Alternatively, you can provide a streaming input using a pipe.

4. Create the command:

```
// Run grep and search for a word
cmd := exec.Command("grep", word)
```

5. Get the input pipe:

```
input, err:=cmd.StdinPipe()
if err!=nil {
  panic(err)
}
```

6. Send the input to the program through the pipe. When done, close the pipe:

```
go func() {
  // Defer close the pipe
  defer input.Close()
  // Open a file
  file, err := os.Open("input.txt")
  if err != nil {
    panic(err)
  }
  defer file.Close()
  io.Copy(input,file)
}()
```

7. Run the program and wait for it to end:

```
if err = cmd.Start(); err != nil {
  panic(err)
}
if err = cmd.Wait(); err != nil {
  panic(err)
}
```

Changing environment variables of a child process

Environment variables are key-value pairs associated with a process. They are useful for passing information specific to the environment, such as the current user's home directory, executable search path, configuration options, and more. In containerized deployments, environment variables are a convenient way to pass the credentials a program needs.

The environment variables for a process are provided by its parent process, but once the process starts, a copy of those provided environment variables is assigned to the child process. Because of this, a parent process cannot change the environment variables of its child process after the child starts running.

How to do it...

- To use the same environment variables as the current process when launching a child process, set Command.Env to nil. That will copy the current process environment variables to the child.

- To start the child process using additional environment variables, append those new variables to the current process variables:

```
// Run the server
cmd:=exec.Command("./server")
// Copy current process environment variables
cmd.Env=os.Environ()
// Append new environment variables
// Set the authentication key as an environment variable
// of the current process
cmd.Env=append(cmd.Env,fmt.Sprintf("AUTH_KEY=%s", authkey))
// Start the server process. Parent process environment is
copied to
cmd.Start()
```

Graceful termination using signals

To gracefully terminate a program, you should do the following:

- No longer accept new requests

- Finish any requests that are accepted but not completed

- Allow a certain amount of time for any long-running processes to finish, and terminate them if they cannot be completed in the given time

Graceful termination is especially important in cloud-based service development because most cloud services are ephemeral and they get replaced by new instances often. This recipe shows how it can be done.

How to do it...

1. Handle interrupt and termination signals. An interrupt signal (SIGINT) is usually initiated by the user (for instance, by pressing *Ctrl + C*), and a termination signal (SIGTERM) is usually initiated by the host operating system, or for a containerized environment, the container orchestration system.

2. Disable acceptance of any new requests.

3. Wait for existing requests to complete with a timeout

4. Terminate the process.

An example is shown next. This is a simple HTTP echo server. When the program starts, it creates a goroutine that listens to a channel responding to SIGINT and SIGTERM signals. When any one of these signals is received, it shuts down the server (which first disables the acceptance of new requests, and then waits for the existing requests to complete up to a timeout), which then terminates the program:

```
func main() {
  // Create a simple HTTP echo service
  http.HandleFunc("/", func(w http.ResponseWriter, r *http.Request) {
    io.Copy(w, r.Body)
  })
  server := &http.Server{Addr: ":8080"}

  // Listen for SIGINT and SIGTERM signals
  // Terminate the server with the signal
  sigTerm := make(chan os.Signal, 1)
  signal.Notify(sigTerm, syscall.SIGINT, syscall.SIGTERM)
  go func() {
    <-sigTerm
    // 5 second timeout for the server to shutdown
    ctx, cancel := context.WithTimeout(context.Background(), 5*time.
    Second)
    defer cancel()
    server.Shutdown(ctx)
  }()

  // Start the server. When the server shuts down, program will end
  server.ListenAndServe()
}
```

13

Network Programming

Network programming is a crucial skill for application developers. An extensive treatise on the topic would be a formidable endeavor, so we will look at some of the select examples you might encounter in your work. An important point to keep in mind is that network programming is the primary means of creating vulnerabilities in an application. Network programs are also inherently concurrent, making correct and safe network programming especially difficult. So, this section will include examples written with security and scalability in mind.

This chapter contains the following recipes:

- Writing TCP servers
- Writing TCP clients
- Writing a line-based TCP server
- Sending/receiving files using a TCP connection
- Writing a TLS client/server
- A TCP proxy for TLS termination and load-balancing
- Setting read/write deadlines
- Unblocking a blocked read or write operation
- Writing UDP clients/servers
- Making HTTP calls
- Running an HTTP server
- HTTPS – setting up a TLS server
- Writing HTTP handlers
- Serving static files on the file system
- Handling HTML forms

- Writing a handler for downloading large files

- Handling HTTP uploaded files and forms as a stream

TCP networking

Transmission Control Protocol (TCP) is a connection-oriented protocol that provides the following guarantees:

- **Reliability**: The sender will know whether the intended recipient received the data

- **Ordering**: Messages will be received in the order they are sent in

- **Error-checked**: Messages will be protected against corruption during transit

Thanks to these guarantees, TCP is relatively easy to work with. It is the basis for many higher-level protocols such as HTTP and WebSockets. In this section, we will look at some recipes that show how to write TCP servers and clients.

Writing TCP servers

A TCP server is a program that listens to connection requests on a network port. Once a connection is established with a client, the communication between the client and the server takes place over a net.Conn object. The server may continue to listen for new connections. This way, a single server can communicate with many clients.

How to do it...

1. Select a port that will connect to the clients server.

    This is usually a matter of application configuration. The first 1,024 (0 to 1023) ports usually require a server program to have root privileges. Most of these ports are reserved for well-known server programs, such as port 22 for ssh, or port 80 for HTTP. Ports 1024 and above are ephemeral ports. Your server program can use any port number of 1,024 and above without additional privileges as long as no other program is listening to it.

    Use port number 0 to let the kernel pick a random unused port. You can create a listener for port 0, and then query the listener to find out what port number was selected.

2. Create a listener. A listener is a mechanism that binds the address:port. Once you create a listener using a port number, no other process on the same host, or within the same container, can use that port number to listen to network traffic.

    The following program snippet shows how to create a listener:

    ```
    // The address:port to listen. If none given, use :0 to select
    // port randomly
    addr:=":8080"
    ```

```
// Create a TCP listener
listener, err := net.Listen("tcp", addr)
if err != nil {
  panic(err)
}
// Print out the address we are listening
fmt.Println("Listening on ", listener.Addr())
defer listener.Close()
```

The program first determines the network address to listen to. The exact format of the address depends on the protocol chosen, which is TCP in this case. If no hostname or IP address is given, the listener will listen to all available unicast IP addresses of the local system. If you give a hostname or IP address, the listener will only listen to the traffic coming from the given IP address. That means if you give localhost:1234, the listener will listen to traffic coming from localhost only. It will not listen to external traffic.

The above example prints listener.Addr(). This is useful if you provide :0 as the listen address, or if you do not provide one at all. In this case, the listener will listen to a random port, and listener.Addr() will return the address that clients can connect to.

3. Listen and accept connections. Accept incoming connections using Listener.Accept(). This is usually done in a loop as follows:

```
// Listen to incoming TCP connections
for {
  // Accept a connection
  conn, err := listener.Accept()
  if err != nil {
    fmt.Println(err)
    return
  }
  // Handle the connection in its own goroutine
  go handleConnection(conn)
}
```

In this example, the listener.Accept call will fail with an error if the listener is closed.

4. Handle the connection in its own goroutine. This way, the listener will continue to accept connections while the server communicates with the connected clients in their own goroutines, using the connections created specifically for those clients.

A connection handler for a simple echo server can be written as follows:

```
func handleConnection(conn net.Conn) {
  io.Copy(conn,conn)
}
```

Here's the complete server program:

```
var address = flag.String("a", ":8008", "Address to listen")

func main() {
    flag.Parse()

    // Create a TCP listener
    listener, err := net.Listen("tcp", *address)
    if err != nil {
        panic(err)
    }
    fmt.Println("Listening on ", listener.Addr())
    defer listener.Close()
    // Listen to incoming TCP connections
    for {
        conn, err := listener.Accept()
        if err != nil {
            fmt.Println(err)
            return
        }
        go handleConnection(conn)
    }
}

func handleConnection(conn net.Conn) {
    io.Copy(conn, conn)
}
```

This program will write everything it reads from the connection back to the connection, forming an echo service. When the client terminates the connection, the read operation will return io.EOF, terminating the copy operation.

How it works...

The net.Conn interface has both the Read([]byte) (int,error) method (which makes it an io.Reader), and Write([]byte) (int,error) (which also makes it an io.Writer). Due to this, whatever is read from the connection is written back to it.

You may notice that because of io.Copy, every byte read will be written back to the connection, so this is not a line-based protocol.

Writing TCP clients

A TCP client connects to a TCP server that is listening on a port of some host. Once the connection is established, communication is bidirectional. In other words, the distinction between a server and a client is based on how the connection is established. When we say "server," we mean the program that waits listening to a port, and when we say "client," we mean the program that connects ("dials") a port on a host that is being listened on by a server. Once the connection is established, both sides send and receive data asynchronously. TCP guarantees that the messages will be received in the order they are sent, and that the messages will not be lost, but there are no guarantees on when a message will be received by the other side.

How to do it...

1. The client side has to know the server address and port. This should be provided by the environment (command line, configuration, etc.).

2. Use net.Dial to create a connection to the server:

    ```
    conn, err := net.Dial("tcp", addr)
    if err != nil {
     // Handle error
     }
    ```

3. Use the returned net.Conn object to send data to the server, or to receive data from the server:

    ```
    // Send a line of text
    text := []byte("Hello echo server!")
    conn.Write(text)
    // Read the response
    response := make([]byte, len(text))
    conn.Read(response)
    fmt.Println(string(response))
    ```

4. Close the connection when done:

    ```
    conn.Close()
    ```

Here is the complete program:

```
var address = flag.String("a", ":8008", "Server address")

func main() {
    flag.Parse()
    conn, err := net.Dial("tcp", *address)
    if err != nil {
        panic(err)
```

```
  }
  // Send a line of text
  text := []byte("Hello echo server!")
  conn.Write(text)
  // Read the response
  response := make([]byte, len(text))
  conn.Read(response)
  fmt.Println(string(response))
  conn.Close()
}
```

This example demonstrates a request-response type of interaction with the server. This is not necessarily always the case. A network connection provides both an io.Writer and an io.Reader interface, and they can be used concurrently.

Writing a line-based TCP server

In this recipe, we will look at a TCP server that works with lines instead of bytes. There are some points you need to be careful about when reading lines from a network connection, especially related to the security of the server. Just because you are expecting to read lines does not mean the client will send well-formed lines.

How to do it...

1. Use the same structure to set up the server as given in the previous section.

2. In the connection handler, use a bufio.Reader or bufio.Scanner to read lines.

3. Wrap the connection with an io.LimitedReader to limit line length.

Let's take a look at how this can work. The following example shows how a connection handler can be implemented:

```
// Limit line length to 1KiB.
const MaxLineLength = 1024

func handleConnection(conn net.Conn) error {
  defer conn.Close()
  // Wrap the connection with a limited reader
  // to prevent the client from sending unbounded
  // amount of data
  limiter := &io.LimitedReader {
    R: conn,
    N: MaxLineLength+1, // Read one extra byte to detect long lines
  }
```

```go
reader := bufio.NewReader(limiter)
for {
  bytes, err := reader.ReadBytes(byte('\n'))
  if err != nil {
    if err != io.EOF {
      // Some error other than end-of-stream
      return err
    }
    // End of stream. It could be because the line is too long
    if limiter.N==0 {
      // Line was too long
      return fmt.Errorf("Received a line that is too long")
    }
    // End of stream
    return nil
  }
  // Reset the limiter, so the next line can be read with
  // newlimit
  limiter.N=MaxLineLength+1

  // Process the line: send it back to client
  if _, err := conn.Write(bytes); err != nil {
    return err
  }
}
}
```

The connection handling routine starts by wrapping the connection in an io.LimitedReader. This is necessary to prevent reader.ReadBytes from reading an unlimited amount of data until it sees the newline character. Without this, a malicious client can send large amounts of data without any newline characters, consuming all the server memory. Putting a hard limit on the line length prevents this attack vector. After reading every line, we reset the limiter.N to its original value so the next line can be read using the same limits. Note that the limiter is set to read one extra byte. This is because the io.LimitedReader returns io.EOF for both a legitimate EOF (which means the client disconnected), and a read exceeding the limit. If the reader exceeds the limit, that means the last line read is at least one byte above the limit, allowing us to decide this is an invalid line.

Sending/receiving files using a TCP connection

Sending and receiving files over a TCP connection demonstrates several important points about network programming, namely the protocol design (which deals with who sends what when) and encoding (which deals with how data elements are represented on the wire). This example will show how to transfer metadata and an octet stream over a TCP connection.

How to do it...

1. Use the same structure to set up the server as in the previous section.

2. On the sender end (client), do the following:

   - Encode file metadata containing the filename, size, and mode and send it.

   - Send the contents of the file.

   - Close the connection.

3. On the receiver end (server), do the following:

   - Decode file metadata. Create a file to store the received file contents with the given mode.

   - Receive file contents and write the file.

   - After all file content is received, close the file.

The first part is the transfer of metadata about the file. There are several ways this can be done: you can work with a text-based encoding scheme such as key-value pairs or JSON, but the problem with such schemes is that they are not fixed length. A simple, effective, and portable encoding scheme is binary encoding using the encoding/binary package. That does not solve the encoding of the filename, which is not a fixed-sized string. So, we include the length of the filename in the file metadata, and encode the filename using exactly the necessary number of bytes.

The fixed-sized fileMetadata structure is as follows:

```
type fileMetadata struct {
    Size    uint64
    Mode    uint32
    NameLen uint16
}
```

This structure is 14 bytes on all platforms (eight bytes of Size, four bytes of Mode, and two bytes of NameLen.) Using binary/encoding.Write, you can encode this fixed-size structure on the wire using either binary.BigEndian or binary.LittleEndian encoding, and the receiving end will decode it successfully.

More detailed information on endianness is included in the next chapter.

The rest of the client is as follows:

```
var address = flag.String("a", ":8008", "Server address")
var file = flag.String("file", "", "File to send")

func main() {
    flag.Parse()
```

```go
    // Open the file
    file, err := os.Open(*file)
    if err != nil {
        panic(err)
    }

    // Connect the receiver
    conn, err := net.Dial("tcp", *address)
    if err != nil {
        panic(err)
    }

    // Encode file metadata
    fileInfo, err := file.Stat()
    if err != nil {
        panic(err)
    }
    md := fileMetadata{
        Size:    uint64(fileInfo.Size()),
        Mode:    uint32(fileInfo.Mode()),
        NameLen: uint16(len(fileInfo.Name())),
    }
    if err := binary.Write(conn, binary.LittleEndian, md); err != nil {
        panic(err)
    }
    // The file name
    if _, err := conn.Write([]byte(fileInfo.Name())); err != nil {
        panic(err)
    }
    // The file contents
    if _, err := io.Copy(conn, file); err != nil {
        panic(err)
    }
    conn.Close()
}
```

Note the use of io.Copy to transfer the actual contents of the file. Using io.Copy, you can transfer arbitrary-size files to the receiver without consuming significant amounts of memory.

Now let's look at the server (receiver):

```go
func handleConnection(conn net.Conn) {
    defer conn.Close()
```

```go
    // Read the file metadata
    var meta fileMetadata
    err := binary.Read(conn, binary.LittleEndian, &meta)
    if err != nil {
        fmt.Println(err)
        return
    }
    // Do not allow file names that are too long
    if meta.NameLen > 255 {
        fmt.Println("File name too long")
        return
    }
    // Read the file name
    name := make([]byte, meta.NameLen)
    _, err = io.ReadFull(conn, name)
    if err != nil {
        fmt.Println(err)
        return
    }
    path:=filepath.Join("downloads",string(name))
    // Create the file
    file, err := os.OpenFile(
        path,
        os.O_CREATE|os.O_WRONLY,
        os.FileMode(meta.Mode),
    )
    if err != nil {
        fmt.Println(err)
        return
    }
    defer file.Close()
    // Copy the file contents
    _, err = io.CopyN(file, conn, int64(meta.Size))
    if err != nil {
        // Remove file in case of error
        os.Remove(path)
        fmt.Println(err)
        return
    }
    fmt.Printf("Received file %s: %d bytes\n", string(name), meta.
Size)
}
```

The first operation is a fixed-size read operation of the file metadata. Then we read the filename. Note the filename length check before reading the filename. It is an important defensive approach to validate and limit all memory allocations involving size read from an external system or user. Here, we reject filenames that are longer than 255 bytes. Then, we create the file using the given mode and use `io.CopyN` to read exact file size bytes from the input. In case of an error, we remove the partially downloaded file.

Writing a TLS client/server

Transport Layer Security (**TLS**) provides end-to-end encryption without revealing the encryption key to prevent man-in-the-middle attacks. It also provides authentication of peers and message integrity guarantees. This recipe shows how to set up a TLS server for securing network communications. However, first, a few words on public key cryptography can be useful.

A cryptographic **key pair** contains a private key and a public key. The private key is kept secret and the public key is published.

This is how a key pair is used to encrypt messages: Since the public key of a party is published, anybody can create a message and encrypt it using the public key, then send it to the party that has the private key. Only the private key owner can decrypt that message. That also means that if the private key is revealed, anybody with that private key can eavesdrop on such messages.

This is how a key pair is used to ensure message integrity: The owner of a private key can create a signature (hash) of a message using its private key. Anybody with a public key can verify the integrity of the message, that is, the public key can be used to validate whether a signature is generated by the corresponding private key.

Public keys are distributed in the form of **digital certificates**. A digital certificate is a file that contains the public key of an entity signed by a trusted third party, a **certificate authority** (**CA**). There are many well-known CAs that publish their own public keys as certificates (root certificates), and these root certificates are shipped with most modern operating systems, so when you get a certificate, you can validate its authenticity using the public key of the CA that signed it. Once you validate that a public key is authentic, you can connect the owner of the public key, which has the corresponding private key, and establish a secure channel.

The root certificate of a CA is usually signed by the CA itself.

If you need to create certificates for your internal servers, you usually create a CA for your environment by creating a self-signed root CA. You keep the private key for that CA secret and publish the public key internally. There are automated tools that will help you create CAs and certificates for your servers.

How to do it...

Here's how you can set up a server and client for TLS:

1. Create or purchase an X.509 certificate for your server. If the server is not an internet-facing server, a self-signed certificate is usually sufficient. If this is an internet-facing server, you either have to get a certificate from one of the CA organizations, or publish your own public key certificate so the clients that want to connect to your servers can use that certificate to authenticate and encrypt traffic.

2. For the server, do the following:

    *   Load the certificate using `crypto/tls.LoadX509KeyPair`.

    *   Create a `crypto/tls.Config` using the certificate.

    *   Create a listener using `crypto/tls.Listen`.

    *   The rest of the server follows the same TCP server layout.

The following code segment illustrates these steps:

```go
var (
    address     = flag.String(
        "a", ":4433", "Address to listen")
    certificate = flag.String(
        "c", "../server.crt", "Certificate file")
    key         = flag.String(
        "k", "../privatekey.pem", "Private key")
)

func main() {
    flag.Parse()

    // 2.1 Load the key pair
    cer, err := tls.LoadX509KeyPair(*certificate, *key)
    if err != nil {
        panic(err)
    }
    // 2.2 Create TLS configuration for the listener
    config := &tls.Config{
        Certificates: []tls.Certificate{cer},
    }
    // 2.3 Create the listener
    listener, err := tls.Listen("tcp", *address, config)
    if err != nil {
        panic(err)
```

```
            return
        }
        defer listener.Close()

        fmt.Println("Listening TLS on ", listener.Addr())
        // 2.4 Listen to incoming TCP connections
        for {
            conn, err := listener.Accept()
            if err != nil {
                fmt.Println(err)
                return
            }
            go handleConnection(conn)
        }
    }
}
```

Note that both the certificate and the private key are necessary to set up the server. Once the TLS listener is set up, the rest of the code is identical to an unencrypted TCP server.

For the client, please follow these steps:

1. If you are using a certificate from a well-known CA, use `crypto/x509.SystemCertPool`. If you have a self-signed certificate or some other custom certificate, create an empty certificate pool using `crypto/x509.NewCertPool`.

2. Load the server certificate, and add it to the certificate pool.

3. Use `crypto/tls.Dial` with a TLS configuration initialized using the certificate pool.

4. The rest of the client follows the same TCP client layout described here.

The following code segment shows these steps:

```
var (
    addr     = flag.String(
      "addr", "", "Server address")
    certFile = flag.String(
      "cert", "../server.crt", "TLS certificate file")
)

func main() {
    flag.Parse()

    // 3.1 Create new certificate pool
    roots := x509.NewCertPool()
    // 3.2 Load server certificate
    certData, err := os.ReadFile(*certFile)
```

```
    if err != nil {
        panic(err)
    }
    ok := roots.AppendCertsFromPEM(certData)
    if !ok {
        panic("failed to parse root certificate")
    }
    // 3.3 Connect the server
    conn, err := tls.Dial("tcp", *addr, &tls.Config{
        RootCAs: roots,
    })
    if err != nil {
        panic(err)
    }
    // 3.4 Send a line of text
    text := []byte("Hello echo server!")
    conn.Write(text)
    // Read the response
    response := make([]byte, len(text))
    conn.Read(response)
    fmt.Println(string(response))
    conn.Close()
}
```

Again, loading the certificate and adding it to a certificate pool is only required if the server certificate is signed by a CA that is not recognized by the operating system. Many websites that use HTTPS have certificates signed by a well-known CA, and that's why you can connect them without installing custom certificates: the operating system already trusts the CA.

> **Note**
> There are examples of this under the book's GitHub (https://github.com/
> PacktPublishing/Go-Recipes-for-Developers/tree/main/src/chp13).

A TCP proxy for TLS termination and load-balancing

Most internet-facing applications use a reverse proxy (ingress) to separate the internal resources from the external world. The reverse proxy is usually connected by the external clients using encrypted connections (TLS), and forwards the requests to backend services via unencrypted channels (*Figure 11.1*) or by re-encrypting the connection using the internal CA. The reverse proxy usually also performs some sort of load-balancing to distribute the work evenly.

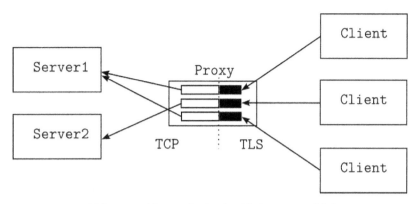

Figure 13.1 – TLS proxy with round-robin load balancing and TLS termination

In this section, we will look at such a reverse proxy that accepts TLS traffic from external hosts, and forwards that traffic to backend servers using unencrypted TCP while distributing the requests to those servers in a round-robin fashion.

As a Go developer, you are unlikely to write your own reverse proxy or load balancer, as there are multiple options available already. However, it is an interesting application and I am including it here to show how something like this can be done in Go, in particular the proxy itself.

How to do it...

Here, we assume that the proxy is given the list of available backend servers. Many times, you will need to use a platform-specific discovery mechanism to find out what the available servers are:

1. Create an external facing TLS receiver using the certificate and key for the proxy host.

2. Listen to incoming TLS connections.

3. When a client connects, select a backend server and connect.

4. Start a proxy goroutine to forward all traffic coming from the external host to the backend server, and traffic coming from the backend server to the external host.

5. Terminate the proxy when one of the connections closes.

The following program illustrates these steps:

```
var (
    tlsAddress      = flag.String(
        "a", ":4433", "TLS address to listen")
    serverAddresses = flag.String(
        "s", ":8080", "Server addresses, comma separated")
    certificate     = flag.String(
        "c", "../server.crt", "Certificate file")
```

```go
    key              = flag.String(
      "k", "../privatekey.pem", "Private key")
)

func main() {
    flag.Parse()

    // 1. Create external facing TLS receiver

    // Load the key pair
    cer, err := tls.LoadX509KeyPair(*certificate, *key)
    if err != nil {
        panic(err)
    }
    // Create TLS configuration for the listener
    config := &tls.Config{
        Certificates: []tls.Certificate{cer},
    }
    // Create the tls listener
    tlsListener, err := tls.Listen("tcp", *tlsAddress, config)
    if err != nil {
        panic(err)
    }
    defer tlsListener.Close()
    fmt.Println("Listening TLS on ", tlsListener.Addr())

    // Listen to incoming TLS connections
    servers := strings.Split(*serverAddresses, ",")
    fmt.Println("Forwarding to servers: ", servers)

    nextServer := 0
    for {
        // 2. Listen to incoming TLS connections
        conn, err := tlsListener.Accept()
        if err != nil {
            fmt.Println(err)
            return
        }
        retries := 0
        for {
            // 3. Select the next server
            server := servers[nextServer]
            nextServer++
            if nextServer >= len(servers) {
```

```
                    nextServer = 0
            }
            // Start a connection to this server
            targetConn, err := net.Dial("tcp", server)
            if err != nil {
                retries++
                fmt.Errorf("Cannot connect to %s", server)
                if retries > len(servers) {
                    panic("None of the servers are available")
                }
                continue
            }
            // 4. Start the proxy
            go handleProxy(conn, targetConn)
        }
    }
}
```

We have already covered the details of setting up a TLS receiver in the previous recipes, so let's take a look at how the backend server is selected. This implementation is given a list of all available backend servers. Every accepted client connection is assigned the next server in the list, pointed to by the nextServer index. The proxy uses net.Dial to connect the selected server, and if the connection fails (the server may be temporarily down), it skips to the next server in the list. If this fails len(servers) times, then all backend servers are unavailable, and the program terminates. However, if one server is selected, a proxy is started and the main goroutine goes back to listening to new connections.

Let's see how the proxy handler is written:

```
func handleProxy(conn, targetConn net.Conn) {
    defer conn.Close()
    defer targetConn.Close()
    // Copy data from the client to the server
    go io.Copy(targetConn, conn)
    // Copy data from the server to the client
    io.Copy(conn, targetConn)
}
```

As I mentioned in the previous sections, a network connection contains two concurrent streams, one going from the client host to the server, and the other going from the server to the client host. Both of these streams can include data in flight at the same time. Due to this, proxying a TCP connection involves two io.Copy operations, one from server to client, and one from client to server. Furthermore, at least one of these has to run in a separate goroutine. In the preceding example, the traffic from the external connection to the backend server is copied in a separate goroutine, and the traffic from the backend server to the external host is copied in the proxy goroutine. The copy operation will terminate if either side closes the connection, which will cause the last copy operation to terminate, closing the other connection as well.

Setting read/write deadlines

If you do not want to wait indefinitely for a connected host to send data, or for the connected host to receive the data you sent, you have to set a deadline.

How to do it...

Depending on your specific protocol, you can set read or write deadlines, and you may choose to set these deadlines for individual I/O operations, or globally:

1. Set the deadline before the operation:

    ```
    conn.SetDeadline(time.Now().Add(timeoutSeconds * timeSecond))
    if n, err:=conn.Read(data); err!=nil {
      if errors.Is(err, os.ErrDeadlineExceeded) {
        // Deadline exceeded.
      } else {
        // Some other error
      }
    }
    ```

2. If you will continue using the connection after a deadline is exceeded, you have to reset the deadline:

    ```
    conn.SetDeadline(time.Time{})
    ```

Or, set a new deadline with a time in the future.

Unblocking a blocked read or write operation

Sometimes, you need to unblock a read or write operation based on an external event. This recipe shows how you can unblock such an I/O operation.

How to do it...

*   If you want to unblock an I/O operation with no intention of reusing the connection again, close the connection asynchronously:

    ```
    cancel:=make(chan struct{})
    done:=make(chan struct{})
    ```

```
    // Close the connection if a message is sent to cancel channel
    go func() {
        select {
            case <-cancel:
                conn.Close()
            case <-done:
        }
    }()
    go handleConnection(conn)
```

• If you want to unblock an I/O operation but not terminate it, set the deadline to now:

```
    unblock:=make(chan struct{})
    // Unblock the connection if a message is sent to unblock
    channel
    go func() {
        <-unblock
        conn.SetDeadline(time.Now())
    }()
    timedout:=false
    if n, err:=conn.Read(data); err!=nil {
        if errors.Is(err,os.ErrDeadlineExceeded) {
            // Reset connection deadline
            conn.SetDeadline(time.Time{})
            timedout=true
            // continue using the connection
        } else {
            // Handle error
        }
    }
    if timedout {
        // Read timedout
    } else {
        // Read did not timeout
    }
```

How it works...

A TCP read operation blocks until there is something available to read, which only happens when some data is received from the peer. A TCP write operation will block when no more data can be buffered on the sending side. The preceding recipe shows two ways you can unblock these calls.

Closing a connection unblocks read/write operations with an error because the connection is closed while waiting for data to arrive, or while waiting for data to be written. Closing a connection discards all unread or unwritten data and destroys all resources allocated for that connection.

Setting the timeout asynchronously will set a deadline for the waiting operation, and when that deadline passes, the operation fails but the connection remains open. You can reset the deadline and retry the operation.

Writing UDP clients/servers

Unlike TCP, UDP is connectionless. That means instead of establishing a connection with another peer and sending data back and forth, you simply send data packets and receive them. There are no delivery or ordering guarantees.

One of the prominent uses of UDP is the **Domain Name Service** (**DNS**) protocol. UDP is also the choice for many streaming protocols (voice over IP, video streaming, etc.) where occasional package loss is tolerable. Network monitoring tools also favor UDP.

Despite being connectionless, the UDP networking APIs offer an interface similar to the TCP networking APIs. Here, we will show a simple client-server UDP echo server to demonstrate how these APIs can be used.

How to do it...

The following steps show how to write a UDP server:

1. Resolve the UDP address the server will listen on using net.ResolveUDPAddr:

    ```
    addr, err := net.ResolveUDPAddr("udp4", *address)
    if err != nil {
      panic(err)
    }
    ```

2. Create a UDP listener:

    ```
    // Create a UDP connection
    conn, err := net.ListenUDP("udp4", addr)
    if err != nil {
      panic(err)
    }
    defer conn.Close()
    ```

    Even though net.ListenUDP returns a *net.UDPConn, the returned object resembles a listener and not a connection. UDP is connectionless, so this call starts listening UDP packets on the given address. The clients technically do not *connect* the server and start a two-way stream; they simply send a packet. That's why, in the next step, the read operation also returns the address of the sender, so a response can be sent.

3. Read from the listener. This will return the remote address of the peer:

```
// Listen to incoming UDP connections
buf := make([]byte, 1024)
n, remoteAddr, err := conn.ReadFromUDP(buf)
if err != nil {
  // Handle the error
}
fmt.Printf("Received %d bytes from %s\n", n, remoteAddr)
```

4. Send the response to the peer using the address obtained in the previous step:

```
if n > 0 {
  _, err := conn.WriteToUDP(buf[:n], remoteAddr)
  if err != nil {
    // Handle the error
  }
}
```

Now let's take a look at the UDP client:

1. Resolve the address of the server:

```
addr, err := net.ResolveUDPAddr("udp4", *serverAddress)
if err != nil {
  panic(err)
}
```

2. Create a UDP connection. This requires a local address and a remote address. If the local address is nil, the local address is automatically chosen. If the remote address is nil, it is assumed to be the local system:

```
// Create a UDP connection, local address chosen randomly
conn, err := net.DialUDP("udp4", nil, addr)
if err != nil {
  panic(err)
}
fmt.Printf("UDP server %s\n", conn.RemoteAddr())
defer conn.Close()
```

Again, UDP is connectionless. The preceding call to `DialUDP` creates a socket that will be used in subsequent calls. It does not create a connection to the server.

3. Send data to the server using `conn.Write`:

```
// Send a line of text
text := []byte("Hello echo server!")
n, err := conn.Write(text)
```

```
if err != nil {
  panic(err)
}
fmt.Printf("Written %d bytes\n", n)
```

4. Read data from the server using conn.Read:

```
// Read the response
response := make([]byte, 1024)
conn.ReadFromUDP(response)
```

Working with HTTP

HTTP is a client-server protocol where the client (a user agent or proxy) sends requests to a server, and the server returns a response. It is an application layer hypertext protocol, and the backbone of the World Wide Web.

Making HTTP calls

The Go standard library offers two basic ways of issuing HTTP calls to interact with websites and web services: if you do not need to configure timeouts, transport properties, or redirect policies, simply use the shared client. If you need to do additional configuration, use http.Client. This recipe demonstrates both.

How to do it...

- The standard library includes a shared HTTP client. You can use that to interact with web servers using the default configuration:

```
response, err := http.Get("http://example.com")
if err!=nil {
  // Handle error
}
// Always close response body
defer response.Body.Close()
if response.StatusCode/100==2 {
  // HTTP 2xx, call was successful.
  // Work with response.Body
}
```

- If you need to apply different timeout values, change the redirect policy, or configure the transport, create a new http.Client, initialize it, and use that:

```
client:=http.Client{
  // Set a timeout for all outgoing calls.
```

```
    // If the call does not complete within 30 seconds, timeout.
    Timeout: 30*time.Second,
}
response, err:=client.Get("http://example.com")
if err!=nil {
  // handle error
}
// Always close response body
defer response.Body.Close()
```

- You can call websites using HTTPS (using TLS) if the operating system already has the certificate for the CA that issued that website's certificate. This is the case for most public websites over the internet:

  ```
  response, err := http.Get("https://example.com")
  ```

- If you are using TLS with a custom CA, or if you are using self-signed certificates, you have to create a http.Client with a Transport containing the certificate.

  - Create a new certificate pool:

    ```
    roots := x509.NewCertPool()
    ```

  - Load the server certificate:

    ```
    certData, err := os.ReadFile(*certFile)
    if err != nil {
      panic(err)
    }
    ```

  - Add the certificate to the certificate pool:

    ```
    ok := roots.AppendCertsFromPEM(certData)
    if !ok {
      panic("failed to parse root certificate")
    }
    ```

  - Create a TLS config:

    ```
    config:=tls.Config{
      RootCAs: roots,
    }
    ```

  - Create an HTTP Transport using the TLS config:

    ```
    transport := &http.Transport {
      TLSClientConfig: &config,
    }
    ```

- Create an HTTP client:

```
client:= &http.Client{
  Transport: transport,
}
```

- Use the client:

```
resp, err:=client.Get(url)
if err!=nil {
  // Handle error
}
defer resp.Body.Close()
```

> **Tip**
> Always close the response body when you are done working with it, and try to read all data available in the body. The `response.Body` represents a streaming connection to the server. The server will reserve resources for the connection as long as there is data in transit and the client keeps the connection open. It also prevents the client from reusing keep-alive connections.

Running an HTTP server

The standard Go library offers an HTTP server with sensible defaults that you can use out of the box, similar to the way HTTP clients are implemented. If you need to configure transport specifics, timeouts, and so on, then you can create a new `http.Server` and work with it. This section describes both approaches.

How to do it...

- Create an `http.Handler` to handle HTTP requests:

```
func myHandler(w http.ResponseWriter, req *http.Request) {
  if req.Method == http.MethodGet {
    // Handle an HTTP GET request
  }
  ...
}
```

- Call `http.ListenAndServe`:

```
err:=http.ListenAndServe(":8080",http.HandlerFunc(myHandler))
log.Fatal(err)
```

- The `ListenAndServe` function either returns immediately due to an error setting up a network listener (for example, if the address is already in use) or successfully starts listening. When the server is asynchronously closed (by calling `server.Close()` or `server.Shutdown()`), it returns `ErrServerClosed`.

- Alternatively, you can use a `http.Server` struct to better control server options:

  - Create an `http.Handler` as described.

  - Initialize an `http.Server` instance:

    ```
    server := http.Server {
      // The address to listen
      Addr: ":8080",
      // The handler function
      Handler: http.HandlerFunc(myHandler),
      // The handlers must read the request within 10 seconds
      ReadTimeout: 10*time.Second,
      // The headers of a request must be read within 5 seconds
      ReadHeaderTimeout: 5*time.Second,
    }
    ```

  - Listen HTTP requests:

    ```
    err:=server.ListenAndServe()
    log.Fatal(err)
    ```

> **Tip**
>
> A common way to create an HTTP handler is to use a request multiplexer. Recipes for using a request multiplexer will be covered later.

HTTPS – setting up a TLS server

To start a TLS server, you need a certificate and a private key. You can either purchase one from a CA or generate our own certificates with your internal CA. Once you have your certificate, you can use the recipes in this section to start your HTTPS server.

How to do it...

To create a TLS HTTP server, use one of the following:

1. Use the `Server.ListenAndServeTLS` method with the certificate and key files:

   ```
   server := http.Server {
     Addr: ":4443",
   ```

```
        Handler: handler,
    }
    server.ListenAndServeTLS("cert.pem", "key.pem")
```

2. To use the default HTTP server, set a handler function (or `http.Handler`) and call `http.ListenAndServeTLS`:

```
    http.HandleFunc("/",func(w http.ResponseWriter, req *http.
    Request) {
      // Handle request
    })
    http.ListenAndServeTLS("cert.pem", "key.pem")
```

3. Or prepare a `http.Transport` with certificates:

   3.1   Load the TLS certificate:

```
    cert, err := tls.LoadX509KeyPair("cert.pem", "key.pem")
    if err!=nil {
      panic(err)
    }
```

   3.2   Create a `tls.Config` using the certificate:

```
    tlsConfig := &tls.Config{
      Certificates: []tls.Certificate{cert},
    }
```

   3.3   Create a `http.Server` using the `tlsConfig`:

```
    server := http.Server{
      Addr:      ":4443",
      Handler:   handler,
      TLSConfig: tlsConfig,
    }
```

   3.4   Call `server.ListenAndServeTLS`

```
    server.ListenAndServeTLS("","")
```

Writing HTTP handlers

When an HTTP request arrives at a server, the server looks at the HTTP method (GET, POST, etc), the hostname the client used (the `Host` header), and the URL to decide how to handle the request. The mechanism that determines which handler should handle such a request is called a **request multiplexer**. The Go standard library comes with one, and there are many third-party open source multiplexers. In this section, we will look at the standard library multiplexer and how it can be used.

How to do it...

1. You can use an anonymous function for simple cases, such as a health-check endpoint:

```
mux := http.NewServeMux()
mux.HandleFunc("GET /health",func(w http.ResponseWriter, req
*http.Request) {
  w.Write([]byte("Ok")
})
...
server := http.Server {
  Handler: mux,
  Addr: ":8080",
  ...
}
server.ListenAndServe()
```

The preceding handler will respond to GET /health endpoint requests with an Ok and HTTP 200 status.

2. You can use a data type that implements the http.Handler interface:

    • Create a new data type, which can be a struct containing information that you will need to implement the handler:

```
// The RandomService reads random data from a source, and
// returns random numbers
type RandomService struct {
  rndSource io.Reader
}
```

    • Implement the `http.Handler` interface:

```
func (svc RandomService) ServeHTTP(w http.ResponseWriter, req
*http.Request) {
  // Read 4 bytes from the random number source, convert it to
string
  data:= make([]byte,4)
  _,err:=svc.rndSource.Read(data)
  if err!=nil {
    // This will return an HTTP 500 error with the error message
    // as the message body
    http.Error(w,err.Error(),http.StatusInternalServerError)
    return
  }
  // Decode random data using binary little endian encoding
  value:=binary.LittleEndian.Uint32(data)
```

```
  // Write the data to the output
  w.Write([]byte(strconv.Itoa(int(value))))
}
```

- Create an instance of the handler type and initialize it

```
file, err:=os.Open("/dev/random")
if err!=nil {
  panic(err)
}
defer file.Close()
svc:=RandomService {
  rndSource: file,
}
```

3. Create a multiplexer:

```
mux:=http.NewServeMux()
```

4. Assign the handler to a pattern. The following example assigns GET requests for /rnd path to the instance constructed at *step 3*.

```
mux.Handle("GET /rnd", svc)
```

5. Start the server.

```
server := http.Server {
  Handler: mux,
  Addr: ":8080",
  ...
}
server.ListenAndServe()
```

6. A more general method involves creating data types with multiple methods as handlers. This pattern is especially useful for web service development because it allows for creating structures that serve all the APIs related to a specific business domain:

- Create a data type. This can be a struct containing all the necessary information to implement handlers, such as database connections, public/private keys, and so on:

```
type UserHandler struct {
  DB *sql.DB
}
```

7. Create methods using the signature for `http.HandlerFunc` to implement multiple API endpoints:

```
func (hnd UserHandler) GetUser(w http.ResponseWriter, req *http.
Request) {
    ...
}
```

8. Create an initialize the handlers.

```
userDb, err:=sql.Open(driver, UserDBUrl)
if err!=nil {
  panic(err)
}

userHandler := UserHandler {
  DB: userDb,
}
```

9. Create a request multiplexer

```
mux := http.NewServeMux()
```

10. Assign handler methods to patterns:

```
mux.Handle("GET /users/{userId}",userHandler.GetUser)
mux.Handle("POST /users", userHandler.NewUser)
mux.Handle("DELETE /users/{userId}", userHandler.DeleteUser)
```

11. Use the multiplexer to start the server.

```
server := http.Server{
    Addr: serverAddr,
    Handler: mux,
}
server.ListenAndServe()
```

The following code snippet illustrates how you can use the standard library request multiplexer tools when writing HTTP handlers:

```
func (hnd UserHandler) GetUser(w http.ResponseWriter, req *http.
Request) {
  // User req.PathValue("userId") to get userId portion of /users/
  // {userId}
  // That is, if this API is invoked with GET /users/123, then after
  // the following line `userId` is assigned to "123"
  userId:=req.PathValue("userId")
```

```
// Get user data from the DB
user, err:=GetUserInformation(hnd.DB,userId)
if err!=nil {
  http.Error(w,err.Error(),http.StatusNotFound)
  return
}
// Marshal user data to JSON
data, err:=json.Marshal(user)
if err!=nil {
  http.Error(w, err.Error(),http.StatusInternalServerError)
  return
}
// Set the content type header. You **must** set all headers before
// writing the body. Once the body is placed on the write, there is
// no way to change a header that is already written.
w.Header().Set("Content-Type","application/json")
w.Write(data)
}
```

Serving static files on the file system

Not all files served by web applications are dynamically generated. JavaScript files, cascading stylesheets, and some HTML pages are usually served verbatim. This section shows several methods to serve such files.

How to do it...

There are several ways a static file can be served via HTTP:

1. To serve all static files under a directory, use `http.FileServer` to create a handler:

    ```
    fileHandler := http.FileServer(http.Dir("/var/www"))
    server:=http.Server{
      Addr: addr,
      Handler: fileHandler,
    }
    http.ListenAndServe()
    ```

    The above snippet will serve the files under /var/www at the root path. That is, a GET /index.html request will serve the /var/www/index.html file with Content-Type: text/html. Similarly, a GET /css/styles.css will serve /var/www/css/styles.css with Content-Type: text/css.

2. To serve all static files under a directory but with a different URL path prefix, use `http.StripPrefix`:

    ```
    fileHandler := http.StripPrefix("/static/", http.
    FileHandler(http.Dir("/var/www")))
    ```

    The above call wraps the given file handler with another that strips the given prefix from the URL path. For a `GET /static/index.html` request, this handler will serve `/var/www/index.html` with `Content-Type: text/html`. If the path does not include the given prefix, this will return `HTTP 404 Not Found`.

3. To add additional logic to URL-filename mapping, implement the `http.FileSystem` interface and use `FileServerFS` with that file system. You can combine this handler with `http.StripPrefix` to further change URL path processing:

    ```
    // Serve only HTML files in the given directory
    type htmlFS struct {
      fs *http.FileSystem
    }

    // Filter file names by their extension before opening them
    func (h htmlFS) Open(name string) (http.File, error) {
      if strings.ToLower(filepath.Ext(name))==".html" {
        return h.fs.Open(name)
      }
      return nil, os.ErrNotFound
    }
    ...

    htmlHandler := http.FileHandler(htmlFS{fs:http.Dir("/var/www"))
    // htmlHandler serves all HTML files under /var/www
    ```

Handling HTML forms

HTML forms are an essential component of capturing data in web applications. An HTML form can be processed on the server side through the use of a `Form` HTML element, or it can be processed on the client side using JavaScript. In this section, we will look at handling HTTP form submissions for server-side processing.

How to do it...

On the client side, do the following.

1. Enclose data input fields in a Form HTML element:

    ```html
    <form method="POST" action="/auth/login">
    <input type="text" name="userName">
    <input type="password" name="password">
    <button type="submit">Submit</button>
    </form>
    ```

    Here, the method attribute determines the HTTP method, which is POST, and the action attribute determines the URL. Note that this URL is relative to the current page URL. When the form is submitted, the client-side processing will prepare a POST request for the given URL, and send the contents of input fields as name-value pairs encoded as application/x-www-form-urlencoded encoding.

2. On the server side, do the following:

    *   Write a handler to process the POST request. In the handler, do the following:

        *   Call http.Request.ParseForm to process submitted data.

        *   Get the submitted information from http.Request.PostForm.

        *   Process the request.

    The following example implements a simple login scenario using the submitted username and password. The handler uses an authenticator that performs the actual user validation and returns a cookie if the login is successful. This cookie contains information to identify the user in the subsequent calls:

    ```go
    type UserHandler struct {
      Auth Authenticator
    }

    func (h UserHandler) HandleLogin(w http.ResponseWriter, req
    *http.Request) {
      // Parse the submitted form. This fills up req.PostForm
      // with the submitted information
      if err:=req.ParseForm(); err!=nil {
        http.Error(w, err.Error(), http.StatusBadRequest)
        return
      }
      // Get the submitted fields
      userName := req.PostForm.Get("userName")
      password := req.PostForm.Get("password")
    ```

```
    // Handle the login request, and get a cookie
    cookie,err:=h.Auth.Authenticate(userName,password);
    if err!=nil {
      // Send the user back to login page, setting an error
      // cookie containing an error message
      http.SetCookie(w,h.NewErrorCookie("Username or password
      invalid"))
      http.Redirect(w, req, "/login.html", http.StatusFound)
      return
    }
    // Set the cookie representing user session
    http.SetCookie(w,cookie)
    // Redirect the user to the main page
    http.Redirect(w,req,"/dashboard.html",http.StatusFound)
}
```

- Register the handler to handle the POST requests for the URL:

```
userHandler := UserHandler {
  Auth: authenticator,
}
mux := http.NewServeMux()
mux.HandleFunc("POST /auth/login", userHandler.HandleLogin)
mux.HandleFunc("GET /login.html", userHandler.ShowLoginPage)
```

> **Tip**
>
> You have to be careful when working with cookies. In our example, a cookie was created by the server application and sent to the client. Subsequent calls to the server will include that cookie for the server to keep track of the user session. However, there is no guarantee that the cookie submitted by the client is a valid cookie. Malicious clients can send forged or expired cookies. Use cryptographic methods to ensure the cookie is created by the server, such as signing a cookie using a secret key, or using a JSON Web Token.

> **Tip**
>
> The preceding example includes another usage of cookies to send status information from one page to another. If login fails, the user is redirected to the login page with a cookie containing the error message. The login page handler can check the presence of this cookie and display the message.

An example implementation is given here:

```
func (h UserHandler) ShowLoginPage(w http.ResponseWriter, req *http.
Request) {
  loginFormData:=map[string]any{}
  cookie, err:= req.Cookie("error_cookie")
  if err==nil {
    loginFormData["error"] = cookie.Value
    // Unset the cookie
    http.SetCookie(w, &http.cookie {
      Name: "error_cookie",
      MaxAge: 0,
    })
  }
  w.Header().Set("Content-Type","text/html")
  loginFormTemplate.Execute(w,loginFormData)
}
```

An implementation of the `NewErrorCookie` method looks like the following:

```
func (h UserHandler) NewErrorCookie(msg string) *http.Cookie {
  return &http.Cookie {
    Name: "error_cookie",
    Value: msg,
    MaxAge: 60, // Cookie lives for 60 seconds
    Path:    "/",
  }
}
```

Writing a handler for downloading large files

When an HTTP client requests a large file, it is usually not feasible to load all the file data and then send it to the client. Use `io.Copy` to stream large content to clients.

How to do it...

This is how you can write a handler to download a large file:

1. Set the `Content-Type` header.
2. Set the `Content-Length` header.
3. Write the file contents using `io.Copy`.

These steps are illustrated here:

```
func DownloadHandler(w http.ResponseWriter, req *http.Request) {
  fileName := req.PathValue("fileName")
  f, err:= os.Open(filepath.Join("/data",fileName))
  if err!=nil {
    http.Error(w,err.Error(),http.StatusNotFound)
    return
  }
  defer f.Close()
  w.Header.Set("Content-Type","application/octet-stream")
  w.Header.Set("Content-Length",  strconv.Itoa(f.Length()))
  io.Copy(w,f)
}
```

Handling HTTP uploaded files and forms as a stream

The standard library provides methods to deal with file uploads. You can call `http.Request.ParseMultipartForm`, and work with uploaded files. There is one problem with this approach: `ParseMultipartForm` processes all uploads up to a given memory limit. It may even use temporary files. This is not a scalable approach if you are dealing with large files. This section describes how you can work with file uploads without creating temporary files or a large memory footprint.

How to do it...

On the client side, do the following:

1. Create an HTML form with `multipart/form-data` encoding.

2. Add the form fields and files that you are planning to upload.

An example is given here:

```
<form action="/upload" method="post" enctype="multipart/form-data">
  <input type="text" name="textField">
  <input type="file" name="fileField">
  <button type="submit">submit</button>
</form>
```

When submitted, this form will create a multipart message containing two parts:

- There's a part with `Content-Disposition: form-data; name="textField"`. The contents of this part will contain the input the user typed for the `textField` input field.

- There's also a part with `Content-Disposition: form-data; name="fileField"; filename=<name of the file user selected>`. The contents of this part will contain the file contents.

On the server side, do the following:

1. Use `http.Request.MultipartReader` to get a multipart body reader from the request. If the request is not a multipart request (multipart/mixes or multipart/form-data), this will fail:

    ```go
    reader, err:=request.MultipartReader()
    if err!=nil {
      http.Error(w,"Not a multipart request",http.StatusBadRequest)
      return
    }
    ```

2. Process the parts of the submitted data one by one by calling `MultipartReader.NextPart`:

    ```go
    for {
      part, err:= reader.NextPart()
      if errors.Is(err,io.EOF) {
        break
      }
      if err!=nil {
        http.Error(w,err.Error(),http.StatusBadRequest)
        return
      }
    }
    ```

3. Check whether the part is form data or file using the `Content-Disposition` header:

    - If `Content-Disposition` is `form-data` without a `filename` parameter, then this part contains a form field.

    - If `Content-Disposition` is `form-data` with a `filename` parameter, then this part is a file. You can read the file contents from the body.

      ```go
      formValues:=make(url.Values)
      if fileName:=part.FileName(); fileName!="" {
        // This part contains a file
        output, err:=os.Create(fileName)
        if err!=nil {
          // Handle error
      ```

```
    }
    defer output.Close()
    if err:=io.Copy(output,part); err!=nil {
      // Handle error
    }
  } else if fieldName := part.FormName(); fieldName!="" {
    // This part contains form data for an input field
    data, err := io.ReadAll(part)
    if err!=nil {
      // Handle error
    }
    formValues[fieldName]=append(formValues[fieldName],
    string(data))
  }
```

14

Streaming Input/Output

There is flexibility and elegance in simplicity. Unlike several languages that decided to implement a feature-rich streaming framework, Go chose a simple capability-based approach: a reader is something from which you read bytes, and a writer is something to which you write bytes. In-memory buffers, files, network connections, and so on are all readers and writers, defined by `io.Reader` and `io.Writer`. A file is also an `io.Seeker`, as you can randomly change the reading/writing location, but a network connection is not. A file and a network connection can be closed, so they are both `io.Closer`, but a memory buffer is not. Such simple and elegant abstractions are the key to writing algorithms that can be used in different contexts.

In this chapter, we will look at some recipes showing how this capability-based streaming framework can be used idiomatically. We will also look at how to work with files and the filesystem. The recipes covered in this chapter are in the following main sections:

- Readers/writers
- Working with files
- Working with binary data
- Copying data
- Working with the filesystem
- Working with pipes

Readers/writers

Remember, Go uses a structural type system. This makes any data type that implements `Read([]byte) (int,error)` an `io.Reader`, and any data type that implements `Write([]byte) (int,error)` an `io.Writer`. There are many uses of this property in the standard library. In this recipe, we will look at some of the common uses of readers and writers.

Reading data from a reader

An io.Reader fills a byte slice you pass to it. By passing a slice, you actually pass two pieces of information: how much you want to read (the length of the slice) and where to put the data that was read (the underlying array of the slice).

How to do it...

1. Create a byte slice large enough to hold the data you want to read:

    ```
    buffer := make([]byte,1024)
    ```

2. Read the data into the byte slice:

    ```
    nRead, err := reader.Read(buffer)
    ```

3. Check how much was read. The number of bytes actually read may be smaller than the buffer size:

    ```
    buffer = buffer[:nRead]
    ```

4. Check the error. If the error is io.EOF, then the reader reached the end of the stream. If the error is something else, handle the error or return it:

    ```
    if errors.Is(err,io.EOF) {
        // End of file reached. Return data
        return buffer, nil
    }
    if err!=nil {
        // Some other error, handle it or return
        return nil,err
    }
    ```

Note the ordering of *steps 3* and *4*. Returning io.EOF is not necessarily an error, it simply means the end of the file has been reached or the network connection has been closed, so you should stop reading. There is probably some data read in the buffer, and you should process that data. The reader returns how much data was read.

Writing data to a writer

1. Encode the data you want to write as a byte slice; for instance, use json.Marshal to get the JSON representation of your data as a []byte:

    ```
    buffer, err:=json.Marshal(data)
    if err!=nil {
        return err
    }
    ```

2. Write the encoded data:

```
_, err:= writer.Write(buffer)
if err!=nil {
  return err
}
```

3. Check and handle errors.

> **Warning**
>
> Unlike a reader, all errors returned from a writer should be treated as errors. A writer does not return io.EOF. Even when there is an error, a write may have written some part of the data.

Reading from and writing to a byte slice

A reader or a writer does not have to be a file or a network connection. This section shows how you can work with byte slices as readers and writers.

How to do it...

- To create a reader from a []byte, use bytes.NewReader. The following example marshals a data structure to JSON (which returns a []byte), then sends that []byte to an HTTP POST request by creating a reader from it:

```
data, err:=json.Marshal(myStruct)
if err!=nil {
  return err
}
rsp, err:=http.Post(postUrl, "application/json", bytes.
NewReader(data))
```

- To use a []byte as a writer, use bytes.Buffer. The buffer will append to the underlying byte slice as you write to it. When you are done, you can get the contents of the buffer:

```
buffer := &bytes.Buffer{}
encoder := json.NewEncoder(buffer)
if err:=encoder.Encode(myStruct); err!=nil {
    return err
}
data := buffer.Bytes()
```

A bytes.Buffer is also an io.Reader, with a separate read location. Writing to a bytes. Buffer appends to the end of the underlying slice. Reading from a bytes.Buffer starts reading from the beginning of the underlying slice. Because of this, you can read the bytes you wrote, as follows:

```
buffer := &bytes.Buffer{}
encoder := json.NewEncoder(buffer)
if err:=encoder.Encode(myStruct); err!=nil {
    return err
}
rsp,err:=http.Post(postUrl, "application/json", buffer)
```

Reading from and writing to a string

To create a reader from a string, use strings.NewReader, as follows:

```
rsp, err:=http.Post(postUrl,"application/json",strings.
NewReader(`{"key":"value"}`))
```

Do *not* use bytes.NewReader([]byte(stringValue)) instead of strings. NewReader(stringValue). The former copies the contents of the string to create a byte slice. The latter accesses the underlying bytes without copying.

To use a string as an io.Writer, use strings.Builder. For instance, as an io.Writer, strings.Builder can be passed to the fmt.Fprint family of functions:

```
query:=strings.Builder{}
args:=make([]interface{},0)
query.WriteString("SELECT id,name FROM users ")
if !createdAt.IsZero() {
  args=append(args,createdAt)
  fmt.Fprintf(&query,"where createdAt < $%d",len(args))
}
rows, err:=tx.Query(ctx,query.String(),args...)
```

Working with files

Files are simply sequences of bytes on a storage system. There are two ways of working with files: as a random access byte sequence or as a stream of bytes. We will look at both types of recipes in this section.

Creating and opening files

To work with the contents of a file, you first have to open it or create it. This recipe shows how that can be done.

How to do it...

To open an existing file for reading, use `os.Open`:

```
file, err := os.Open(fileName)
if err!=nil {
  // handle error
}
```

You can read data from the returned file object, and when you are done, you should close it using `file.Close()`. So, you can use it as an `io.Reader` or `io.ReadCloser` (there are more interfaces that `*os.File` implements!)

If you attempt to write to the file, you will receive an error from the write operation. On my Linux system, this error is a `*fs.PathError` message saying `bad file descriptor`.

To create a new file or to overwrite an existing one, use `os.Create`:

```
file, err := os.Create(fileName)
if err!=nil {
  // handle error
}
```

If the above call is successful, the returned file can be read from or written to. The file is created with `0o666 & ^umask`. If the file already existed before this call, it will be truncated to a length of 0.

Tip

`umask` defines the set of permissions applications cannot set on files. In the preceding text, `0o666` means that the owner, group, and others can read and write the file. A `umask` value of `0o022`, for instance, will change the file mode from `0o666` to `0o644`, which means the owner can read and write, but the group and others can only read.

To open an existing file for reading/writing, use `os.OpenFile`. This is the most general form of the open/create family of functions:

- To open an existing file for both reading and writing, use the following:

  ```
  file, err := os.OpenFile(fileName,os.O_RDWR, 0)
  ```

  The last argument is 0. This argument is only used when creating the file is an option. We will see this case later shortly.

- To open an existing file for reading only, use the following:

  ```
  file, err := os.OpenFile(fileName,os.O_RDONLY, 0)
  ```

- To open an existing file for writing only, use the following:

```
file, err := os.OpenFile(fileName,os.O_WRONLY, 0)
```

- To open an existing file for appending only, use the following:

```
file, err := os.OpenFile(fileName,os.O_WRONLY|os.O_APPEND, 0)
```

Trying to write somewhere other than the end of the file will fail.

- To open an existing file or to create one if it does not exist, use the following:

```
file, err := os.OpenFile(fileName,os.O_RDWR|os.O_CREATE, 00644)
```

The above operation will open the file for reading and writing if it exists. If the file does not exist, it will be created using the 00644 & ^umask permission bits. 00644 means the owner can read/write (06), users from the same group can read (04), and other users can read (04).

The following is equivalent to os.Create; that is, truncate and open the file if it exists but create if it does not:

```
file, err:= os.Open(fileName, os.O_RDWR|os.O_CREATE|os.O_TRUNC,00644)
```

If you want to create the file only if it does not exist, use the "exclusive" bit:

```
file, err := os.Open(fileName, os.O_RDWR|os.O_CREATE|os.O_EXCL,00644)
```

This call will fail if the file already exists.

Tip

This is a common way of ensuring a single instance of a process is running, or to lock a resource if it is not locked. For instance, if you want to lock a directory, you can use this call to create a lock file. It will fail if some other process already locked it (created the file before you.)

Closing a file

There are two reasons why you should always explicitly close files you open:

- All data stored in buffers are flushed when you close the file.
- There are limits to how many files you can keep open at any given time. These limits change from platform to platform.

The following steps show how you can do this consistently.

How to do it...

When you are done working with a file, close it. Use `defer file.Close()` where possible:

```
file, err:=os.Open(fileName)
if err!=nil {
  // handle error
}
defer file.Close()
// Work with the file
```

Do *not* rely on `defer` if you are working with many files. Do not do this:

```
for _,fileName:=range files {
   file, err:=os.Open(fileName)
   if err!=nil {
     // handle error
   }
   defer file.Close()
   // Work with file
}
```

Deferred calls will execute when the function returns, not when the block in which you used them ends. The above code will keep all the files open until the function returns, and if there is a large number of files, `os.Open` will start failing once you pass the open file limit. You can do one of two things. The first is to explicitly close the file for all exit points:

```
for _,fileName:=range files {
   file, err:=os.Open(fileName)
   if err!=nil {
     return err
   }
   // Work with file
   err:=useFile(file)
   if err!=nil {
     file.Close()
     return err
   }
   err:=useFileAgain(file)
   if err!=nil {
     file.Close()
     return err
   }
   // Do more work
   file.Close()
}
```

The second is to use a closure with `defer`:

```
for _,fileName:=range files {
    file, err:=os.Open(fileName)
    if err!=nil {
        return err
    }
    err=func() error {
        defer file.Close()
        // Work with file
        err:=useFile(file)
        if err!=nil {
            return err
        }
        err:=useFileAgain(file)
        if err!=nil {
            return err
        }
        // Do more work
        return nil
    }()
    if err!=nil {
        return err
    }
}
```

> **Tip**
>
> Files are garbage collected. If you open/create files and then work with file descriptors directly instead of using `*os.File`, the garbage collector is not your friend. Use `runtime.KeepAlive(file)` to prevent the garbage collector from closing the file while you're working with it through the file descriptor and/or syscalls. Avoid relying on the garbage collector to close your files. Always close files explicitly.

Reading/writing data from/to files

When you open a file for reading and writing, the operating system keeps the **current location** within the file. Read and write operations are performed at that current location, and once you read or write some data, the current location advances to accommodate the data read or written. For instance, if you open a file for reading, the current location is set to an offset of 0. Then if you read 10 bytes from the file, the current location becomes 10 (assuming the file is larger than 10 bytes). The next time you read from the file or write to it, you will read the contents or write starting from an offset of 10. Keep this behavior in mind, especially if you are mixing reads and writes to a file.

How to do it...

- To read some data starting from the current location, use `file.Read`:

```
file, err:=os.Open(fileName)
if err!=nil {
  return err
}
// Current location: 0
buffer:=make([]byte,100)
// Read 100 bytes
n, err:=file.Read(buffer)
// Current location: n
// n tells how many bytes actually read
data:=buffer[:n]
if err!=nil {
  if errors.Is(err, io.EOF) {
  }
}
```

The ordering of checking for n (the number of bytes read) and checking whether there was an error is important. An `io.Reader` may do a partial read and return the number of bytes read along with an error. That error may be `io.EOF`, signifying that the file has less data than you attempted to read. For instance, a file with 10 bytes will return n=10 and err=io.EOF. Also note that this behavior is dependent on the current location of the file. The following code segment reads the file as a slice of byte slices:

```
slices := make([][]byte,0)
for {
  buffer:=make([]byte,1024)
  n, err:=file.Read(buffer)
  if n>0 {
    slices=append(slices,buffer[:n])
    buffer=make([]byte,1024)
  }
  if err!=nil {
    if errors.Is(err,io.EOF) {
      break
    }
    return err
  }
}
```

If the current location in the file is 0 when the preceding code begins, after every read operation, the current location will progress by n. Note that all the byte slices will be 1024 bytes except the last. The last slice can be anywhere from 1 to 1024 bytes, depending on the file size.

- Writing to a file is done similarly:

```
buffer:=[]byte("Hello world!")
n, err:=io.Write(buffer)
if err!=nil {
   return err
}
```

A write operation will not return io.EOF. If you write past the end of the file, the file will be enlarged to accommodate the written bytes. If the write operation cannot write all the given bytes, the error will always be non-nil, and you should check and handle the error.

If the current location is 0 at the beginning, it will be n after the write operation.

- To read everything from a file, use os.ReadFile:

```
data, err:= os.ReadFile("config.yaml")
if err!=nil {
   // Handle error
}
```

> **Tip**
>
> Be careful when using os.ReadFile. It allocates a []byte that is the size of the file. Use this function only if you are sure the file you are reading is of a reasonable size.

- To read a large file in fixed-size chunks, allocate a fixed-size buffer and read iteratively until io.EOF is returned:

```
// Read file in 10K chunks
buf:=make([]byte,10240)
for {
   n, err:=file.Read(buf)
   if n>0 {
     // Process buffer contents:
     processData(buf[:n])
   }
   // Check for errors. Check for io.EOF and handle it
   if err!=nil {
     if errors.Is(err,io.EOF) {
       // End of file. We are done
       break
     }
     // Some other error
     return err
   }
}
```

- To write a byte slice to a new file, use os.WriteFile:

```
err:=os.WriteFile("config.yaml", data, 0o644)
```

Reading/writing from/to a specific location

We talked about the concept of the **current location** previously. This section is about moving the current location to start reading or writing from a random location in a file.

How to do it...

You may change the current location using File.Seek.

- To set the current location relative to the beginning of the file, use the following:

```
// Move to offset 100 in file
newLocation, err := file.Seek(100,io.SeekStart)
```

The returned newLocation is the new current location of the file. Subsequent read or write operations will read from or write to that location.

- To set the current location relative to the end of the file, use the following:

```
// Move to the end of the file:
newLocation, err := file.Seek(0,io.SeekEnd)
```

This is also a quick way of determining the current file size, as newLocation is 0 bytes ahead of the end of the file.

- You can seek beyond the end of the file. Reading from such a location will read 0 bytes. Writing to such a location will extend the file size to accommodate the data written at that location:

```
// Go to 100 after the end of file and write 1 byte
newLocation, err:=file.Seek(100, io.SeekEnd)
if err!=nil {
  panic(err)
}
// Write 1 byte.
file.Write([]byte{0})
// The file is 101 bytes larger now.
```

> **Tip**
>
> When you extend a file like this, the area between the end of the file and the newly written bytes is filled with 0s. The underlying platform may implement this as a **hole**; that is, the area that is not written may not be actually allocated.

- os.File supports additional methods for such random access. File.WriteAt will write data to the given location (relative to the beginning of the file) without moving the current location. File.ReadAt will read from the given location without moving the current location:

```
// Go to offset 1000
_,err:=file.Seek(1000,io.SeekStart)

// Write "Hello world" to offset 10.
n, err:=file.WriteAt([]byte("Hello world!"),10)
if err!=nil {
  panic(err)
}

// Write to offset 1000, because WriteAt does not move
// the current location
_,err:=file.WriteAt([]byte{"offset 1000")

buffer:=make([]byte,5)
file.ReadAt(buffer,10)
fmt.Println(string(buffer))
// Prints "Hello"
```

Changing the file size

Extending a file is usually achieved by writing more data to the end of it, but how can you shrink an existing file? This recipe describes different ways to change the file size.

How to do it...

- To truncate a file to a size of 0, you can open a file with the truncate flag:

```
file, err:=os.OpenFile("test.txt", os.O_RDWR|os.O_TRUNC,0o644)
// File is opened and truncated to 0 size
```

- If the file is already open, you can use File.Truncate to set the file size. File.Truncate works both ways – you can extend a file or you can shrink it:

```
// Truncate the file to 0-size
err:=file.Truncate(0)
if err!=nil {
  panic(err)
}

// Extend the file to 100-bytes
err=file.Truncate(100)
```

```
if err!=nil {
  panic(err)
}
```

- You can also extend a file by appending to it. You can do this in one of two ways. You can open the file for append-only:

```
file, err:=os.OpenFile("test.txt", os.O_WRONLY|os.O_APPEND,0)
// File is opened for writing, current location is set to the
// end of the file
```

If you open a file append-only, you cannot read/write from other locations of the file, you can only append to it.

- Alternatively, you can seek the end of the file and start writing there:

```
// Seek to the end
_,err:=file.Seek(0,io.SeekEnd)
if err!=nil {
  panic(err)
}
// Write new data to the end of the file
_,err:=file.Write(data)
```

Finding the file size

If the file is open, you can obtain the file size as follows:

```
fileSize, err:= file.Seek(0,io.SeekEnd)
```

This will return the current file size, including any data that was appended but not yet flushed.

The above operation will move the file pointer to the end of the file. To preserve the current location, use the following:

```
// Get current location
currentLocation, err:=file.Seek(0,io.SeekCurrent)
if err!=nil {
  return err
}
// Find file size
fileSize, err:=file.Seek(0,io.SeekEnd)
if err!=nil {
  return err
}
// Move back to the saved location
```

```
_,err:=file.Seek(currentLocation,io.SeekStart)
if err!=nil {
  return err
}
```

If the file is not open, use os.Stat:

```
fileInfo, err:=os.Stat(fileName)
if err!=nil {
  return err
}
fileSize := fileInfo.Size()
```

> **Tip**
>
> If you have the file open and you appended data to the file, the file size reported by os.Stat may be different from the file size you obtained by File.Seek. The os.Stat function reads the file information from the directory. The File.Seek method uses process-specific file information that may not have been reflected in the directory entry yet.

Working with binary data

If you need to send a piece of data over a network connection or store it in a file, you first have to encode it (or serialize it, or marshal it.) This is necessary because the system at the other end of the network connection or the application that will read the file you wrote may be running on a different platform. A portable, easy-to-debug but not necessarily efficient way to do this is to use text-based encodings such as JSON. If performance is paramount or when the use case demands it, you use binary encoding.

There are many high-level binary encoding schemes. Gob (https://pkg.go.dev/encoding/gob) is a Go-specific encoding scheme that can be used for networking applications. Protocol buffers (https://protobuf.dev) provide a language-neutral, extensible, schema-driven mechanism for encoding structured data. There are more. Here, we will look at the basics of binary encoding that every software engineer should know about.

Encoding data involves transforming data elements into a stream of bytes. If you have a data element that is a single byte or a data element that is already a sequence of bytes, you can encode them verbatim. When working with multi-byte data types (int16, int32, int64, etc.), how you order those bytes becomes important. For example, if you have an int16 value of 0xABCD, how should you encode those bytes as a []byte? There are two options:

- **Little-endian**: 0xABCD is encoded as []byte{0xCD, 0xAB}
- **Big-endian**: 0xABCD is encoded as []byte{0xAB, 0xCD}

Similarly, a 32-bit integer, `0x01234567`, encoded in little-endian byte order gives `[]byte{0x-67,0x45,0x23,0x01}` and encoded in big-endian byte ordering gives `[]byte{0x01,0x-23,0x45,0x67}`. Most modern hardware uses little-endian byte ordering to represent values in memory. Network protocols (such as IP) tend to use big-endian.

How to do it...

There are two main approaches to encoding binary data:

- The first is using a fixed structure. In this approach, the ordering and type of data fields are fixed. For instance, the IPv4 header defines where every header field starts and ends. There is no way to omit a field or add extensions in this approach. An example is shown in *Figure 14.1*.

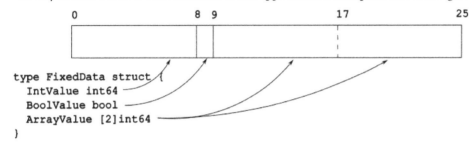

Figure 14.1: Fixed-length encoding example

- The second is using a dynamic encoding scheme, such as **length value (LV)** or **tag length value (TLV)**. In this scheme, the encoded data is not fixed in length, but it is self-describing. A tag defines the data type and/or data element, an optional length defines the length of data, and value is the value of the data element. For instance, a common approach to LV encoding strings is to first encode the length of the string, and then the bytes of the string itself. A TLV encoding of the string would first write a tag denoting the value as a `string` field, then the length, and then the string itself. An example TLV encoding scheme is shown in *Figure 14.2*.

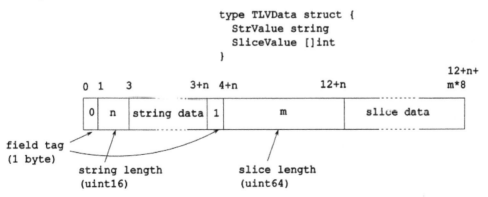

Figure 14.2: TLV encoding example

This example uses 16-bit string length and 64-bit slice length encoding.

Use encoding/binary to encode data in big-endian or little-endian byte ordering.

For fixed-length encoding, you can use encoding.Write to encode, and encoding.Read to decode data:

```go
type Data struct {
  IntValue int64
  BoolValue bool
  ArrayValue [2]int64
}

func main() {
  output := bytes.Buffer{}
  data:=Data{
    IntValue: 1,
    BoolValue: true,
    ArrayValue: [2]int64{1,2},
  }
  // Encode data using big endian byte order
  binary.Write(&output, binary.BigEndian, data)
  stream := output.Bytes()
  fmt.Printf("Big endian encoded data    : %v\n", stream)
  // Decode data
  var value1 Data
  binary.Read(bytes.NewReader(stream), binary.BigEndian, &value1)
  fmt.Printf("Decoded data: %v\n", value1)

  // Encode data using little endian byte order
  output = bytes.Buffer{}
  binary.Write(&output, binary.LittleEndian, data)
  stream = output.Bytes()
  fmt.Printf("Little endian encoded data: %v\n", stream)
  // Decode data
  var value2 Data
  binary.Read(bytes.NewReader(stream), binary.LittleEndian, &value2)
  fmt.Printf("Decoded data: %v\n", value2)
}
```

This program outputs the following:

```
Big endian encoded data   : [0 0 0 0 0 0 0 1 1 0 0 0 0 0 0 0 1 0 0 0 0
0 0 0 2]
Decoded data: {1 true [1 2]}
Little endian encoded data: [1 0 0 0 0 0 0 0 1 1 0 0 0 0 0 0 0 2 0 0 0
0 0 0 0]
Decoded data: {1 true [1 2]}
```

Take special care when defining the Data structure. You cannot use variable length or platform-specific types if you want to use encoding.Read or encoding.Write:

- No int because the size of int is platform-specific

- No slices

- No maps

- No strings

How can we encode these values, then? Let's take a look at an LV encoding scheme to encode a string value:

```go
func EncodeString(s string) []byte {
    // Allocate the output buffer for string length (int16) +
    // len(string)
    buffer:=make([]byte, 0, len(s)+2)
    // Encode the length little endian - 2 bytes
    binary.LittleEndian.PutUint16(buffer,uint16(len(s)))
    // Copy the string bytes
    copy(buffer[2:],[]byte(s))
    return buffer
}
```

Here is one to decode a string value:

```go
func DecodeString(input []byte) (string, error) {
    // Read the string length. It must be at least 2 bytes
    if len(input) < 2 {
        return "", fmt.Errorf("invalid input")
    }
    n := binary.LittleEndian.Uint16(input)
    if int(n)+2 > len(input) {
        return "", fmt.Errorf("invalid input")
    }
    return string(input[2 : n+2]), nil
}
```

Copying data

io.Copy reads data from a reader and writes it to a writer until one of the operations fails or the reader returns io.EOF. There are many use cases where you need to get chunks of data from a reader and send it to a writer. io.Copy works at an abstract layer that allows you to copy data from a file to a network connection, or from a string to a file. It also performs capability-based optimizations to minimize data copying. For instance, if the platform supports the splice system call, io.Copy can use it to bypass buffer usage. In this section, we will see some uses of io.Copy.

Copying files

How to do it...

To copy a file, follow these steps:

1. Open the source file.

2. Create the target file.

3. Use io.Copy to copy data.

4. Close both files.

These steps are illustrated here:

```
sourceFile, err:=os.Open(sourceFileName)
if err!=nil {
  panic(err)
}
defer sourceFile.Close()
targetFile, err:=os.Create(targetFileName)
if err!=nil {
  panic(err)
}
defer targetFile.Close()
if _,err:=io.Copy(targetFile,sourceFile);err!=nil {
  panic(err)
}
```

Since io.Copy works with io.Reader and io.Writer, any object implementing these interfaces can be used as the source or the target. For example, the following code segment returns a file as a response to an HTTP request:

```
// Handle GET /path/{fileName}
func HandleGetImage(w http.ResponseWriter, req *http.Request) {
  // Get the file name from the request
```

```
file, err:=os.Open(req.PathValue("fileName"))
if err!=nil {
  http.Error(w,err.Error(),http.StatusNotFound)
  return
}
defer file.Close()
// Write file contents to the response writer
io.Copy(w,file)
}
```

Working with the filesystem

There are many aspects of filesystems that are platform-specific. This section talks about portable ways of working with filesystems.

Working with filenames

Use `path/filepath` package to work with filenames in a portable way.

How do to it...

- To build a path from several path segments, use `filepath.Join`:

  ```
  fmt.Println(filepath.Join("/a/b/","/c/d")
  // Prints /a/b/c
  fmt.Println(filepath.Join("/a/b/c/d/","../../x")
  // Prints a/b/x
  ```

  Note that `filepath.Join` does not allow consecutive separators, and interprets `".."` correctly.

- To split a path to its directory and filename parts, use `filepath.Split`:

  ```
  fmt.Println(filepath.Split("/home/bserdar/work.txt"))
  // dir: "/home/bserdar" file: "work.txt"
  fmt.Println(filepath.Split("/home/bserdar/projects/"))
  // dir: "/home/bserdar/projects/" file: ""
  ```

- Avoid using path separators (/ and \) in your code. Use `filepath.Separator`, which is a platform-specific rune value.

Creating temporary directories and files

Sometimes, you will need to create unique directory names and filenames, mostly for temporary data.

How to do it...

- To create a temporary directory under the platform-specific default directory for temporary files, use os.MkdirTemp("",prefix):

```
dir, err:=os.MkdirTemp("","tempdir")
if err!=nil {
  // Handle error
}
// Clean up when done
defer os.RemoveAll(dir)
fmt.Println(dir)
// Prints /tmp/example10287493
```

The created name is unique. If there are multiple calls to create a temporary directory, each will generate a unique name.

- To create a temporary directory under a specific directory, use os.MkdirTemp(dir,prefix):

```
// Create a temporary directory under the current directory
dir, err:=os.MkdirTemp(".","tempdir")
if err!=nil {
  // Handle error
}
// Cleanup when done
defer os.RemoveAll(dir)
```

- To create a temporary directory with the random part of the name not as a suffix, use *. The random string replaces the last * character:

```
dir, err:=os.MkdirTemp(".", "myapp.*.txt")
if err!=nil {
  // Handle error
}
defer os.RemoveAll(dir)
fmt.Println(dir)
// Prints ./myapp.13984873.txt
```

- To create a temporary file, use os.CreateTemp. A unique file is created and opened for reading and writing. The name of the created file can be obtained from the returned file. Name value:

```
file, err:=os.CreateTemp("","app.*.txt")
if err!=nil {
  // Handle error
}
fmt.Println("Temp file", file.Name)
```

```
// Cleanup when done
defer os.Remove(file.Name)
defer file.Close()
```

Similar to os.MkdirTemp, if the filename contains *, a random string is inserted in place of the last * character. If the filename does not contain *, the random string is appended at the end of the name.

Reading directories

Use os.ReadDir to list or discover files under a directory.

How to do it...

- Call os.ReadDir to get the contents of a directory. This returns directory entries in order sorted by name:

```
entries, err:=os.ReadDir(".")
if err!=nil {
  // handle error
}
for _, entry:=range entries {
    // Name contains the file name only, not the directory
    name := entry.Name()
    if entry.IsDir() {
      // This is a directory
    } else {
      // This is not a directory. Does not mean it is a regular
      // file Can be a named pipe, device, etc.
    }
}
```

You may notice that os.ReadDir is not your best bet if you are dealing with potentially large directories. It returns an unbounded slice, and it also spends time sorting it.

- For performance and memory-conscious applications, open the directory and read it using File.ReadDir:

```
// Open the directory
dir, err:= os.Open("/tmp")
if err!=nil {
  panic(err)
}
defer dir.Close()

// Read directory entries unordered, 10 at a time
for {
```

```
entries, err:=dir.ReadDir(10)
// Are we done reading
if errors.Is(err, io.EOF) {
  break
}
if err!=nil {
  panic(err)
}
// There are at most 10 fileInfo entries
for _,entry:=range entries {
  // Process the entry
}
}
```

- To recursively iterate directory entries in a portable way, use io.fs.WalkDir. This function uses "/" as the path separator regardless of the platform. The following example prints all the files under /tmp, skipping directories:

```
err:=fs.WalkDir(os.DirFS("/"), "/tmp", func(path string,d
fs.DirEntry,err error) error {
  if err!=nil {
    fmt.Println("Error during directory traversal", err)
    return err
  }
  if !d.IsDir() {
    // This is not  a directory
    fmt.Println(filepath.Join(path,d))
  }
  return nil
})
```

- To recursively iterate directory entries, use filepath.WalkDir. This function uses a platform-specific path separator. The following example prints all directories under /tmp recursively:

```
err:=filepath.WalkDir("/tmp", func(path string,d fs.DirEntry,err
error) error {
  if err!=nil {
    fmt.Println("Error during directory traversal", err)
    return err
  }
  if d.IsDir() {
    // This is a directory
    fmt.Println(filepath.Join(path,d), " directory")
  }
  return nil
})
```

Working with pipes

If you have a piece of code that expects a reader and another piece of code that expects a writer, you can connect the two using io.Pipe.

Connecting code expecting a reader with code expecting a writer

A good example of this use case is preparing an HTTP POST request, which requires a reader. If you have all of the data available, or if you already have a reader (such as os.File), you can use that. However, if the data is produced by a function that takes a writer, use a pipe.

How to do it...

A pipe is a synchronously connected reader and writer. That is, if you write to a pipe, there must be a reader consuming from it concurrently. So make sure you put the data-producing side (where you use the writer) in a different goroutine than the data-consuming side (where you use the reader).

- Create a pipe reader and pipe writer using io.Pipe:

```
pipeReader, pipeWriter := io.Pipe()
```

pipeReader will read everything written to pipeWriter.

- Use pipeWriter to produce data in a goroutine. When everything is written, close pipeWriter:

```
go func() {
  // Close the writer side, so the reader knows when it is done
  defer pipeWriter.Close()
  encoder:=json.NewEncoder(pipeWriter)
  if err:=encoder.Encode(payload); err!=nil {
    if errors.Is(err,io.ErrClosedPipe) {
      // The reader side terminated with error
    } else {
      // Handle error
    }
  }
}()
```

- Use pipeReader where a reader is needed. If the function fails and not everything in the pipe can be consumed, close pipeReader so the writer can terminate:

```
if _, err:= http.Post(serverURL, "application/json",
pipeReader); err!=nil {
  // Close the reader, so the writing goroutine terminates
  pipeReader.Close()
  // Handle error
}
```

Above, the goroutine that encodes the JSON data will block until the POST request establishes a connection and streams the data. If there is an error during this process, `pipeReader.Close()` ensures that the goroutine that encodes JSON data does not leak.

Intercepting a reader using TeeReader

In plumbing, a tee pipe is a fitting that has a T shape. It splits the flow into two. TeeReader takes its name from that. An `io.TeeReader(r io.Reader, w io.Writer) io.Reader` function returns a new reader that reads from r at the same time as writing whatever it read to w. This is very useful for intercepting the data going through a reader.

How to do it...

1. Create a pipe:

    ```
    pipeReader, pipeWriter := io.Pipe()
    ```

2. Create a TeeReader from another reader, using `pipeWriter` as the writer that will receive data:

    ```
    file, err:=os.Open(dataFile)
    if err!=nil {
      // Handle error
    }
    defer file.Close()
    tee := io.TeeReader(file, pipeWriter)
    ```

    At this stage, reading some data from `tee` will read data from `file` and write that data to `pipeWriter`.

3. Use `pipeReader` in a separate goroutine to process data read from the original reader:

    ```
    go func() {
      // Copy the file to stdout
      io.Copy(os.Stdout,pipeReader)
    }()
    ```

4. Use the TeeReader to read the data:

    ```
    _,err:=http.Post(serverURL, "text/plain", tee)
    if err!=nil {
      // Make sure pipe is closed
      pipeReader.Close()
    }
    ```

Note that working with a pipe requires at least one other goroutine where writing to or reading from the pipe happens. In case of error, make sure all goroutines working with the pipe terminate by closing one end of the pipe.

15
Databases

Most applications have to work with at least one type of database. SQL databases are common enough that the Go standard library offers a unified way to connect and use them. This chapter shows some of the patterns you can use to work with the standard library implementation of the SQL package.

Many databases offer nonstandard extensions, in terms of both functionality and query language. Even if you use the standard library to interface with a database, you should always check the vendor-specific database driver to understand potential limitations, implementation differences, and the supported SQL dialect.

Here, it might be useful to mention NoSQL databases. The Go standard library does not offer a NoSQL database package. This is because, unlike SQL, most NoSQL databases have nonstandard query languages that are purpose-built for the specific database. NoSQL databases built for specific workloads perform much better than a general-purpose SQL database. If you are using such a database, refer to its documentation. However, many of the concepts presented in this chapter will apply to some degree to NoSQL databases as well.

This chapter has the following recipes:

- Connecting to a database
- Running SQL statements
- Running SQL statements without explicit transactions
- Running SQL statements with transactions
- Running prepared statements within a transaction
- Getting values from a query
- Dynamically building SQL statements
- Building UPDATE statements
- Building WHERE clauses

Connecting to a database

There are two ways you can incorporate a database into your applications: you can use a database server or an embedded database. Let's start by defining what those are.

A database server runs as a separate process on the same or a different host but is independent of your application. Usually, your application connects to this database server through a network connection, so you have to know its network address and port. There is usually a library you have to import into your program, a "database driver" specific to the database server you use. This driver provides the interface between your application and the database by managing the connections, queries, transactions, and so on.

An embedded database is not a separate process. It is included in your application as a library and runs in the same address space. A database driver acts as an adapter that presents a standard interface (i.e., using the database/sql package) to the application. When using an embedded database, you have to be mindful of the resources you share with other processes. Many embedded databases will not let multiple programs access the same underlying data.

Before performing any operations, you must connect to the database server (such as a MySQL or PostgreSQL server) or to the embedded database engine (such as SQLite).

> **Tip**
> This page contains a list of SQL drivers: https://go.dev/wiki/SQLDrivers.

How to do it...

Find the database-specific driver you need. This driver may be provided by the database vendor or published as an open source project. Import this database driver in the main package.

You need a driver-specific driver name and connection string to connect to the database server or the embedded database engine. If you are connecting to a database server, this connection string usually includes the host/port information, authentication information, and connection options. If this is an embedded database engine, it may include filename/directory information. Then, you either call sql.Open or use a driver-specific connection function that returns a *sql.DB.

A database driver may defer the actual connection to the first database operation. That is, connecting to a database using sql.Open may not actually connect immediately. To ensure you are connected to the database, use DB.Ping. An embedded database driver usually would not require a ping.

The following is an example showing a connection to a MySQL database:

```
package main

import (
```

```go
    "fmt"
    "database/sql"
    "context"

    // Import the mysql driver
    _ "github.com/go-sql-driver/mysql"
)

func main() {
    // Use mysql driver name and driver specific connection string
    db, err := sql.Open("mysql", "username:password@tcp(host:port)/
    databaseName")
    if err != nil {
        panic(err.Error())
    }
    defer db.Close()

    // Check if database connection succeeded, with 5 second timeout
    ctx, cancel := context.WithTimeout(context.
    Background(),5*time,Second)
    defer cancel()
    if err:=db.PingContext(ctx); err!=nil {
        panic(err)
    }

    fmt.Println("Success!")
}
```

The following is an example showing a connection to an in-memory SQLite database using a local file:

```go
package main

import (
    "database/sql"
    "fmt"
    "os"
    // Import the database driver
    _ "github.com/mattn/go-sqlite3"
)

func main() {
    // Open the sqlite database using the given local file ./database.
    // db
    db, err := sql.Open("sqlite3", "./database.db")
```

```
    if err != nil {
        log.Fatal(err)
    }
    defer db.Close()

    // You don't need to ping an embedded database
}
```

> **Tip**
>
> Note the use of blank identifier, _, for the database driver import. That means the package is imported only for its side effects, which, in this case, are the init() functions that register the database driver. For instance, importing the go-sqlite3 package in main causes the init() function declared in go-sqlite3 to register itself with the name sqlite3.

Running SQL statements

After acquiring an instance of *sql.DB, you can run SQL statements to modify or query data. These queries are simply SQL strings, but the flavor of SQL varies between database vendors.

Running SQL statements without explicit transactions

When interacting with a database, an important consideration is determining transaction boundaries. If you need to perform a single operation, such as inserting a row or running a query, you usually do not need to create a transaction explicitly. You can execute a single SQL statement that will start and end the transaction. However, if you have multiple SQL statements that should either run as an atomic unit or not run at all, you have to use a transaction.

How to do it...

1. To run a SQL statement to update data, use DB.Exec or DB.ExecContext:

    ```
    result, err:=db.ExecContext(ctx, `UPDATE users SET user.last_
    login=? WHERE user_id=?",time.Now(), userId)
    if err!=nil {
        // Handle error
    }
    n, err:=result.RowsAffected()
    if err!=nil {
        // Handle error
    }
    if n!=1 {
        return errors.New("Cannot update last login time")
    }
    ```

To run the same statement multiple times with different values, use a prepared statement. A prepared statement usually sends the statement to the database server where it is parsed and prepared. Then, you can simply run this parsed statement with different arguments, bypassing the parsing and optimization stages of the database engine.

You should close the prepared statement when you are done using it:

```go
func AddUsers(db *sql.DB, users []User) error {
    stmt, err := db.Prepare(`INSERT INTO users (user_name,email)
    VALUES (?,?)`)
    if err!=nil {
        return err
    }
    // Close the prepared statement when done
    defer stmt.Close()
    for _,user:=range users {
        // Run the prepared statement with different arguments
        _, err := stmt.Exec(user.Name,user.Email)
        if err!=nil {
            return err
        }
    }
    return nil
}
```

> **Tip**
> You can create prepared statements after connecting to the database and use them in your program until the program ends. Prepared statements can be executed from multiple goroutines concurrently.

To run a query that returns results, use DB.Query or DB.QueryContext. To run a query that is expected to return at most one row, you can use the DB.QueryRow or DB.Query-RowContext convenience functions.

The DB.Query and DB.QueryContext methods return a *sql.Rows object that is essentially a uni-directional cursor over the results of a query. This provides an interface that allows you to process large result sets without loading all results to the memory. Database engines usually return the results in batches, and the *sql.Rows object allows you to go through the result rows one by one, fetching results in batches as necessary.

Another thing to keep in mind is that many database engines defer the actual execution of the query until you start fetching the results. In other words, just because you ran a query, does not mean that the query is actually evaluated by the server. The query evaluation may happen when you fetch the first result row:

```go
func GetUserNamesLoggedInAfter(db *sql.DB, after time.Time) ([]
string,error) {
```

```
rows, err:=db.Query(`SELECT users.user_name FROM users WHERE
last_login > ?`, after)
if err!=nil {
  return nil,err
}
defer rows.Close()
names:=make([]string,0)
for rows.Next() {
  var name string
  if err:=rows.Scan(&name); err!=nil {
    return nil,err
  }
  names=append(names,name)
}
// Check if iteration produced any errors
if err:=rows.Err(); err!=nil {
  return nil,err
}
return names,nil
}
```

If the expected result set has at most one row (in other words, you are looking for a specific object that may or may not be there), you can shorten the above pattern by using DB.QueryRow or DB.QueryRowContext. You can determine whether the operation found the row by checking whether the returned error is sql.ErrNoRows:

```
func GetUserByID(db *sql.DB, id string) (*User, error) {
  var user User
  err:=db.QueryRow(`SELECT user_id, user_name, last_login FROM
  users WHERE user_id=?`,id).
    Scan(&user.Id, &user.Name, &user.LastLogin)
  if errors.Is(err,sql.ErrNoRows) {
    return nil,nil
  }
  if err!=nil {
    return nil,err
  }
  return &user,nil
}
```

Never use values provided by a user, read from a configuration file, or received from an API request to build a SQL statement without validating first. Use query arguments to avoid SQL injection attacks.

Running SQL statements with transactions

If you need to perform multiple updates atomically, you must execute those updates in a transaction. In this context, atomically means either all updates complete successfully or none of them complete.

The transaction isolation level determines how other concurrent transactions see the updates performed within a transaction. You can find many resources that describe transaction isolation levels. Here, I will provide a summary to help you decide which isolation level is best for your use case:

- `sql.LevelReadUncommitted`: This is the lowest transaction isolation level. A transaction may see uncommitted changes performed by another transaction. Another transaction may read some uncommitted data and perform business logic based on what was read. and the uncommitted data may be rolled back, invalidating the business logic.

- `sql.ReadCommitted`: A transaction reads only committed changes performed by another transaction. That means if one transaction attempts to read/write data that is being modified by another transaction, the first transaction has to wait until the second transaction completes. However, once a transaction in the ReadCommitted isolation level reads data, another transaction may change it.

- `sql.RepeatableRead`: A transaction reads only committed changes performed by another transaction. Furthermore, the value read by the transaction in the RepeatableRead isolation level is guaranteed to remain unchanged until the transaction is committed or rolled back. Any other transaction attempting to modify data read by a repeatable-read transaction will wait until the repeatable-read transaction ends. However, this isolation level does not prevent another transaction from inserting rows into a table that satisfy the query criteria of a repeatable-read transaction, so querying the same table with range queries may yield different results.

- `sql.Serializable`: This is the highest transaction isolation level. A serializable transaction reads only committed changes, prevents other transactions from modifying data it reads, and prevents other transactions from inserting/updating/deleting rows that match the criteria of any of the queries performed within the transaction.

Level of concurrency decreases as the transaction isolation level increases. This also affects the performance: lower transaction isolation levels are faster. You have to select the isolation level carefully: choose the lowest isolation level that is safe for the operation. Usually, there is a driver-specific default isolation level that will be used if you do not specify a level explicitly.

How to do It...

Start a transaction with the desired isolation level:

```
ctx, cancel := context.WithCancel(context.Background())
defer cancel()
// 1. Start transaction
tx, err := db.BeginTx(ctx, &sql.TxOptions{
```

```
    Isolation: sql.LevelReadCommitted,
    })
if err!=nil {
  // Handle error
}
// 2. Call rollback with defer, so in case of error, transaction
// rolls back
defer tx.Rollback()
```

Make sure the transaction either commits or rolls back. You can do this by deferring `tx.Rollback`. This causes the transaction to roll back if the function returns without committing it. If the transaction is successful, you commit the transaction. Once a transaction is committed, the deferred rollback does not have any effect.

Perform database operations using the transaction. All database operations performed using the methods of `*sql.Tx` will be done within the transaction:

```
_, err:= tx.Exec(`UPDATE users SET user.last_login=? WHERE user_
id=?",time.Now()`, userId)
if err!=nil {
  // Do not commit, handle error
}
```

If there are no errors, commit the transaction:

```
tx.Commit()
```

> **Tip**
> Some database drivers may roll back and cancel a transaction when a query cannot complete due to a constraint violation, such as a duplicate value on a unique index. Check your driver documentation to see whether it performs an auto-rollback.

Running prepared statements within a transaction

A statement can be prepared by calling the `*sql.Tx.Prepare` or `*sql.Tx.PrepareContext` method of the transaction struct. The prepared statement returned by these two will be associated with that transaction only. That is, you cannot prepare a statement using one transaction and use that statement for another transaction.

How to do it...

There are two ways you can use prepared statements in a transaction.

The first is using a statement prepared by `*DB`:

1. Prepare the statement using `DB.Prepare` or `DB.PrepareContext`.

2. Get a transaction-specific copy of the transaction:

   ```
   txStmt := tx.Stmt(stmt)
   ```

3. Run the operations using the new statement.

4. The second is using a statement prepared by `*Tx`:

5. Prepare the statement using `Tx.Prepare` or `Tx.PrepareContext`.

6. Run the operations using this statement.

Getting values from a query

A SQL query returns `*sql.Rows`, or if you use the `QueryRow` methods, it returns `*sql.Row`. The next thing you have to do is iterate over the rows and scan the values into Go variables.

How to do it...

Running `Query` or `QueryContext` implies you are expecting zero or more rows from the query. Because of that, it returns `*sql.Rows`.

For the code snippets in this section, we use the following `User` struct:

```
type User struct {
  ID        uint64
  Name      string
  LastLogin time.Time
  AvatarURL string
}
```

This is used with the following table definition:

```
CREATE TABLE users (
  user_id int not null,
  user_name varchar(32) not null,
  last_login timestamp null,
  avatar_url varchar(128) null
)
```

Iterate through the rows and work with each individual result row. In the following example, the query returns zero or more rows. The first call to `rows.Next` moves to the first row in the result set, and each subsequent call to `rows.Next` moves to the next row. This allows for the use of a `for` statement, as in the following example:

```go
rows, err := db.Query(`SELECT user_id, user_name, last_login, avatar_
url FROM users WHERE last_login > ?`, after)
if err!=nil {
  return err
}
// Close the rows object when done
defer rows.Close()
for rows.Next() {
  // Retrieve data from this row
}
```

For each row, use `Scan` to copy data into Go variables:

```go
users:=make([]User,0)
for rows.Next() {
  // Retrieve data from this row
  var user User
  // avatar column is nullable, so we pass a *string instead of string
  var avatarURL *string

  if err:=rows.Scan(
    &user.ID,
    &user.Name,
    &user.LastLogin,
    &avatarURL);err!=nil {
      return err
    }
    // avatar URL can be nil in the db
    if avatarURL!=nil {
      user.AvatarURL=*avatarURL
    }
    users=append(users,user)
}
```

The order of arguments to `Scan` must match the order of columns retrieved from the `SELECT` statement. That is, the first argument, `&user.ID`, corresponds to the `user_id` column; the next argument, `&user.Name`, corresponds to the `user_name` column; and so on. The number of arguments to `Scan` thus must be equal to the number of columns fetched.

The SQL driver performs the translation from database-native types to Go data types. If the translation results in data or precision loss, the driver usually returns an error. For instance, if you try to scan a large integer value into an `int16` variable and the translation cannot represent the value, `Scan` returns an error.

If the database column is defined as nullable (in this example, `avatar_url varchar(128) NULL`), and if the data value retrieved from the database is null, then the Go value must be able to accommodate the null value. For instance, if we used `&user.AvatarURL` in `Scan` and the value in the database was null, then `Scan` would have returned an error complaining that a null value cannot be scanned to a string. To prevent such errors, we used `*string` instead of `string`. In general, if the underlying database column is nullable, you should use a pointer in `Scan` for that column.

Check for errors after fetching all rows:

```
// Check if there was an error during iteration
if err:=rows.Err(); err!=nil {
  return err
}
```

Close `*sql.Rows`. This is usually done with a `defer rows.Close()` statement as previously.

Running `QueryRow` or `QueryRowContext` implies you are expecting zero or one row from the query. Then, return a `*sql.Row` object that you can use to scan values and check for errors.

Run `QueryRow` or `QueryRowContext`, and scan the values as described previously:

```
var user User
row:=db.QueryRow(`SELECT user_id, user_name, last_login, avatar_url
FROM users WHERE user_id = ?`, id)
if err:=row.Scan(
    &user.ID,
    &user.Name,
    &user.LastLogin,
    &avatarURL);err!=nil {
  return err
}
return user
```

If there is an error during query execution, it will be returned by the row.

Dynamically building SQL statements

In any nontrivial application using a SQL database, you will have to build SQL statements dynamically. This becomes necessary for cases such as the following:

- Using flexible search criteria that may change based on user input or requests
- Optionally joining multiple tables based on requested fields

- Selectively updating a subset of columns

- Inserting a variable number of columns

This section shows several common methods to build SQL statements for different use cases.

> **Tip**
> There are many open source query builder packages. You might want to explore those packages before writing your own.

Building UPDATE statements

If you need to update a given number of columns of a table without modifying others, you can follow the pattern given in this section.

How to do it...

1. You need two pieces of information to run an UPDATE statement:

   - **The data to update**: A common way of describing such information is to use pointers to represent updated values. Consider the following example:

     ```
     type UpdateUserRequest struct {
         Name *string
         LastLogin *time.Time
         AvatarURL *string
     }
     ```

     Here, a column will only be updated if the corresponding field is not null. For instance, with the following instance of UpdateUserRequest, only the LastLogin and AvatarURL fields will be updated:

     ```
     now:=time.Now()
     urlString:="https://example.org/avatar.jpg"
     update:=UpdateUserRequest {
         LastLogin: &now,
         AvatarURL: &urlString,
     }
     ```

   - **The record locator**: This is usually the unique identifier of the row that needs to be updated. However, it is also common to use a query that will locate multiple records.

With this information, a common way to write an update function is as follows:

```
func UpdateUser(ctx context.Context, db *sql.DB, userId uint64,
req *UpdateUserRequest) error {
    ...
}
```

In the preceding code, the record locator is `userId`.

- Use `strings.Builder` to build the statement while keeping track of the query arguments in a slice:

```
query:=strings.Builder{}
args:=make([]interface{},0)
// Start building the query. Be mindful of spaces to separate
// query clauses
query.WriteString("UPDATE users SET ")
```

2. Create a SET clause for each column that needs to be updated:

```
if req.Name != nil {
  args=append(args,*req.Name)
  query.WriteString("user_name=?")
}
if req.LastLogin!=nil {
  if len(args)>0 {
    query.WriteString(",")
  }
  args=append(args,*req.LastLogin)
  query.WriteString("last_login=?")
}
if req.AvatarURL!=nil {
  if len(args)>0 {
    query.WriteString(",")
  }
  args=append(args,*req.AvatarURL)
  query.WriteString("avatar_url=?")
}
```

3. Add the WHERE clause:

```
query.WriteString(" WHERE user_id=?")
args=append(args,userId)
```

4. Run the statement:

```
_,err:=db.ExecContext(ctx,query.String(),args...)
```

Not all database drivers use ? for query arguments. For example, one of the Postgres drivers uses $n, where n is a number starting from 1 giving the order of the argument. The algorithm is a bit different for such drivers:

```
if req.Name != nil {
  args=append(args,*req.Name)
  fmt.Fprintf(&query,"user_name=$%d",len(args))
}
if req.LastLogin!=nil {
  if len(args)>0 {
    query.WriteString(",")
  }
  args=append(args,*req.LastLogin)
  fmt.Fprintf(&query,"last_login=$%d",len(args))
}
if req.AvatarURL!=nil {
  if len(args)>0 {
    query.WriteString(",")
  }
  args=append(args,*req.AvatarURL)
  fmt.Fprintf(&query,"avatar_url=$%d",len(args))
}
```

Building WHERE clauses

A WHERE clause can be a part of a SELECT, UPDATE, or DELETE statement. Here, I will show a SELECT example, and you can extend this to apply to UPDATE and DELETE. Be careful with the arguments as an UPDATE statement will include arguments for update column values as well.

How to do it...

This example shows the case where AND is used in the search criteria:

1. You need a data structure that gives which columns to include in the WHERE clause. Take the following example:

    ```
    type UserSearchRequest struct {
      Ids             []uint64
      Name            *string
      LoggedInBefore  *time.Time
      LoggedInAfter   *time.Time
      AvatarURL       *string
    }
    ```

With this structure, the search function looks as follows:

```
func SearchUsers(ctx context.Context, db *sql.DB, req
*UserSearchRequest) ([]User,error) {

   ...

}
```

2. Use `strings.Builder` to build the statement parts while keeping track of the query arguments in a slice:

```
query:=strings.Builder{}
where:= strings.Builder{}
args:=make([]interface{},0)
// Start building the query. Be mindful of spaces to separate
// query clauses
query.WriteString("SELECT user_id, user_name, last_login,
avatar_url FROM users ")
```

3. Build a predicate for each search item:

```
if len(req.Ids)>0 {
  // Add this to the WHERE clause with an AND
  if where.Len()>0 {
     where.WriteString(" AND ")
   }
  // Build an IN clause.
  // We have to add one argument for each id
  where.WriteString("user_id IN (")
  for i,id:=range req.Ids {
    if i>0 {
      where.WriteString(",")
    }
    args=append(args,id)
    where.WriteString("?")
  }
  where.WriteString(")")
}
if req.Name!=nil {
  if where.Len()>0 {
    where.WriteString(" AND ")
  }
  args=append(args,*req.Name)
  where.WriteString("user_name=?")
}
if req.LoggedInBefore!=nil {
  if where.Len()>0 {
```

```
    where.WriteString(" AND ")
  }
  args=append(args,*req.LoggedInBefore)
  where.WriteString("last_login<?")
}
if req.LoggedInAfter!=nil {
  if where.Len()>0 {
    where.WriteString(" AND ")
  }
  args=append(args,*req.LoggedInAfter)
  where.WriteString("last_login>?")
}
if req.AvatarURL!=nil {
  if where.Len()>0 {
    where.WriteString(" AND ")
  }
  args=append(args,*req.AvatarURL)
  where.WriteString("avatar_url=?")
}
```

4. Build and run the query:

```
if where.Len()>0 {
  query.WriteString(" WHERE ")
  query.WriteString(where.String())
}
rows, err:= db.QueryContext(ctx,query.String(), args...)
```

Again, not all database drivers use the ? marker. See the previous section for an alternative if your database driver is one of those.

16

Logging

Printing log messages from a program can be an important tool for troubleshooting. Log messages tell you what is going on at any given moment, and provide much-needed contextual information when something goes wrong. Go standard library provides convenient packages to generate and manage log messages from programs. Here, we will look at using the `log` package, which can be used to generate text messages, and the `slog` package, which can be used to generate structured log messages from programs.

This chapter contains the following recipes:

- Using the standard logger

    - Writing log messages

    - Controlling format

    - Changing where to log

- Using the structured logger

    - Logging using the global logger

    - Writing structured logs using different levels

    - Changing log level at runtime

    - Using loggers with additional attributes

    - Changing where to log

    - Adding logging information from the context

Using the standard logger

The standard library logger is defined in the `log` package. It is a simple logging library that can be used to print formatted log messages that show the progression of a program. For most practical purposes, the standard library logger functionality is too limited, but it can be a useful tool that requires minimal setup for proof-of-concepts and smaller programs. Use the structured logger `log/slog` package for any nontrivial project.

Writing log messages

The standard logger is a simple logging implementation to print diagnostic messages. It does not offer structured output or multiple log levels but can be useful for programs where log messages are geared toward the end users or developers.

How to do it...

You can use the default logger to print log messages:

```
log.Println("This is a log message similar to fmt.Println")
log.Printf("This is a log message similar to fmt.Printf")
```

Here is the output:

```
2024/09/17 23:05:26 This is a log message similar to fmt.Println
2024/09/17 23:05:26 This is a log message similar to fmt.Printf
```

The above functions use a singleton instance of `log.Logger`, which can be obtained by `log.Default()`. In other words, calling `log.Println` is equivalent to calling `log.Default().Println`.

You can also create a new logger, configure it, and pass it around:

```
logger := log.New(os.Stderr, "", log.LstdFlags)
logger.Println("This is a log message written to stderr")
```

Here is the output:

```
2024/09/17 23:10:34 This is a log message written to stderr
```

Other than `log.Println` and `log.Printf`, you can use `log.Fatal` or `log.Panic` to stop a program:

```
log.Fatal("Fatal error")
```

This will terminate the program with exit code 1 and output the following:

```
2024/09/17 23:05:26 Fatal error
```

We can observe something similar with the following:

```
log.Panic("Fatal error")
```

This will panic and generate the output that follows:

```
2024/09/17 23:05:26 Fatal error
panic: Fatal error

goroutine 1 [running]:
log.Panic({0xc000104f30?, 0xc00007c060?, 0x556310?})
    /usr/local/go-faketime/src/log/log.go:432 +0x5a
main.main()
    /tmp/sandbox255937470/prog.go:8 +0x38
```

Controlling format

You can control the output format of the logger using bit flags. You can also define a prefix for the subsequent log messages.

How to do it...

You can create a new logger with a prefix as follows:

```
logger := log.New(log.Writer(), "prefix: ", log.LstdFlags)
logger.Println("This is a log message with a prefix")
```

This outputs the following:

```
prefix: 2024/09/17 23:10:34 This is a log message with a prefix
```

You can also set the prefix of an existing logger:

```
logger.SetPrefix("newPrefix")
logger.Println("This is a log message with the new prefix")
```

Here is the output:

```
newPrefix: 2024/09/17 23:10:34 This is a log message with the new
prefix
```

The output fields and how they are printed are controlled by the flags. The `log.LstdFlags` tells the logger that the date and time of the log should also be written.

The `log.Lshortfile` prints the file name and line number showing where the log statement is:

```
logger.SetFlags(log.LstdFlags | log.Lshortfile)
logger.Println("This is a log message with a prefix and file name")
```

This gives the following output:

```
prefix: 2024/09/17 23:10:34 main.go:17: This is a log message with a
prefix and file name
```

The `log.Llongfile` prints the full path:

```
logger.SetFlags(log.LstdFlags | log.Llongfile)
logger.Println("This is a log message with a prefix and long file name")
```

Here is the output:

```
prefix: 2024/09/17 23:10:34 /home/github.com/PacktPublishing/Go-
Recipes-for-Developers/blob/main/src/chp16/stdlogger/main.go:19: This
is a log message with a prefix and long file name
```

You can combine multiple flags using the bitwise | OR operator. The `log.Lmsgprefix` moves
the prefix string (if one exists) to the beginning of the message from the beginning of the log line:

```
logger.SetFlags(log.LstdFlags | log.Lshortfile | log.Lmsgprefix)
logger.Println("This is a log message with a prefix moved to the
beginning of the message
```

Here's the output::

```
2024/09/17 23:10:34 main.go:21: prefix: This is a log message with a
prefix moved to the beginning of the message
```

The following flags print the time and date in UTC, as well as the short file name:

```
logger.SetFlags(log.LstdFlags | log.Lshortfile | log.LUTC)
logger.Println("This is a log message with with UTC time") ```
```

This outputs the following:

```
prefix: 2024/09/18 05:10:34 main.go:23: This is a log message with
with UTC time
```

Changing where to log

By default, the logging output goes to standard error (`os.Stderr`), but it can be changed without
affecting the logging directives.

How to do it...

You can create a logger with a given output using `log.NewLogger`. The following example creates
`logger` to print its output to standard error:

```
logger := log.New(os.Stderr, "", log.LstdFlags)
```

You can then change the logging target using `Logger.SetOutput`:

```
output, err := os.Create("log.txt")
if err != nil {
    log.Fatal(err)
}
defer output.Close()
logger.SetOutput(output)
logger.Println("This is a log message to log.txt")
logger.SetOutput(os.Stderr)
logger.Println("Message to log.txt was written")
```

Use `io.Discard` as the log output to stop logging:

```
logger.SetOutput(io.Discard)
logger.Println("This message will not be logged")
```

Using the structured logger

Since the standard logger has limited practical use, many third-party logging libraries were developed by the community. Some of the patterns that emerged from these libraries emphasized structured logging and performance. The structured logging package was added to the standard library with these usage patterns in mind. The `log` package is still a useful tool for development as it provides a simple interface for developers and the users of the program, but the `log/slog` package is a production quality library that enables automated log analysis tools while providing a simple-to-use and flexible interface.

Logging using the global logger

Similar to the `log` package, there is a global structured logger accessible via the `slog.Default()` function. You can simply configure a global logger and use that in your program.

> **Tip**
> It is advisable to pass an instance of a logger around for any nontrivial project. The logging requirements may change from environment to environment, so having a dedicated logger helps.

How to do it...

Use `slog` logging functions to write logs:

```
slog.Debug("This is a debug message")
slog.Info("This is an info message with an integer field", "arg", 42)
slog.Info("This is another info message with an integer field", slog.
Int("arg",42))
```

You cannot modify the settings of the default logger, but you can create a new one and set it as the default. The following example shows how you can set a JSON logger as the default logger:

```
logger := slog.New(slog.NewJSONHandler(os.Stderr, &slog.
HandlerOptions{
        Level: slog.LevelDebug,
    },
))
slog.SetDefault(logger)
```

> **Tip**
>
> `slog.SetDefault()` also sets the `log` package default logger, so the `log` package functions call the `slog` functions. Use `slog.SetLogLoggerLevel` to set the level of the log package messages.

Writing structured logs using different levels

The structured logger allows you to log messages at different levels. For instance, you can log detailed messages at the `slog.LevelDebug` level, warning messages at the `slog.LevelWarn` level, and error messages at the `slog.LevelError` level, and set the logging level of your program from a configuration or command line argument.

How to do it...

1. Create a `slog.Handler` with `slog.HandlerOptions.Level` set to the desired level. The following example creates a text log handler that prints every log message as a separate line of text. It uses `os.Stderr` as the output, and the logging level is set to `slog.LevelDebug`:

    ```
    handler:= slog.NewTextHandler(os.Stderr, &slog.HandlerOptions{
        Level: slog.LevelDebug,
    })
    ```

2. Create a logger using the handler:

    ```
    logger := slog.New(handler)
    ```

3. Use the logger to create messages at different levels. Only those messages that are equal to or above the level determined by the handler options will be printed to the output:

    ```
    logger.Debug("This is a debug message")
    logger.Info("This is an info message with an integer argument",
    "arg", 42)
    logger.Warn("This is a warning message with a string argument",
    "arg", "foo")
    ```

4. If logging performance is a concern, you can check whether a specific logging level is enabled:

```
// Checking if logging is enabled for a specific level
if logger.Enabled(context.Background(), slog.LevelError) {
   logger.Error("This is an error message", slog.String("arg",
"foo"))
}
```

Changing log level at runtime

Most applications set up a logger at the beginning of the application using a command line option or a configuration file and do not change logging at runtime. However, the ability to set log levels at runtime can be an invaluable tool to identify production problems. You can set the debug level of a running server to slog.LevelDebug, record logs to find out about a troubling behavior, and set it back to its original level. This recipe shows how you can do this.

How to do it...

1. Use a slog.LevelVar to wrap a log level value (this is called **boxing** a variable):

```
level = new(slog.LevelVar)
```

2. Set the initial log level:

```
level.Set(slog.LevelError)
```

3. Create a handler using the boxed level:

```
handler:=slog.NewTextHandler(os.Stderr, &slog.HandlerOptions{
        Level: level,
    })
```

4. Create a logger using the handler:

```
logger:=slog.New(handler)
```

5. Change level to control the log level:

```
level.Set(slog.LevelDebug)
// Now all loggers will start printing debug level messages
```

Using loggers with additional attributes

Let's say you have a server where you handle requests using functions that are shared among multiple request handlers. When the request is received, you can log which handler is running, but when you pass that logger to the common functions, they lose that information. They don't know which request handler called. Instead of passing this information to those common functions (after all, they don't really need that information), you can decorate a logger with such information and pass the logger.

How to do it...

1. Create a new logger using `Logger.With`, and attach additional attributes:

```go
func HandlerA(w http.ResponseWriter, req *http.Request) {
  reqId:=getRequestIdFromRequest(req)
  // Create a new logger with additional attributes
  logger:=slog.With(slog.String("handler", "a"),slog.
  String("reqId",reqId))
  logger.Debug("Start handling request")
  defer logger.Debug("Completed request")
```

2. Use this logger to log messages:

```go
HandleRequest(logger, w,req)
```

This will output a log message that looks like this:

```
{"time":"2024-09-19T14:49:42.064787730-06:00","level":"DEBUG","m
sg":"Start handling request","handler":"a","reqId":"123"}
{"time":"2024-09-19T14:49:42.308187758-
06:00","level":"DEBUG","msg":"This is a debug
message","handler":"a","reqId":"123","key":"value"}
{"time":"2024-09-19T14:49:42.945674637-06:00","level":"DEBUG","m
sg":"Completed request","handler":"a","reqId":"123"}
```

Changing where to log

The default logger writes to `os.Stderr`, and similar to the `log` package, this can be changed when you create the logger.

How to do it...

The logger output is determined by the `slog.Handler`. The following example creates `logger` to print its output to standard error:

```go
logger := slog.New(slog.NewTextHandler(os.Stderr, &slog.
HandlerOptions{
      Level: slog.LevelDebug,
   }))
```

Unlike the `log` package, you cannot change where to log after creating a logger, unless you write your own handler.

Adding logging information from the context

Often, the information you need to log is available in the context. Every `slog` logging function has two variants, one with context and one without. If you use the variants with context, you can write a handler that can extract information from that context containing information from the call site.

How to do it...

Create a new handler, potentially wrapping an existing one. The following code snippet shows a handler that will extract an `id` from the context by wrapping a `slog.Handler`:

```
type ContextIDHandler struct {
    slog.Handler
}
```

Define the `Handle` method. Extract information from the context, modify the log record, and pass it to the wrapped handler:

```
func (h ContextIDHandler) Handle(ctx context.Context, r slog.Record)
error {
    // If the context has a string id, retrieve it and add it to the
    // record
    if id, ok := ctx.Value("id").(string); ok {
        r.Add(slog.String("id", id))
    }
    return h.Handler.Handle(ctx, r)
}
```

Use the logging functions that take `context.Context`:

```
func Handler(w http.ResponseWriter, req *http.Request) {
    logger.Debug(req.Context(),"Handler started")
    ...
```

This will add the `id` from the request context to the log message if there is one:

```
{"time":"2024-09-19T15:02:12.163787730-06:00","level":"DEBUG","msg":"H
andler started","id":"123"}
```

17

Testing, Benchmarking, and Profiling

Having tests and benchmarks for your code will help you in several ways. During development, tests ensure that what you are developing works and that you do not break existing functionality as part of your development work. Benchmarks ensure that your program stays within certain resource and time constraints. After the development is complete, the same tests and benchmarks will ensure that any maintenance work (bug fixes, feature enhancements, etc.) does not introduce bugs in existing functionality. So, you should consider writing tests and benchmarks as a core development activity, and develop both your program and its tests together.

Testing should focus on testing the expected behavior when everything works ("happy path testing") as well as when things fail. It should not focus on testing all possible execution paths. Tests developed to exercise all possible implementation choices quickly become harder to maintain than the program itself. You should find a balance between practicality and test coverage.

This section shows idiomatic ways of dealing with several common testing and benchmarking scenarios. These are the topics covered in this chapter:

- Working with unit tests
- Writing unit tests
- Running unit tests
- Logging in tests
- Skipping tests
- Testing HTTP servers
- Testing HTTP handlers
- Checking test coverage

- Benchmarking

- Writing benchmarks

- Writing multiple benchmarks with different input sizes

- Running benchmarks

- Profiling

Working with unit tests

We will work on an example function that sorts time.Time values in ascending or descending order, which is given here:

```go
package sort

import (
  "sort"
  "time"
)

// Sort times in ascending or descending order
func SortTimes(input []time.Time, asc bool) []time.Time {
  output := make([]time.Time, len(input))
  copy(output, input)
  if asc {
    sort.Slice(output, func(i, j int) bool {
      return output[i].Before(output[j])
    })
    return output
  }
  sort.Slice(output, func(i, j int) bool {
    return output[j].Before(output[i])
  })
  return output
}
```

We will use the built-in testing tools provided by the Go build system and the standard library. For this, let's suppose we stored the preceding function in a file called sort.go. Then, the unit tests for this function will be in a file called sort_test.go in the same directory as sort.go. The Go build system will recognize source files that end with _test.go as unit tests, and will exclude them from regular builds.

Writing a unit test

A unit test ideally tests whether a single unit (a function, a group of interrelated functions, or the methods of a type) behaves as expected.

How to do it...

1. Create unit test files with the `_test.go` suffix. For `sort.go`, we create `sort_test.go`. The files that end with `_test.go` will be excluded from a regular build:

    ```
    package sort
    ```

> **Tip**
>
> You can also write tests in a separate test package that ends with `_test`. In this example, it becomes `package sort_test`. Writing tests in a separate package allows you to test the functions of a package as they are seen from the outside because you will not have access to the unexported names of the package under test. You will have to import the package under test.

2. The Go testing system will run functions that follow the `Test<Feature>(*testing.T)` pattern. Declare a test function that fits this pattern, and write a unit test that exercises a behavior:

    ```go
    func TestSortTimesAscending(t *testing.T) {
        // 2.a Prepare input data
        input := []time.Time{
            time.Date(2023, 2, 1, 12, 8, 37, 0, time.Local),
            time.Date(2021, 5, 6, 9, 48, 11, 0, time.Local),
            time.Date(2022, 11, 13, 17, 13, 54, 0, time.Local),
            time.Date(2022, 6, 23, 22, 29, 28, 0, time.Local),
            time.Date(2023, 3, 17, 4, 5, 9, 0, time.Local),
        }
        // 2.b Call the function under test
        output := SortTimes(input, true)
        // 2.c Make sure the output is what is expected
        for i := 1; i < len(output); i++ {
            if !output[i-1].Before(output[i]) {
                t.Error("Wrong order")
            }
        }
    }
    ```

3. The layout of a test function usually follows this structure:

   - Prepare input data and any necessary environment in which the function under test will run

   - Call the function under test with the necessary input

   - Make sure the function under test returned the correct result or behaved as expected

4. If the test detects errors, notify the testing system that the test failed using the `t.Error` family of functions.

Running unit tests

Use the Go build system tools to run unit tests.

How to do it...

1. To run all unit tests in the current package, input the following:

```
go test
PASS
ok   github.com/PacktPublishing/Go-Recipes-for-Developers/src/
chp17/sorting/sort    0.001s
```

2. To run all unit tests in a package, input the following:

```
go test <packageName>
```

Or, input the following:

```
go test ./<folder>
```

Here is an example:

```
go test github.com/PacktPublishing/Go-Recipes-for-Developers/
src/chp17/sorting/sort
```

Or, you can input the following:

```
go test ./sorting
```

3. To run all unit tests in all packages of a module recursively, input the following:

```
go test ./...
```

Do this from the root directory of the module.

4. To run a single test in the current package, input the following:

```
go test -run TestSortTimesAscending
```

This form treats the test name after the -run flag as a regular expression and runs all tests that contain that string. For instance, go test -run Sort will run all tests whose name has Sort in them. If you want to run a specific test only, construct the regular expression accordingly:

```
go test -run ^TestSortTimesAscending$
```

Here, ^ denotes the string beginning and $ denotes the string end symbols used in regular expressions.

For instance, the following will run all tests that end with Ascending:

```
go test -run Ascending$
```

Logging in tests

Often additional logging functionality is useful for tests to show the state of critical variables, especially if a failure occurs. By default, the Go test executor does not print any logging information if tests pass, but if a test fails, the logging information is also included in the output.

How to do it...

1. Use testing.T.Log and testing.T.Logf functions to record log messages in tests:

    ```
    func TestSortTimeAscending(t *testing.T) {
        ...
        t.Logf("Input: %v",input)
        output:=SortTimes(input,true)
        t.Logf("Output: %v", output)
    ```

2. Run the tests. If the test passes, no log information will be printed. If the test fails, logs will be printed.

    To run the tests with logs, use the -v flag:

    ```
    $ go test -v
    === RUN    TestSortTimesAscending
        sort_test.go:17: Input: [2023-02-01 12:08:37 -0700 MST 2021-
    05-06 09:48:11 -0600 MDT 2022-11-13 17:13:54 -0700 MST 2022-06-
    23 22:29:28 -0600 MDT 2023-03-17 04:05:09 -0600 MDT]
        sort_test.go:19: Output: [2021-05-06 09:48:11 -0600 MDT
    2022-06-23 22:29:28 -0600 MDT 2022-11-13 17:13:54 -0700 MST
    2023-02-01 12:08:37 -0700 MST 2023-03-17 04:05:09 -0600 MDT]
    --- PASS: TestSortTimesAscending (0.00s)
    ```

Skipping tests

You can skip certain tests based on an input flag. This feature lets you have a quick test where only a subset of the tests are run and a comprehensive test where all the tests are run.

How to do it...

1. Check the `testing.Short()` flag for tests that should be excluded from short test runs:

```go
func TestService(t *testing.T) {
  if testing.Short() {
    t.Skip("Service")
  }
  ...
}
```

2. Run tests with the `test.short` flag:

```
$ go test -test.short -v
=== RUN    TestService
      service_test.go:15: Service
--- SKIP: TestService (0.00s)
=== RUN    TestHandler
--- PASS: TestHandler (0.00s)
PASS
```

Testing HTTP servers

The `net/http/httptest` package complements the `testing` package by providing HTTP server testing facilities that allow you to create test HTTP servers quickly.

For this section, suppose we extend our sorting function by converting it to an HTTP service, as given here:

```go
package service

import (
    "encoding/json"
    "io"
    "net/http"
    "time"

    "github.com/PacktPublishing/Go-Recipes-for-Developers/src/chp17/
    sorting/sort"
)

// Common handler function for parsing the input, sorting, and
// preparing the output
func HandleSort(w http.ResponseWriter, req *http.Request, ascending
bool) {
    var input []time.Time
```

```
    data, err := io.ReadAll(req.Body)
    if err != nil {
        http.Error(w, err.Error(), http.StatusBadRequest)
        return
    }
    if err := json.Unmarshal(data, &input); err != nil {
        http.Error(w, err.Error(), http.StatusBadRequest)
        return
    }
    output := sort.SortTimes(input, ascending)
    data, err = json.Marshal(output)
    if err != nil {
        http.Error(w, err.Error(), http.StatusInternalServerError)
        return
    }
    w.Header().Set("Content-Type", "application/json")
    w.Write(data)
}

// Prepares a multiplexer that handles POST /sort/asc and POST /sort/
// desc endpoints
func GetServeMux() *http.ServeMux {
    mux := http.NewServeMux()
    mux.HandleFunc("POST /sort/asc", func(w http.ResponseWriter, req
    *http.Request) {
        HandleSort(w, req, true)
    })
    mux.HandleFunc("POST /sort/desc", func(w http.ResponseWriter, req
    *http.Request) {
        HandleSort(w, req, false)
    })
    return mux
}
```

The GetServeMux function prepares a request multiplexer that handles POST /sort/asc and POST /sort/desc HTTP endpoints for ascending and descending sort requests respectively. The input is a JSON array of time values. The handler returns a sorted JSON array.

How to do it...

1. Use the net/http/httptest package that includes support for a test server:

    ```
    import (
        "net/http/httptest"
    ```

```
        "testing"
        ...
)
```

2. In the test function, create a handler or multiplexer, and use that to create a test server. Make sure the server shuts down when the test ends -- use `defer server.Close()`:

```
func TestService(t *testing.T) {
    mux := GetServeMux()
    server := httptest.NewServer(mux)
    defer server.Close()
```

3. Call the server using `server.URL`. This is initialized to use an unallocated local port by the `httptest.NewServer` function. In the following example, we are sending an invalid input to the server to verify if the server returns an error:

```
rsp, err := http.Post(server.URL+"/sort/asc", "application/
json", strings.NewReader("test"))
if err != nil {
    t.Error(err)
    return
}
// Must return http error
if rsp.StatusCode/100 == 2 {
    t.Errorf("Error was expected")
    return
}
```

Note that the `http.Post` function does not return an error. An error from `http.Post` would mean the `POST` operation failed. In this case, the `POST` operation was successful, but an HTTP error status was returned.

4. You can issue multiple calls to the server to test different inputs and check the output:

```
data, err := json.Marshal([]time.Time{
    time.Date(2023, 2, 1, 12, 8, 37, 0, time.Local),
    time.Date(2021, 5, 6, 9, 48, 11, 0, time.Local),
    time.Date(2022, 11, 13, 17, 13, 54, 0, time.Local),
    time.Date(2022, 6, 23, 22, 29, 28, 0, time.Local),
    time.Date(2023, 3, 17, 4, 5, 9, 0, time.Local),
})
if err != nil {
    t.Error(err)
    return
}
rsp, err = http.Post(server.URL+"/sort/asc", "application/json",
bytes.NewReader(data))
```

```
if err != nil {
  t.Error(err)
  return
}
defer rsp.Body.Close()

if rsp.StatusCode != 200 {
  t.Errorf("Expected status code 200, got %d", rsp.StatusCode)
  return
}

var output []time.Time
if err := json.NewDecoder(rsp.Body).Decode(&output); err != nil
{
  t.Error(err)
  return
}
for i := 1; i < len(output); i++ {
  if !output[i-1].Before(output[i]) {
    t.Errorf("Wrong order")
  }
}
```

Testing HTTP handlers

The net/http/httptest package also contains ResponseRecorder, which can be used as http.ResponseWriter for HTTP handlers to test a single handler without creating a server.

How to do it...

1. Create ResponseRecorder:

   ```
   func TestHandler(t *testing.T) {
     w := httptest.NewRecorder()
   ```

2. Call the handler, passing the response recorder instead of http.ResponseWriter:

   ```
   data, err := json.Marshal([]time.Time{
     time.Date(2023, 2, 1, 12, 8, 37, 0, time.Local),
     time.Date(2021, 5, 6, 9, 48, 11, 0, time.Local),
     time.Date(2022, 11, 13, 17, 13, 54, 0, time.Local),
     time.Date(2022, 6, 23, 22, 29, 28, 0, time.Local),
     time.Date(2023, 3, 17, 4, 5, 9, 0, time.Local),
   })
   ```

```
if err != nil {
  t.Error(err)
  return
}
req, _ := http.NewRequest("POST", "localhost/sort/asc", bytes.
NewReader(data))
req.Header.Set("Content-Type", "application/json")
HandleSort(w, req, true)
```

3. The response recorder stores the HTTP response built by the handler. Validate that the response is correct:

```
if w.Result().StatusCode != 200 {
  t.Errorf("Expecting HTTP 200, got %d", w.Result().StatusCode)
  return
}
var output []time.Time
if err := json.NewDecoder(w.Result().Body).Decode(&output); err
!= nil {
  t.Error(err)
  return
}
for i := 1; i < len(output); i++ {
  if !output[i-1].Before(output[i]) {
    t.Errorf("Wrong order")
  }
}
```

Checking test coverage

A test coverage report shows which lines of source code were covered by tests.

How to do it...

1. To get a quick coverage result, run tests with the cover flag:

```
$ go test -cover
PASS
coverage: 76.2% of statements
```

2. To write a test coverage profile to a separate file so you can get detailed reports on it, give the test run a cover profile file name:

```
$ go test -coverprofile=cover.out
PASS
coverage: 76.2% of statements
```

Then, you can see the coverage report in your browser using:

```
$ go tool cover -html=cover.out
```

This command opens the browser and allows you to see which lines were covered by tests.

Benchmarking

Unit tests check correctness while benchmarks check performance and memory usage.

Writing benchmarks

Similar to a unit test, benchmarks are stored in the _test.go files, but these functions start with Benchmark instead of Test. A benchmark is given a number N where you repeat the same operation N times while the runtime is measuring the performance.

How to do it...

1. Create a benchmark function in one of the _test.go files. The following example is in the sort_test.go file:

```
func BenchmarkSortAscending(b *testing.B) {
```

2. Do the setup before the benchmark loop, otherwise, you will be benchmarking the setup code as well, not the actual algorithm:

```
input := []time.Time{
  time.Date(2023, 2, 1, 12, 8, 37, 0, time.Local),
  time.Date(2021, 5, 6, 9, 48, 11, 0, time.Local),
  time.Date(2022, 11, 13, 17, 13, 54, 0, time.Local),
  time.Date(2022, 6, 23, 22, 29, 28, 0, time.Local),
  time.Date(2023, 3, 17, 4, 5, 9, 0, time.Local),
}
```

3. Write a for loop iterating b.N times and perform the operation that will be benchmarked:

```
for i := 0; i < b.N; i++ {
  SortTimes(input, true)
}
```

> **Tip**
> Avoid logging or printing data in benchmark loops.

Writing multiple benchmarks with different input sizes

You usually want to see the behavior of your algorithms with different input sizes. The Go testing framework only provides the number of times a benchmark should run, not with what input size. Use the following pattern to exercise different input sizes.

How to do it...

1. Define an unexported parameterized benchmark function that accepts input size information or inputs of different sizes. The following example gets the number of items and sort direction as arguments, and creates a randomly shuffled input slice with the given size before performing the benchmark:

```
func benchmarkSort(b *testing.B, nItems int, asc bool) {
    input := make([]time.Time, nItems)
    t := time.Now().UnixNano()
    for i := 0; i < nItems; i++ {
        input[i] = time.Unix(0, t-int64(i))
    }
    rand.Shuffle(len(input), func(i, j int) { input[i], input[j]
    = input[j], input[i] })
    for i := 0; i < b.N; i++ {
        SortTimes(input, asc)
    }
}
```

2. Define exported benchmark functions by calling the common benchmark with different values:

```
func BenchmarkSort1000Ascending(b *testing.B)   {
benchmarkSort(b, 1000, true) }
func BenchmarkSort100Ascending(b *testing.B)    {
benchmarkSort(b, 100, true) }
func BenchmarkSort10Ascending(b *testing.B)     {
benchmarkSort(b, 10, true) }
func BenchmarkSort1000Descending(b *testing.B) {
benchmarkSort(b, 1000, false) }
func BenchmarkSort100Descending(b *testing.B)   {
benchmarkSort(b, 100, false) }
func BenchmarkSort10Descending(b *testing.B)    {
benchmarkSort(b, 10, false) }
```

Running benchmarks

Go tooling runs unit tests before running benchmarks -- there is no point in benchmarking failing code.

How to do it...

1. Use the go test -bench=<regexp> tool. To run all benchmarks, use the following command:

   ```
   go test -bench=.
   ```

2. Enter a benchmark regular expression if you want to run a subset of the benchmarks. The following only runs benchmarks containing 1000 in their names:

   ```
   go test -bench=1000
   goos: linux
   goarch: amd64
   pkg: github.com/PacktPublishing/Go-Recipes-for-Developers/src/
   chp17/sorting/sort
   cpu: AMD Ryzen 5 7530U with Radeon Graphics
   BenchmarkSort1000Ascending-12                    9753        105997 ns/
   op
   BenchmarkSort1000Descending-12                   9813        105192
   ns/op
   PASS
   ```

Profiling

A profiler samples a running program to find how much time is spent in certain functions. You can profile a benchmark, create a profile, and then inspect that profile to find bottlenecks in your programs.

How to do it...

To get a CPU profile and analyze it, follow these steps:

1. Run benchmarks with the cpuprofile flag:

   ```
   $ go test -bench=1000Ascending --cpuprofile=profile
   goos: linux
   goarch: amd64
   pkg: github.com/PacktPublishing/Go-Recipes-for-Developers/src/
   chp17/sorting/sort
   cpu: AMD Ryzen 5 7530U with Radeon Graphics
   BenchmarkSort1000Ascending-12                   10000        106509 ns/
   op
   ```

2. Start the pprof tool using the profile:

   ```
   $ go tool pprof profile
   File: sort.test
   Type: cpu
   ```

3. Use the `topN` command to see the top N samples in the profile:

```
(pprof) top5
Showing nodes accounting for 780ms, 71.56% of 1090ms total
Showing top 5 nodes out of 47
      flat  flat%   sum%        cum   cum%
     250ms 22.94% 22.94%      360ms 33.03%  github.com/
PacktPublishing/Go-Recipes-for-Developers/src/chp17/sorting/
sort.SortTimes.func1
     230ms 21.10% 44.04%      620ms 56.88%  sort.partition_func
     120ms 11.01% 55.05%      120ms 11.01%  runtime.memmove
      90ms  8.26% 63.30%      340ms 31.19%  internal/
reflectlite.Swapper.func9
      90ms  8.26% 71.56%      230ms 21.10%  internal/
reflectlite.typedmemmove
```

This shows that most time is spent in the anonymous function that compares two time values. The `flat` column shows how much time is spent in a function, excluding the time spent in functions called by it. `cum`, which stands for cumulative, includes the time spent in a function, defined as the point in time the function returned minus the point in time the function started running. That is, the cumulative value includes the time spent in the functions called by the function. For example `sort.partition_func` ran for `620ms`, but only `230ms` of that time was spent in `sort.partition_func` and the remaining time was spent in functions called by `sort.partition_func`.

4. Use the web command to see a visual representation of the call graph and how much time is spent on each function.

To get a memory profile and analyze it, follow these steps:

1. Run benchmarks with the `memprofile` flag:

```
$ go test -bench=1000Ascending --memprofile=mem
goos: linux
goarch: amd64
pkg: github.com/PacktPublishing/Go-Recipes-for-Developers/src/
chp17/sorting/sort
cpu: AMD Ryzen 5 7530U with Radeon Graphics
BenchmarkSort1000Ascending-12              10000            106509 ns/
op
```

2. Start the `pprof` tool using the profile:

```
$ go tool pprof mem
File: sort.test
Type: alloc_space
```

3. Use the `topN` command to see the top N samples in the profile:

```
pprof) top5
Showing nodes accounting for 493.37MB, 99.90% of 493.87MB total
Dropped 2 nodes (cum <= 2.47MB)
      flat  flat%   sum%        cum   cum%
 492.86MB 99.80% 99.80%    493.36MB 99.90%  github.com/
PacktPublishing/Go-Recipes-for-Developers/src/chp17/sorting/
sort.SortTimes
    0.51MB   0.1% 99.90%    493.87MB   100%  github.com/
PacktPublishing/Go-Recipes-for-Developers/src/chp17/sorting/
sort.benchmarkSort
        0     0% 99.90%    493.87MB   100%  github.com/
PacktPublishing/Go-Recipes-for-Developers/src/chp17/sorting/
sort.BenchmarkSort1000Ascending
        0     0% 99.90%    493.87MB   100%  testing.(*B).launch
        0     0% 99.90%    493.87MB   100%  testing.(*B).runN
```

Similar to the CPU profile output, this table shows how much memory was allocated to each function. Again, `flat` refers to memory allocated in that function only, and `cum` refers to memory allocated in that function and any function called by that function. Here, you can see that `sort.SortTimes` is the function that allocates most of the memory. This is because it first creates a copy of the slice and then sorts it.

4. Use the `web` command to see a visual representation of the memory allocations.

See also

- The definitive guide to profiling Go Programs is available at `https://go.dev/blog/pprof`

- The `pprof` README explains the node and edge representations: `https://github.com/google/pprof/blob/main/doc/README.md`

Index

`packtpub.com`

Subscribe to our online digital library for full access to over 7,000 books and videos, as well as industry leading tools to help you plan your personal development and advance your career. For more information, please visit our website.

Why subscribe?

- Spend less time learning and more time coding with practical eBooks and Videos from over 4,000 industry professionals

- Improve your learning with Skill Plans built especially for you

- Get a free eBook or video every month

- Fully searchable for easy access to vital information

- Copy and paste, print, and bookmark content

Did you know that Packt offers eBook versions of every book published, with PDF and ePub files available? You can upgrade to the eBook version at packtpub.com and as a print book customer, you are entitled to a discount on the eBook copy. Get in touch with us at customercare@packtpub.com for more details.

At www.packtpub.com, you can also read a collection of free technical articles, sign up for a range of free newsletters, and receive exclusive discounts and offers on Packt books and eBooks.

Other Books You May Enjoy

If you enjoyed this book, you may be interested in these other books by Packt:

System Programming Essentials with Go

Alex Rios

ISBN: 978-1-80181-344-0

- Understand the fundamentals of system programming using Go
- Grasp the concepts of goroutines, channels, data races, and managing concurrency in Go
- Manage file operations and inter-process communication (IPC)
- Handle USB drives and Bluetooth devices and monitor peripheral events for hardware automation
- Familiarize yourself with the basics of network programming and its application in Go
- Implement logging, tracing, and other telemetry practices
- Construct distributed cache and approach distributed systems using Go

Domain-Driven Design with Golang

Matthew Boyle

ISBN: 978-1-80461-926-1

- Get to grips with domains and the evolution of Domain-driven design
- Work with stakeholders to manage complex business needs
- Gain a clear understanding of bounded context, services, and value objects
- Get up and running with aggregates, factories, repositories, and services
- Find out how to apply DDD to monolithic applications and microservices
- Discover how to implement DDD patterns on distributed systems
- Understand how Test-driven development and Behavior-driven development can work with DDD

Packt is searching for authors like you

If you're interested in becoming an author for Packt, please visit `authors.packtpub.com` and apply today. We have worked with thousands of developers and tech professionals, just like you, to help them share their insight with the global tech community. You can make a general application, apply for a specific hot topic that we are recruiting an author for, or submit your own idea.

Share Your Thoughts

Now you've finished *Go Recipes for Developers*, we'd love to hear your thoughts! Scan the QR code below to go straight to the Amazon review page for this book and share your feedback or leave a review on the site that you purchased it from.

https://packt.link/r/1835464394

Your review is important to us and the tech community and will help us make sure we're delivering excellent quality content.

Download a free PDF copy of this book

Thanks for purchasing this book!

Do you like to read on the go but are unable to carry your print books everywhere?

Is your eBook purchase not compatible with the device of your choice?

Don't worry, now with every Packt book you get a DRM-free PDF version of that book at no cost.

Read anywhere, any place, on any device. Search, copy, and paste code from your favorite technical books directly into your application.

The perks don't stop there, you can get exclusive access to discounts, newsletters, and great free content in your inbox daily

Follow these simple steps to get the benefits:

1. Scan the QR code or visit the link below

https://packt.link/free-ebook/978-1-83546-439-7

2. Submit your proof of purchase
3. That's it! We'll send your free PDF and other benefits to your email directly

www.ingramcontent.com/pod-product-compliance
Lightning Source LLC
Chambersburg PA
CBHW080618060326
40690CB00021B/4732